VALUING MUSIC IN EDUCATION

"I was not satisfied as a teacher with merely passing on the culture. I wanted a role in creating it. The classroom is not just a place for learning about yesterday, but a laboratory for inventing tomorrow."

Charles B. Fowler

Valuing Music in Education

A CHARLES FOWLER READER

Edited with Critical Commentary by *Craig Resta*

OXFORD
UNIVERSITY PRESS

OXFORD
UNIVERSITY PRESS

Oxford University Press is a department of the University of Oxford. It furthers
the University's objective of excellence in research, scholarship, and education
by publishing worldwide. Oxford is a registered trade mark of Oxford University
Press in the UK and certain other countries.

Published in the United States of America by Oxford University Press
198 Madison Avenue, New York, NY 10016, United States of America.

Library of Congress Cataloging-in-Publication Data
Names: Fowler, Charles, 1931–1995, author. | Resta, Craig, editor.
Title: Valuing music in education : a Charles Fowler reader / edited by Craig Resta.
Description: New York City : Oxford University Press, 2017. |
Includes bibliographical references and index.
Identifiers: LCCN 2016014890 (print) | LCCN 2016023430 (ebook) |
ISBN 9780199944361 (cloth : alk. paper) | ISBN 9780199944385 (pbk. : alk. paper) |
ISBN 9780199944378 (updf) | ISBN 9780190619787 (epub)
Subjects: LCSH: Music—Instruction and study—Social aspects—United States. |
Music—Instruction and study—United States—History. |
Arts—Study and teaching—United States.
Classification: LCC MT3.U5 F69 2016 (print) |
LCC MT3.U5 (ebook) | DDC 780.71—dc23
LC record available at https://lccn.loc.gov/2016014890

9 8 7 6 5 4 3 2 1

Paperback printed by WebCom, Inc., Canada
Hardback printed by Bridgeport National Bindery, Inc., United States of America

For Charles—who made us pay attention to music education;
And Jay—who embodies it every day.

Contents

Foreword

CHARLES FOWLER'S VOICE of reform resounded in publications, speeches, and leadership roles over more than three decades, setting him apart as one of the most powerful advocates for arts education in the late twentieth century, whose ideas have lost none of their bracing pertinence. Grounded in music, but passionate about all the arts and committed to their role in education broadly conceived, his unsurpassed gift for articulating the perennial values of the arts in education reached a variety of audiences. Always engaging, he challenged readers to look beyond existing curricular restraints in an ongoing quest to move the arts from their peripheral status to a position of central importance in the general education of all students.

Fowler urged arts educators to direct their message not to their colleagues, but to the public. He himself modeled such action by offering reasoned arguments to school administrators that forcefully show why systemic inclusion of the arts in education makes for strong schools, and by sharing his ideas in forums beyond the arts education mainstream. He addressed his final summative work, *Strong Arts, Strong Schools*, published posthumously in 2001, to the general reader.

While *Strong Arts, Strong Schools* brings together the major themes of his career and represents his thinking during the final years of his life, this volume, *Valuing Music in Education*, culls from an earlier exposition of Fowler's principal themes: namely, his 164 essays written over 20 years as education editor of *Musical America*. Craig Resta has done an invaluable service by selecting 50 of those essays, organizing them according to the central themes of Fowler's opus, and providing critical commentary. Those themes are: music pedagogy and schooling; advocacy and arts education policy; arts, culture, and community; music education and professional reform, and; diversity and pluralism in music education. Resta's selections reflect the breadth of topics that Fowler addressed, from school to community to nation, illustrating how Fowler viewed arts education as integral to American culture, not as a separate institution. The content of the pieces also reveals Fowler as a writer whose compelling vision speaks through the decades, as fresh today as they were at the time of publication. His message is relevant in the twenty-first century, and it can inspire arts educators not to give up the fight that Fowler waged before them.

Craig Resta has engaged deeply with Charles Fowler's legacy for more than a decade. In this book he brings to light some of Fowler's important contributions to the literature on arts education, providing a contemporary sounding board for Fowler's voice of reform. Other arts educators are fortunate to have access to the Charles B. Fowler Papers held in the Special Collections in Performing Arts of the Michelle Smith Library at the University of Maryland, College Park, where Resta did his research. The wealth of materials there supports further investigation, discourse, and publication, to further extend understanding of the arts experience into the public arena.

Marie McCarthy
University of Michigan

Bruce D. Wilson
University of Maryland

Preface

IN THE PREFACE to his most notable book, *Strong Arts, Strong Schools: The Promising Potential and Shortsighted Disregard of the Arts in American Schooling*, Charles Fowler said that it was a book he wanted to write for a long time. With the present volume, I would suggest that this is a book he took a long time to write. Indeed, the articles highlighted here were his capstone work, articulating more than forty years of insight on the value of arts and music education in schools and communities.

Fowler was a prolific writer and wrote for numerous publications and outlets; *Musical America* was just one of many. The articles here, however, represent fifteen years of contribution that advocated passionately for the importance of the arts in schools, and described what was happening at the time (1974–1989). While these pieces were written decades ago, they are just as relevant today as in the 1970s and 1980s. In fact, they may be more important today than ever: we are still struggling with understandings about music and the arts, and the roles they play in schools. It is hoped this volume will provide insight to current practitioners by offering the clear and direct arguments by Fowler, and his experience. Indeed, few voices have written (or are writing today) with the depth, clarity, focus, and wisdom that Charles offered as his gift to us.

I have been researching the work of Charles Fowler since 2003. The bulk of my investigation has been a thorough, first look and analysis into his life and writings, as this had not been previously conducted. An important purpose of the research is to reacquaint the profession with Charles and his contributions, and more widely disseminate Fowler's writings and his unique and important view of music education and its possibilities. To this end, I have selected significant articles from his years at

Musical America for their unique connection to music education, and the fight to keep it vibrant in the United States. They have been organized by principal themes that relate to the content, and Fowler's beliefs and philosophical worldview. Finally, I have written introductions for each article to provide an overview, set the context, offer some analysis, and engage the reader on these topics which are so important to the profession of music teaching and learning.

During my research I have spent hundreds of hours collecting and analyzing documents—as many as 11,000+ pages during the period of my doctoral study and later work (of which this book represents a small portion). I have also conducted interviews with important scholars in the field who knew Charles and his work, received a good deal of commentary on why he was important to the field, and came away with a strong understanding of the need to promote his ideas to the current community of scholars and teachers in music education. Further, I have thought carefully about the context of the times in which he lived and worked, and reflected on his messages not only historically, but on the relevance of his writings in current times. Imagine the strength and success of our field had we actually listened those many years ago.

In this fiftieth year since the Tanglewood Symposium (1967–2017) that started the most important era of reform in the history of music education, I am of the feeling that considering Fowler and his writings is more critical than ever. Charles was right there through all of it, and kept the clarion call strongly present for another thirty years. The wealth of material available and the important and unique messages he created and promoted from the mid–1950s to the mid–1990s, is a valuable addition to the literature and the profession. It is hoped that this text will be a useful contribution to K12 music and higher education scholarship, practicing teachers in the field, and anyone interested in moving music education forward in the coming decades.

Acknowledgments

MY SINCERE GRATITUDE goes to all who have helped with this book project. No work of this magnitude could be completed by one alone, and I am most thankful to those who have contributed along the way. These include Charles Fowler, Marie McCarthy, Bruce Wilson, and Philip Moeller. Others are Jay White, Regina Carlow, Patricia Grutzmacher, Terri Brown Lenzo, Kristin Hruby, Vin Novara, and Bonnie Jo Dopp. Special thanks to Stephanie Challener and *Musical America*. Further, this project would not have been possible without the support and collaboration of the Michelle Smith Performing Arts Library, Special Collections in the Performing Arts, and Charles B. Fowler Papers, all of the University of Maryland College Park. To everyone here, and those whom I have undoubtedly missed, I appreciate your unending efforts and encouragement.

Acknowledgments

MY SINCERE GRATITUDE goes to all who have helped with this book...

VALUING MUSIC IN EDUCATION

INTRODUCTION

AN INTRODUCTION TO CHARLES FOWLER AND HIS WRITINGS

Music education advocacy has become an important tool in the development of quality K–12 music programs in the United States. While many steadfastly support the value of music in public schools, there is still a need to maintain a campaign to keep music education strong and dynamic in the curricula in American education. The benefits to children who participate in music education are addressed and debated on many levels, but the overall power of music to change the lives of children and society in a positive way is often not understood by those outside of the music education profession. An important figure who articulated the value of music in schooling is the noted music education advocate Charles Bruner Fowler (1931–1995). While he was a prolific writer on all matters musical and pedagogical, this collection represents fifteen years of his work with the well-regarded classical music publication, *Musical America*.

Before his writing at *Musical America*, Fowler spent twenty-five years of his career expressing the message that music and arts education are not only vital to the education of children in schools, but also an important component of a civilized society.[1]

---

[1] Charles Fowler, *Strong Arts, Strong Schools: The Promising Potential and Shortsighted Disregard of the Arts in American Schooling* (New York: Oxford University Press, 1996/2001); Charles Fowler, *Can We Rescue the Arts for America's Children? Coming to Our Senses–10 Years Later* (New York: American Council for the Arts, 1988); Charles Fowler, "A Reconstructionist Philosophy of Music Education" (PhD diss., Boston University, 1964).

Why, then, is the study of Charles Fowler and his writings an valuable endeavor? Few other figures can claim the distinction of working for such a large and varied number of influential organizations that represent culture and the humanities in the United States and around the world. For example, Fowler worked for the Music Educators National Conference, The Rockefeller Foundation, The Getty Center for Education in the Arts, Walt Disney Productions, Epcot Center, The Kennedy Center, Radio City Music Hall, New York Philharmonic, Metropolitan Opera, National Endowment for the Arts, National Public Radio, and later his own organization, National Cultural Resources.

During his career, Fowler published, wrote, or edited roughly 230 articles, books, and other works with publishing houses such as Oxford University Press, Musical America, McGraw-Hill, Hinshaw Music, American Council for the Arts, Music Educators National Conference (National Association for Music Education), Wadsworth Publishing, Macmillan, and several others.[2] While Fowler is lesser known today, it is evident from these lists alone that his output was prolific and valuable. Further, determining his contribution to music education in the later decades of the twentieth century is an important and timely task that is explored in this study. The content of the work is the primary focus, and various levels of analysis focus on the important messages Fowler attempted to convey through his publications and output.

Analysis involved looking at all of the articles he wrote or edited at *Musical America* (164), then narrowing the list to those he wrote (137), and finally further reducing the list to those (50) in this volume. Following extensive reading and content analysis over several years, emerging themes were considered, along with connection to the larger organizational topics included in the collection. From there, works were summarized and placed into context relative to the philosophical and pragmatic underpinnings on the value of music and arts education in school and community settings. While deciding which work to include in a collection such as this is never easy—especially when working with so much rich material—I believe that the selected articles best represent the important advocacy and educational messages that Fowler hoped to deliver to his readers, and others who needed to hear them.

While Fowler was mostly known as an advocate for music education and the other arts during his career, it is important to note the philosophical background that instilled his belief that music education could empower children to improve their lives and change the societal conditions around them. Fowler grounded his music education advocacy in a philosophy of reconstructionism, which suggested that education can be a social change agent. Through his advocacy efforts, Fowler wished to create more in-depth cultural awareness, more effective education, greater appreciation of music for its own sake, deeper aesthetic understandings, and stronger empowerment of the self, among others. For Fowler, advocacy was the mechanism by which to promote the powerful value of music in education. A strong weapon in his arsenal was his ability to

---

[2] Gale Reference Team, "Charles Bruner Fowler," *Contemporary Authors Online* (Farmington Hills, MI: Thomson and Gale, 2004).

write in a clear and succinct way. The articles collected here are excellent examples, and carry just as much weight in contemporary context as when they were first written.

A PERSONAL INTEREST

My interest in this topic stems from personal experience, and belief that the role of a music teacher is not only that of an educator who develops musical ability, but also one who advocates for the importance of music and its larger purpose in the education of a child and in the development of a civil society. I have thought for many years that music teachers, as a community of educators, have a role in articulating the power of their message to anyone who will listen. Most notably, those who most need to hear that message are generally those with the authority to influence educational policy and values: superintendents, principals, school board members, other academic teachers, community members, and parents. This message was consistently relayed by Fowler throughout his career.

Charles Fowler spent a significant portion of his career expressing why the arts are an invaluable asset to society. It seems that many of his core ideas are still not understood and appreciated in the mainstream of American education and society even in the early twenty-first century. This highlights the rationale for undertaking a study such as this, in order to clarify and classify his writings and evaluate the way he reframed the purpose of music education. The journey of research into Fowler's prolific work has informed and changed my view of music in education and the role of the arts in society.

While my representation of his unique voice will never match the power of his own writing, I have endeavored to do my best to emphasize and clarify that power throughout my analysis and commentary of his output and vision. Thus, a principal purpose of this book is to examine and reveal Charles Fowler's works that illustrate how he advocated for and valued music education, all the while echoing and pushing forward other important voices in the field. He did this consistently, reinforcing the main thesis of his work: namely, that music education has a larger purpose in schooling and society, as an agent of social change and progressive improvement.

A BIOGRAPHICAL SKETCH

In order to better understand the individual who is central to the study—Charles Fowler—a biographical sketch is useful. Based on a thorough search of related literature, limited information has been published about Fowler's life in biographical form. Two short pieces exist: an electronic biography released by Thomson and Gale Publishers,[3] and the finding aid from *The Charles Fowler Papers in the Special Collections*

---

[3] Ibid.

in the Performing Arts at the University of Maryland.[4] I have also added information based on my research into Fowler and his life, in addition to numerous conversations with those who knew and worked with him over the years.

Charles Fowler was born on May 12, 1931, in Peekskill, New York, the son of Charles and Mabel Fowler. He began college in 1948 at the State University of New York (SUNY), Potsdam, and graduated in 1952 with a Bachelor of Science in Music Education. He taught in the public schools of Rochester, New York, from 1952 to 1956, working with K–8 music students. In 1956 he began his graduate studies at Northwestern University, where he earned his Master of Music degree. He then worked as Assistant Professor of Music at Mansfield State College (now Mansfield University) from 1957 to 1962 and at the same time served as Supervisor of Vocal Music to the Mansfield Junior and Senior High Schools.[5] While his career as a writer, for which he is primarily known, did not begin until the mid-1960s, one can begin to see some of his thinking in class papers he wrote as a graduate student in the mid-1950s and early 1960s. These included a paper discussing creative approaches to preparing elementary music teachers.[6] Another example was a paper surveying principal philosophical concepts in education and music, from the Romans to the Renaissance.[7] In these papers, he began to show an interest in the broader picture of music teaching as it related to education and society in general.

In 1962, Fowler moved to Boston and began work toward a Doctor of Musical Arts (DMA) in Music Education at Boston University.[8] His doctoral dissertation, titled "A Reconstructionist Philosophy of Music Education," was completed in 1964 and offered the first full-scale glimpse into his thinking about music education as it related to society.[9] In this nearly 600-page manuscript, Fowler explored the philosophy of reconstructionism as it applied to music education. He argued for greater support and understanding of music education in the greater community and the valuable role music could play in improving society.

Once Fowler completed his doctorate, he took a position for one year at Northern Illinois University at DeKalb, where he began to work on publications that represent important early works. A principal article he prepared that year was on the poor

---

[4] Lynn Jacobsen and Bonnie Jo Dopp, *Charles Fowler Papers Finding Aid* (University of Maryland Libraries, 1999). The Finding Aid is an index of the contents found in an individual historical archive or special library collection. It generally includes scope and content, series descriptions, topical contents, a chronology, and a detailed listing of the specific documents housed within the collection of archival materials. In this case, there is also a brief biography of Charles Fowler, along with the index and list of holdings. This particular document was prepared well and aided by the fact that Fowler himself was involved in the donation of his materials to the University of Maryland Special Collections in the Performing Arts.

[5] Jacobsen and Dopp, *Charles Fowler Papers Finding Aid*; Gale Reference Team, "Charles Bruner Fowler."

[6] Charles Fowler, "Some Creative Approaches to the Musical Training of the Prospective Elementary Teacher: A Practical Guide" (unpublished manuscript, 1961).

[7] Charles Fowler, "Survey of the Main Philosophical Concepts in Education and Music from the Romans Through the Renaissance" (Class Paper from Boston University, 1962).

[8] Jacobsen and Dopp, *Charles Fowler Papers Finding Aid*; Gale Reference Team, "Charles Bruner Fowler."

[9] Charles Fowler, "A Reconstructionist Philosophy of Music Education" (PhD diss., Boston University, 1964).

quality of elementary and junior-high music textbooks commonly used in school music classes.[10] This article, which was quite controversial at the time, launched his publishing career and was influential in earning him the position of editor of the *Music Educators Journal (MEJ)* at the Music Educators National Conference (MENC). Shortly before publication of the article, Fowler received a letter from Bonnie Kowall, then editor of the *MEJ*, discussing the comments of the editorial board. In a letter to Kowall, Fowler wrote back that he was pleased with the discussion the article was creating.[11] This seems to indicate that he was not afraid to raise controversial issues if he believed they were important and contributed to the greater good of music education.

Although his primary responsibility at MENC from 1965 to 1971 was as editor-in-chief of the *Music Educators Journal,* he also published several important articles that more clearly demonstrated his interest in what we know today as music education advocacy. They included articles about the discovery method and its relevance to education[12]; another in which he argued that music education was not reacting to current trends of the time and needed to be more relevant in mainstream education[13]; and an article on aesthetic evaluation published in *The Journal of Aesthetic Education.*[14] The fact that he was now beginning to write about the arts in journals outside of his primary field of music education is indicative of his view concerning the importance of the arts in general education and society. Toward the end of his time as editor, he published "Facing the Music in Urban Education," which brought to light the issues specific to urban and minority students studying music in the late 1960s.[15]

Although many have said that the *MEJ* enjoyed some of its most productive and intellectually compelling years during Fowler's tenure,[16] in 1971 he moved on to become an independent consultant. During the years 1971 to 1973, he published two articles related to arts education. One addressed the editor as advocate and the role an editor plays in shaping the viewpoint of publications. Another was an interview he gave to the American Association of University Women (*AAUW Journal*) about the arts in American schools.[17] He also completed a brochure for the Pennsylvania Department

---

[10] Charles Fowler, "The Misrepresentation of Music: A View of Elementary and Junior High School Music Materials," *Music Educators Journal* 51 (May 1965): 38–42.

[11] Charles Fowler to Bonnie Kowall, Washington, DC, February 28, 1965, Charles Fowler Papers.

[12] Charles Fowler, "Discovery: One of the Best Ways to Teach a Musical Concept," *Musical Educators Journal* 57 (February 1970): 25–30.

[13] Charles Fowler, "Music Education: Joining the Mainstream," *Music Educators Journal* 54 (November 1967): 49–80.

[14] Charles Fowler, "Perspectivism: An Approach to Aesthetic Evaluation," *The Journal of Aesthetic Education* 2 (January 1968): 87–99.

[15] Charles Fowler, ed., "Facing the Music in Urban Education," Special Report, *Music Educators Journal* 56, no. 5 (January 1970).

[16] Craig Resta, "A Publication, an Editor, a Progressive Voice: Charles Fowler at Music Educators Journal from 1964 to 1971," *Journal of Historical Research in Music Education* 32/2 (April 2011): 145–168; Craig Resta, "Charles Fowler: An *MEJ* Editor Who Changed the Profession," *Music Educators Journal* 100, no. 2 (December 2013): 23–24.

[17] Charles Fowler, "The Arts in American Schools: A Conversation," *AAUW Journal* 66 (February 1972): 2–6.

of Education on the arts process in basic education.[18] By this time, his interest in arts education and advocacy had expanded not only to visual artists, musicians, and arts teachers, but also to those outside the field—administrators, superintendents, school board and community members, and business people, among others—who were influencing arts policy and thinking in the larger field of general education.

As a result of meeting Norman Redmon, then editor of *High Fidelity/Musical America (HiFi/MA)* in the late 1960s, Fowler considered writing a column for the magazine. This decision illustrates his desire to reach others outside of music education and expand his message to a wider audience. Several years later, in 1974, Fowler began what would become some of his most widely known work over the next fifteen years, as editor of the "On Education" column for *Musical America*.[19] (At this time, *Musical America* was published inside *High Fidelity*. Fowler wrote only for *Musical America*.)

In a note he wrote to himself around 1969, he stated that in order to be published in *Musical America (MA)* he would have to create articles that would interest readers.[20] Even though this would seem to be a given, there had been no articles or columns about education in *Musical America* before, so he realized that to create a regular segment about music in education, he must understand how to reach this audience. Fowler had determined that the way to a broader understanding and acceptance of the arts in education and general society was to reach audiences outside of arts education. Writing the arts education column for *MA* contributed to accomplishing this task.

During his time at *Musical America,* he wrote an average of ten articles a year on numerous topics relating to music education, advocacy, and its importance in the schools. He also published other important works during this time, including a follow-up text to the Arts, Education, and Americans Panel funded by the Rockefeller Foundation, titled *Coming to Our Senses: The Significance of the Arts for American Education.*[21] Fowler's book, titled *Can We Rescue the Arts for America's Schoolchildren? Coming to Our Senses— 10 Years Later,* was published in 1988.[22]

During the last six years of his life, Fowler completed two capstone works: a general music textbook titled *Music! Its Role and Importance in Our Lives,*[23] and a detailed

[18] Charles Fowler, *The Arts Process in Basic Education* (Harrisburg, PA: Pennsylvania Department of Education, 1973).

[19] Jacobsen and Dopp, *Charles Fowler Papers Finding Aid*. An editorial note about how these articles are organized in the bibliography. Given that there are fifteen years' worth of articles at the same publication almost all by Fowler, they have been listed in chronological order rather than alphabetized.

[20] Charles Fowler, Note about meeting Norman Redmon at MA regarding possible future MUED articles, July 1969, Charles Fowler Papers. Fowler had met Norman Redmon, then editor of *High Fidelity/Musical America,* and considered writing articles that would interest readers of this combined publication. This note is another instance of how Fowler was constantly thinking of how to reach a larger and broader audience.

[21] Arts, Education, and Americans Panel, *Coming to Our Senses: The Significance of the Arts for American Education* (New York: McGraw-Hill, 1977).

[22] Charles Fowler, *Can We Rescue the Arts for America's Children?*

[23] Charles Fowler, Timothy Gerber, and Vincent Lawrence, *Music! Its Role and Importance in Our Lives* (New York: Glencoe Publishers, 1994).

volume discussing the role of the arts in American education titled *Strong Arts, Strong Schools: The Promising Potential and Shortsighted Disregard of the Arts in American Schooling*, which was published posthumously.[24] On June 11, 1995, Charles Fowler died at the age of sixty-four in Washington, DC, where he had lived for much of his career, since the mid-1960s.

In addition to scholar, writer, and advocate, Fowler played many other roles during his long and productive career. He was an activist, educator, clinician, presenter, editor, advisor, speaker, and consultant to multiple arts and educational organizations. Fowler was a broad, intense thinker who relished debate and dialogue about music education and the role of the arts in society. This passion for life, discussion, and substantive change was evident in the way he lived and in the ideas he presented in his writings and other works. Fowler's love of the arts was paramount to who he was as an individual, and how his vision was portrayed to colleagues and others who encountered his work.

IMPORTANCE OF THE COLLECTION

These articles are important for several reasons. First, they address critical issues related to music education that were not only relevant during his time, but remain timely in the early twenty-first century. Second, these articles were compact, well researched, thoughtfully prepared, and powerfully written. They were addressed to all participants in the process of music education: teachers, parents, administrators, performers, community members, business leaders, arts advocates, scholars, and professors. Third, these pieces can be useful advocacy tools for the same audiences and current practitioners and supporters.

Fourth, the critical commentary provides additional background to these works and places them in a context that clarifies the benefit of their message to music and arts education. Finally, these articles have never been compiled into a single, user-friendly anthology that can provide multiple uses for various audiences and purposes. They are only available in paper form from the original publications, and only in libraries that may keep open archives of magazines dating to the 1970s or earlier. They are not available anywhere else in any thematic format, as presented here.

The intended audience is hoped to be wide and varied. Fowler was a unique figure in that he was schooled at well-regarded institutions for music education and earned his terminal degree working with one of the top scholars in the field at that time. He worked as teacher, administrator, professor, writer, editor, advocate, and consultant, at every level of education from elementary through professional. This allowed him to reach and speak with the voice of numerous populations.

---

[24] Charles Fowler, *Strong Arts, Strong Schools*.

The articles for *Musical America* were geographically and musically wide and far-reaching. Their audience was well educated and interested in the arts and music, and appreciated the value of music education in the schools. In essence, Fowler prepared pieces with scholarly rigor, a teacher-centered understanding of the issues, and in a language that layperson and specialist alike would appreciate, value, and understand.

I envision practicing teachers using this book to find relevant articles for advocacy reasons: school board presentations, parent newsletters, musical programs, and the like. I see school administrators and other school-related personnel (parents, teachers, booster-club members) finding an interest in reading about school music activities that address many success-based practices. Arts advocates and leaders can use this volume to grasp a quick view of historical tradition based on real situations in arts education, which can be used as comparison for advocacy and grant-writing efforts to support struggling programs. It is also a useful reference for university scholars interested in music and arts education to understand history and tradition, theory and practice, and internal and external views of music education as relates to current classroom music contexts.

ORGANIZATION OF THE BOOK

This text includes a select number of articles from Fowler's time at *Musical America* (for which he published a total of 164). In addition to the many pieces he wrote (137), he also edited a good number (27), and invited guest authors to write several more. The articles included in this collection are only those written solely by him, and those focused on music education and its role in education and society. Of those that he wrote, the selections here (50) have been organized into five central themes that represent important topics for Fowler, and the profession of music teaching and learning.

These themes and sections are: 1. Music Pedagogy and Schooling; 2. Advocacy and Arts Education Policy; 3. Arts, Culture, and Community; 4. Music Education and Professional Reform, and; 5. Diversity and Pluralism in Music Education. The Preface and Introduction help to set the context and history of Charles Fowler, his times, and the articles. From there, all sections are structured by topic and include brief commentary about each work, followed by the articles themselves in least to most recent order. The citation information is found in the bibliography at the end of the book, by chapter and article. This format emphasizes the equal importance of all the articles, and shows the historical patterns of Fowler's writing, thinking, and context over time.

The opening comments to the articles are intended to serve several purposes. One is to introduce the reader to the article, and in many cases, contextualize the writing. They also start the conversation in the reader's mind about the topics and content, and perhaps energize the material even further. The comments also provide ideas for additional thought, and perhaps more discussion among students, colleagues, and others. And, perhaps these commentaries will encourage the reader to pass on a particular article to a friend, allow a professor to better engage with students in a class setting, help a scholar to better group works together for additional writing, or offer material for additional research.

Further, these remarks and articles might give a parent or teacher a stronger defense in communicating with administrators or school board members, support arts advocates in their tireless efforts to promote music education in school settings, or simply help more people to understand the vital role that arts and music education can have in the development of children and communities. In all, it is hoped that these sources will be a valuable and useful addition to music education scholarship, and will promote the important message that music is a critical part of the education of all students, every school in which they study, and every community in which they live. Finally, what will your role be in promoting this noble goal, which Charles so admirably articulated at *Musical America* and in his many years as an author, educator, and advocate?

Music Pedagogy and Schooling

1

NATIONAL SURVEY OF MUSICAL PERFORMANCE

MUSICAL AMERICA 24 (August 1974)

The National Assessment of Educational Progress (NAEP) included music for the first time in 1971–1972. The construction and administration of the exam, and the involvement of the music education profession, were problematic, leading to low scores and disgruntled views. While it was important for music to be formally assessed, and perhaps considered more seriously and alongside traditional academic topics, the results and the ensuing concerns over them caused trouble for the Music Educators National Conference (MENC), practicing music teachers, and those otherwise engaged in the field. Allen Britton, then Dean of the University of Michigan School of Music, prepared a strong dissent against the administrators of the NAEP, and the design of the exam altogether. It is interesting to note that MENC was preparing national standards at the time, and perhaps the NAEP results would have differed had they been in place. Of course, national standards have changed at least twice since then, and debates over their effectiveness and implementation remain today. Assessment is presently at the forefront of music and education, and perhaps a lesson learned from 1974 could help avoid similar troubles today.

—CR

* * *

CONSIDERABLE controversy has arisen over the results, released in March, of the first national survey of music performance in the United States. The survey, based on a two-year study of a random sampling of 90,000 persons representative of the entire population, revealed that, "When it comes to over-all ability to perform musically, Americans score low."

On the surface, at least, the report of the survey couldn't have been more bleak. Some of the findings: "Fewer than 15 percent of any age group could sight-read even the simplest line of music. . . . Only one American in ten was able to repeat acceptably a simple melodic phrase. . . ."

In one part of the test participants were asked to sing a selection of their own choice. Again the results were low. "Only 20 percent of the nine-year-olds, 30 percent of the thirteen-year-olds, 25 percent of the seventeen-year-olds and 45 percent of young adults made acceptable vocal performances."

One music critic, reacting to the report, was prompted to write: "Obviously, the country is suffering from a galloping case of musical illiteracy. One is forced to conclude that there must be something radically wrong with a system of music education that produces such a disastrous result."

Instrumental performance seemingly fares no better. The report states that 25 percent of the nine-year-olds, 35 percent of the thirteen-year-olds, 25 percent of the seventeen-year-olds and 15 percent of the young adults "claimed" to play an instrument. The investigators asked this sizable group to come back with their instruments and play any selection of their own choosing. Only half were willing to demonstrate, and, of those, only half "performed an easy piece acceptably."

A DEAN DEBUNKS

Since considerable time and effort has been expended in the public schools on teaching performance skills, the report fell hard on the music education profession. But not without reaction. Music educators questioned the criteria used to distinguish the expectations of our population musically. In a letter to the National Assessment of Educational Progress, the group which conducted the survey, Allen P. Britton, dean of the School of Music at the University of Michigan, asked why a negative rather than positive approach was employed in stating the results. "Where in the world," he asked, "could you find a population in which anything like fifteen percent could sight-read even the simplest line of music? Where in the world could twenty-five percent of the nine-year-olds even think of claiming to play a musical instrument? Where in the world could even half of this number actually play a musical instrument? Where in the world could even half of that number perform an easy piece acceptably on a musical instrument?"

If Americans "scored low," Britton asked, "low in relation to what?" Music educators, at least the ones I talked to, were clearly outraged. They pointed to the present generation as the most musical in our nation's history: "Someone must be doing something right."

But if they were hurt—and they were—they also surfaced questions that probed the validity of the results. Sight reading even a simple line of music has never been acknowledged as a national goal of music education, a skill essential to every American. Only now is the National Commission on Instruction within the Music Educators National Conference readying a set of national standards for music education.

Ultimately the survey focus, with its implicit goals, refired a basic issue that has plagued music education from the beginning: How much musical skill should we logically expect of every American citizen? The spin-offs from this question are many: If, say, appreciation of music is the fundamental goal of music education, how much technical knowledge or skill is a necessary prerequisite? And if the skill to read music is accepted as a legitimate educational goal, are the taxpayers, school administrators, and other teachers, let alone the students, willing to give this goal the priority, resources, time, devotion, and energy that would be required to achieve it?

The debate will certainly wage on in the coming months, especially as the educators await the NAEP's forthcoming survey report on musical notation and terminology, instrumental and vocal media, music history and literature, and attitudes toward music.

CONTROVERSIAL VIEWPOINT

The NAEP is a project of the Education Commission of the States, a Denver-based education organization formed in 1966 "to promote cooperative action among governors, legislators and educators in improving education at all levels, preschool through postsecondary." The results of this first round of music tests are all the more provocative, since the assessment tests were devised in consultation with a group of music educators who evidently have taken a definite, though controversial, point of view in regard to the standards and goals of music education.

The NAEP, functioning under a grant from the U.S. Office of Education, has so far released assessments of science, citizenship, writing, reading, literature, and social studies. These assessments, they say, are designed "to provide education policy-makers with information on how successfully young Americans have mastered subjects traditionally emphasized in school programs, and what approaches in research and curriculum reform are likely to provide the public with full value for its education dollar." The tests, in essence, are a tool for measuring a teacher's accountability. As such, they could have a vast influence over the future course of music education. All the more reason why, if these tests are misfocused, music teachers will tend to be sharp critics of them.

2

MUSIC IN OUR SCHOOLS DAY:

AN OPPORTUNITY TO TAKE STOCK

MUSICAL AMERICA 25 (March 1975)

One of the hopes of the Music Educators National Conference (MENC) is to grow music programs in schools. (Note that MENC is now NAFME, the National Association for Music Education.) One of their more interesting ideas was put into practice in March 1975. The plan was to demonstrate what was happening musically in schools, to increase awareness and garner more public support for music education. Aspects of the program highlighted music teaching in the schools, goals and processes, student progress, musical achievement, and other measures of success. To help better understand music education and happenings in the schools, Fowler offers a broad overview of several techniques and practices common at the time. He also takes the opportunity to emphasize that more children need to be involved with music, not just the talented few. In short, Fowler espouses a wider democratic view that exposes more students, parents, schools, and communities to the benefits of musical learning.

—CR

* * *

MUSIC EDUCATORS are always trying to garner increased public support. And with good reason. Their subject is among the last to be funded and the first to be eliminated. The public often seems doggedly determined to keep the schools totally focused on the "basic" subjects, forgetting that learning is as broad as life itself.

Faced with this situation, it is no wonder that in 1966 the Music Educators National Conference, representing some 62,000 music teachers throughout the United States, became the first of the National Education Association's many affiliated organizations to hire its own public relations director. Since that time they have become increasingly astute at gaining public attention for an area of the curriculum that within the hierarchy of educational respectability is too often considered bottom rung. In the past the MENC has produced public service radio and television "spots," posters, and even bumper stickers to ask the public to "Support Music in Your Schools."

LOCAL AWARENESS

Now they have come up with an ambitious plan to bring local awareness in each community of just what constitutes music education. Borrowing an idea pioneered successfully by New York State in 1973, MENC is sponsoring a national "Music In Our Schools Day" on March 13, 1975. The idea is to focus public attention on the goals, processes, and achievements of music education in the schools. The observance will involve activities in schools and communities throughout the United States to give heightened visibility to the educational aspects of today's broad, comprehensive music program from kindergarten through the twelfth grade.

Notice that the emphasis is on the *educational* aspects of music education. Most people view music education as equatable to the band, chorus, and, if they are fortunate, the orchestra program. School performing groups, like the basketball team in physical education, are often all the public ever sees of the music education curriculum. If a community has a good band, they assume they have a good music education program. This conclusion is not altogether wrong, because a band, like a chorus or orchestra, is one product of music education. But these performing organizations simply do not tell the whole story. Not by far.

What the music educators would like to do is to give the public the opportunity to get acquainted with what actually goes on in the music classroom. They want to be able to demonstrate music teaching techniques and to show the many kinds of activities that constitute a music education program designed for every student, the lesser as well as the most talented. These "consciousness raising" activities might be a day long, or a week long, depending on the particular community. Parents and other interested persons will be invited into the schools to acquaint themselves with the day-to-day activities of music learning.

THE CHANGES

The experience should be an eye-opener. Music education, like education in other subject matters, has been quietly but profoundly changing during the past decade. It would not be exaggerating to characterize these developments as revolutionary, although most are a mix of old as well as new elements. In music education programs today, for example, there are electronic music laboratories where children compose their own music using electronic sound sources; there are guitar and piano classes; there are classroom experiences in jazz and popular music; there are new ways of teaching children to read music, one of which incorporates the techniques of Zoltan Kodály, the Hungarian composer and educator; there are violin classes using the Suzuki methods imported from Japan; there is an increased emphasis on exploring a wider range of music including the ethnic musics of the world; there are "related arts" courses that encourage students to view the arts as a vast area of human communication; there is the Carl Orff approach from Germany which uses his specially developed instruments to induce children to learn music creatively and by ear; there are programs in which music has become an integral part of much of the subject matters in the entire curriculum.

To be sure, not all of these innovative developments are ongoing in any one location, but some new approaches should be observed just about everywhere. Many of these developments arc described in a 64-page pamphlet entitled, appropriately, *The Music Revolution,* published by the American Music Conference, 150 East Huron, Chicago, Illinois 60611. It provides impressive information for parents, school administrators, and boards of education about the operation of innovative music education programs throughout the United States.

This first national "Music In Our Schools Day" has been over a year in the planning. Elaborate steps have been taken to involve the entire country. Each state has appointed a chairman; county committees have been developed; and suggestions for possible activities have been made available to every music teacher. Some schools will offer more elaborate observances than others, but activities will range from open-house demonstrations of music education in action, demonstrations of interfacing music with other subject areas, and choral and instrumental festivals, to exhibits and displays, programs by local professional groups dedicated to "music in our schools," and tributes and salutes by community leaders.

THE POWER STRUCTURE

All this brings to mind the basic question of just what constitutes support for the arts. Patronage, which is an old American tradition, is largely focused on the box office. The power structure in the arts—the boards of trustees of the nation's art centers, symphony orchestras, and opera companies, the foundations, and even the National Endowment for the Arts—looks primarily to the professional artist as the key to culture. There is even contempt for the amateur among some of these opinion leaders. Unfortunately the schools, too, often emphasize arts for the talented few. Most high school music programs, for example, only reach about twenty percent of the students, mainly those who can perform in the band, chorus, or orchestra.

This emphasis on the talented and the professional to the neglect of the audience and the amateur is a serious threat to any musical culture that would call itself vital. One can hear the loud "Hurrah!" from some professional musicians, who judge the success of music education programs solely by the success of their box office. They would make the fundamental objective of music education the development of an audience to support their enterprise. But the aims of music education cannot be defined so simply. The schools do not exist primarily to fill the opera and concert halls with satisfied and dependable auditors, or, for that matter, to provide professional musicians for American performing groups. True, they serve both these purposes, but the main goal of music education is much broader. School music programs exist essentially to bring to all people enough understanding of the vast panorama of musical communication to ensure their enjoyment of it for as long as they live.

IT'S FOR EVERYBODY

In showcasing the educational aspects of music education, "Music In Our Schools Day" is demonstrating that music can and should be for everybody, the amateur as well as the professional, the less as well as the most talented, the poor as well as the best performers. Out of the many opportunities provided, students will naturally gravitate to their own preferred tastes, their own type of involvement, and their own particular degree of commitment.

Music educators are developing musical consumers, but not as their number one priority. Robert Klotman, president-elect of the Music Educators National Conference made this point in an address to symphony orchestra members at the national conference of the American Symphony Orchestra League. He sees music educators as "broadening the base in every conceivable way to try to reach more students with more different kinds of musical experiences." Music programs have become more comprehensive, and that broadened spectrum permits "every child an opportunity to become actively involved in music-making, listening, organizing sounds, and all other forms of musical experience."

Like it or not, the American schools are democratic institutions that serve the needs of all students, and the music education program, as part of that situation, also must serve students of varying backgrounds, interests, abilities, and ambitions. That's no easy undertaking.

The future of American musical culture stirs embryonically in the public schools. Innovative programs are available to the public that wants them. Increased public support is necessary to assure that every child has the broadest possible opportunities for involvement in music. That is what "Music In Our Schools Day" on March 13 is all about.

3

THE ACCOUNTABILITY DILEMMA

MUSICAL AMERICA 26 (August 1976)

How we evaluate students in music classrooms is just as relevant in 2016 as it was in 1976. The difference of course, is that in 1976 the topic was coming to serious attention, and the profession had big decisions to make in a short period of time. Who should be assessed, and what are the best methods for assessment? What measures should be used, and who is to design them? Should teachers be evaluated on student performance, or is process as important as product? What is the role of behaviorism and psychology in testing students? Will more evaluation lead to *teaching to the test*? These and other questions are posed with directness and clarity, and one only wishes the music education profession took more heed at the time. An interesting note is that Robert Stake, longtime professor at University of Illinois and known today for his quantitative and qualitative research expertise, had just published, in 1975, a book titled *Evaluating the Arts in Education*. Would we be better off today had we read up and listened?

—CR

* * *

SHOULD MUSIC teachers, or any teachers for that matter, be held accountable for their work in the same way as a roofer, a dentist, or the manufacturer of an automobile? Are choral and instrumental directors or private music teachers responsible for stipulating results, reporting their degree of success in achieving those results, and measuring the cost effectiveness of their efforts?

Among the many people who answer such questions in the affirmative are those test-conscious parents who note with rising alarm the twelve-year-long decline in Scholastic Aptitude Test scores and the steady erosion of reading skills among American students during the past ten years. Teachers, they say, should be accountable for *results*.

A QUESTIONABLE ASSUMPTION

In a letter to the editor of *The Washington Star* a high school junior stated: "Teachers are asking for more money. What have they done to earn it? Most promotions and raises are given because of better work. Test results are down, so it follows that most teachers aren't doing their jobs."

Not everyone agrees. Teachers, after all, cannot control all the extraneous factors that influence a student's will or ability to learn, factors such as home conditioning, psychological state, and innate intelligence. The current debate, then, centers not upon *whether* the school system and its staff should be held accountable, but rather upon what basis and within what framework accountability should be determined.

While the terminology may be new, accountability has been a concern of music teachers since music teaching began. School performing groups have always demonstrated their proficiencies or lack of them to the public. Parents can usually tell whether or not their child is making adequate progress on a musical instrument. If the music teacher does not inspire interest in general music, that is known, too. Still, the accountability movement poses special dilemmas for music education.

Music educators have a built-in resistance to applying a business-management approach—MacNamara tactics—to education. Dr. Russell P. Getz, director of arts and humanities, Pennsylvania State Department of Education, questions "whether a budgeting system for the Pentagon should be adapted to the education of children." He asks, "If it worked for Ford Motor Company, will it work in public schools?" The point is that education deals with humans, not automobiles.

Achievement tests, which are the major means of assessing learning, have also been criticised as being inadequate and unfair tools in the accountability process. Standardized tests may appear to be scientific, but they are not, says Bernard H. McKenna of the National Education Association. "The College Entrance Examination Board and the Educational Testing Service are reluctant to develop alternatives to testing as long as what they have sells. To overhaul the approach is like tearing down the Ford Motor Company and creating a new kind of car." The problem, he says, is that "high schools teach what the testers test."

ARTS ARE SLIGHTED

The arts suffer in this situation because they are not considered to be of any real significance by the test manufacturers. Since the arts are given, at best, only cursory attention on standardized tests, they are, likewise, given only negligible attention in the curriculum. Inevitably, arts teachers are left in a position of having to construct their own tests, no easy task considering the nature of these subjects. It is one thing to measure factual knowledge or familiarity with basic concepts (quantitative factors) and quite another to measure aesthetic sensitivity, expressive ability, creative development, or musical attitudes, preference, and values (qualitative factors). In music, not only thinking and doing, but *feeling* is important. Those areas—the so-called "affective domain"—are difficult, if not impossible, to measure. Yet they constitute centrally important and often unique learning areas in the arts.

But accountability is far more than just tests. It is responsibility for achieving results. Dr. Leon M. Lessinger, a leader in the accountability movement, points to the important change in attitude accountability brings to the process of instruction: "If the students do not learn, if the instructional system does not attain the objectives set for it, the system is reworked and redesigned until it does. That may mean looking at the methods, the training, the materials, the support; the object is to get where you want to go. . . . The instructional system's job is to achieve specified learning, and if it does not meet expectations, it is changed and rechecked until it does."

The accountability movement began in the U.S. Office of Education in 1969 as a result of the American people's concern for the improvement of education for the poor and disadvantaged, who were not properly being served by the school system. It has resulted in teachers paying considerably more attention to objectives and to the behavioral changes that signify when learning has taken place. During the 1970s music teachers throughout the United States have industriously revised their curricular strategies, setting up "behavioral objectives" and carefully planning the activities that could achieve the desired ends.

BEHAVIORISTIC PSYCHOLOGY

Behavioristic psychology, which has overtaken the schools and the accountability movement, has been eagerly embraced and applied with a passion to music education. No matter that in its very essence it is hostile to the idea of individual freedom and self-determination. The foremost proponent of behaviorism, Harvard psychologist B.F. Skinner, believes that freedom must be replaced with control over man, his conduct, and his culture. In his book, *Beyond Freedom and Dignity*, Skinner states that the idea that man is autonomous, that by his own free will he initiates, originates, and creates, is mistaken. Such acts are conditioned by environment.

The Skinnerian idea of psychological predestination rules out any belief in the possibility of inner, willful choice. The approach is incompatible with spontaneous action, improvisation, and discovery. Human behavior is shaped by reinforcement—rewards—and by "aversive conditioning"—lack of reward or punishment. Skinner admits to not being able to identify the contingent reinforcements that act upon the human being to produce a musical creation, but he says that doesn't mean they aren't there or that they won't be identified by scientists someday.

It is precisely in such areas that arts educators have felt frustrated by the behavioral approach. Teachers can presume to arrange environments favorable to creativity, or developing appreciation, or experiencing the emotional charge of the artistic experience, but how can they be certain they are on the right track and how can they measure the real effects of such experiences on every student? The science of behaviorism is still too imprecise in the affective realms.

Music teachers have been slow to reconcile themselves to these limitations. They have felt constrained to adopt behavioristic methodologies like other teachers, not realizing that the nature of their subject, unlike science or mathematics, is fundamentally tied to those very areas not yet fully explored or proven in behaviorist theory. Their mistake has been that they have begun to teach only what they can test, with the result that they have tended to slight the affective areas. They have met public and administrative pressures to be accountable by distorting their art, making it conform to a system that cannot accommodate the whole of what music learning is about. The fact is that behavioral objectives and measurement techniques cannot as yet be formulated for matters of the spirit, appreciation, or feelings. This is not to say that behavioral objectives are useless. They may be fine for planning, carrying out, and measuring the learning of factual knowledge, technical ability, and certain concrete musical concepts. The flaw is not in accountability, but in the limitations of the notion that everything taught must be couched in terms of behavioral objectives.

GOOD PRACTICE

The answer to the problem lies, as Lessinger suggests, in recognizing that accountability must focus more upon good practice than upon outcomes. Music teachers must be responsible more for their performance than results. It is the teacher's responsibility to teach and the learner's responsibility to learn. Teachers are mistaken when they usurp responsibility which is not rightfully theirs. Music teachers are responsible for the consequences of their actions primarily in terms of the objectives they pursue, the methodologies and materials they employ, and the environment they create to induce learning. To accept trivial and inadequate objectives because of the limitations of measurement techniques is simply a sign of a bankrupt imagination.

As an alternative to objective achievement tests, Robert Stake, in his brief book *Evaluating the Arts in Education* (Charles E. Merrill, 1975), describes "a responsive approach" to evaluation which is more subjective and relies on observation. This approach orients more directly to program activities than to program intents. It determines a program's merits and shortcomings while taking into account the fact that the value of a music program will be different for different people for different purposes.

Accountability, it should be remembered, is not married to behavioral objectives, nor to assembly-line learning sequences. The spine-tingling experience of music is educational in and of itself. The same holds true for the creative act. Who is to say what these experiences mean for the individual or how they will affect behavior?

Perhaps arts teachers should take a cue from humanistic psychology and supplement their list of behavioral objectives with another devoted to perceptual objectives covering those internal experiences in the realms of feelings, values, attitudes, personal meanings, and creativity that are not open to direct investigation at present, but which lie at the center of aesthetic experience. In any case, music teachers are responsible for providing educational experiences which provoke or reveal these aspects, and school programs should be held accountable for including them in the education of every child.

4

ARTS IN THE SCHOOLS: A COMPREHENSIVE VIEW

MUSICAL AMERICA 31 (December 1981)

A book edited by Jerome Hausman called *Arts and the Schools* is the focus here. Hausman presented a fairly comprehensive look at how music and the arts can be, and are, incorporated into school settings. The contributors are notable for being well-known scholars, such as John Goodlad, Howard Gardner, Jack Morrison, Dennis Wolf, and even Bennett Reimer. Readers familiar with music education scholarship may find Fowler's review of Reimer's viewpoints quite interesting— turns out not all music education advocates and writers agree on everything! For those who are debating the important role of music in our schools, and how arts education can benefit children, this should be an interesting read. I suspect, too, it may help strengthen your own current arguments about the critically valuable nature of music teaching and learning.

—CR

* * *

ONLY OCCASIONALLY does a book cross my desk that warrants wide attention. *Arts and the Schools,* edited by Jerome J. Hausman (New York: McGraw-Hill Book Company) is such a volume. This work addresses the issue of the arts in public education from an all-arts point of view, and there is much to be gained by this collaborative approach.

The work represents a cooperative, broadly wrought outlook which, in the concerted effort of its authors, exemplifies the idea that the arts can—and should be—treated as a comprehensive area of the curriculum, just like the sciences. This is all the more remarkable since each author is an expert in a particular discrete arts discipline. Given the bigness of view, which is both sensible and stimulating, the impact of this study can be as great for the educator in music as for the teacher in any other art.

HUMAN GROWTH

The viewpoint here is grounded in humanism and developmental psychology—how the arts in education can contribute to human growth. John Goodlad and Jack Morrison set forth a rationale for the arts in education: "While the arts have contributions to make to the learning of fundamental skills, vocational preparation, and social responsibility, it is in the interpretation of life experiences and continuous reconstruction of the self that they come into their own." They maintain that "It is virtually impossible for individuals to develop in whole and healthy fashion without the arts and aesthetics playing a part."

This first chapter presents compelling arguments in support of arts education, arguments that are stronger for being focused on *all* the art forms.

In the second chapter, Jerome J. Hausman, editor of the volume, presents a view of arts education from the perspective of contemporary arts. He traces the explosion of expressive forms and styles of arts in the modern period and draws implications for arts education. "The lesson being taught us by the artists of our own day," he says, "is that the very 'ground rules' for what constitutes 'art' have undergone change. There must be a similar opening-up of possibilities for students who learn about and experience the arts in school." He maintains that there should be a balance of emphasis between the past and the contemporary and that the latter requires arts education to be "conceived and carried out in a larger and more flexible setting."

ARTISTIC EVOLUTION

In an extraordinary exposition of the stages of artistic growth, Dennie Wolf and Howard Gardner complement Housman's account with a view of arts education from the perspective of developmental psychology. I have heard Gardner talk about his findings as co-director of Harvard's Project Zero on more than one occasion and have been both amazed and perplexed; I find this account refreshingly simple and concise, though as the authors admit, one "drawn with excessive sharpness."

Wolf and Gardner explain what every artist knows to be true, that creativity is both inspired and reasoned—both subjectively imaginative and objectively technical. But they articulate the stages the child goes through to attain this ultimate integration, and they dovetail these insights with education in a way that is both revealing and useful.

In the early years, for example, they recommend "giving free rein to natural tendencies," while in middle childhood, "a more active type of instruction or intervention may be desirable; not rigid exercises but rather situations which give the child tools and techniques..."

I have only one minor reservation. The authors tell us that it is in adolescence that some children have difficulty meeting their own standards and require help to accept their own limitations and continue to forge ahead. I question whether such a condition should be limited to adolescence, and suggest that the authors might find justification for indicating levels of artistic development that extend into adulthood. For example: risk-taking—the need to live vibrantly rather than merely safely—is a lesson that the true artist understands, but one that may not be learned during adolescence.

From here on the book gets down to the practical matters of classroom practice (Chapter 4), designing effective arts programs (Chapter 5), and developing productive community/school relationships (Chapter 6), all of which relate to the fundamentals of human psychology set forth earlier. A final chapter by Goodlad explains the strategies involved in matching "the rhetoric of promise and the reality of performance in arts education."

Obviously the authors spent considerable effort working together to assure that they were on the same wave length. The chapters are complementary and proceed logically, each building on the one before until a kind of universe of arts education is achieved.

A JARRING NOTE

I must mention a particularly jarring note in this otherwise consistent presentation. In his explanation of the "three major modes" of programming—"(1) autonomous arts study; (2) interdisciplinary arts study; and (3) arts study that is integrated within the general curriculum"—Bennett Reimer assumes an either/or stance that runs counter to the comprehensive view set forth in the rest of the book.

Speaking of the "mode" that infuses the arts into general education, Reimer says, "It is unreasonable to expect it to fill all the needs of aesthetic education." I would argue that none of the proponents of that particular approach ever intended it to do so. As a matter of fact, I believe that it is just as unreasonable to expect discrete arts programs to satisfy all those needs, let alone interdisciplinary study. In my view, none of these "modes" should constitute the whole of an arts program in the public schools but, rather, they should be thought of as worthy parts or components of a total—comprehensive—arts education program.

Nor do I see the value in Reimer's treatise against innovation: "What the field of aesthetic education needs most of all is not 'innovation' but full-scale implementation of program elements that are fairly well accepted as proven..." Reimer's fellow authors seem to take exception to this view, as well. Goodlad, for example, says that arts education programs "require much more than mere improvement on what already exists" (p. 229), and "What we are talking about . . . is rather fundamentally changing an institution. . . . There simply is no way of implementing what is required in arts education without affecting and infecting the entire social system of the school" (p. 221).

From my point of view, educators do not need to be given the message to be wary of innovation. The stagnation of much that is called education—at every level—would seem to point to the need for educators to learn to take the risks of trying to operate in innovative ways.

CONCRETE EXAMPLES

But one of the joys of this book, Reimer notwithstanding, are the many concrete examples of innovative programs that are described. Most of the important points made in the course of the lively theoretical discussions are immediately illustrated through brief case studies that take the reader into schools all across the country.

Given these reservations which are modest considering the whole, the book provides an exceptional overview of the arts education field from a humanistic point of view. It is essentially a blueprint for educational change with arts education as the focus. It would make an excellent text for college students studying to be arts educators and is highly recommended reading for administrators, curriculum specialists, members of boards of education, arts teachers, and interested parents.

One wonders how such a humanistic approach will fare now that the Moral Majority has declared war on secular humanism with particular focus on what they consider to be the pervasive influence of humanism in the public schools. But perhaps we can take assurance from the fact that this book and the effort behind it demonstrate that the arts are beginning to pull together, for with that union they will have greater power and wherewithal to withstand such onslaughts now and in the future.

5

HIGH SCHOOLS OF THE ARTS

MUSICAL AMERICA 32 (March 1982)

Specialized schools for students in music and the visual and performing arts are cause for celebration and debate. Which students should have the opportunity to study at such schools? What is their role in school systems? Will artistic and creative students be removed from other schools? What about students who wish to participate, but have programs removed because a magnet school is in their district? Is a career in music or the arts viable, and if not, is an arts high school a responsible choice? These and related questions are explored here, with voices from those working in these schools represented. Several nationally notable schools and their teachers or administrators are highlighted, and some interesting information is revealed. At the time when Fowler wrote this, approximately sixty-five schools around the United States focused on arts education. It would be an interesting question to see how students, parents, and teachers feel about arts high schools today.

—CR

* * *

SINCE NEW YORK CITY opened its High School of Music and Art in 1948, similar schools have sprung up in cities throughout the country, particularly during the past decade. The growing numbers of these schools could have a significant impact on the arts.

At a meeting of the Mid-Atlantic Chapter of the American Theatre Association at Essex Community College near Baltimore last October, theater teachers held an open discussion with representatives from four high schools of the arts. While the discussion focused on theater, the questions and replies have implications for all the arts.

A teacher from the Baltimore School of the Arts (opened in December 1980) raised the question of whether these schools are glutting an already glutted market. "Are we assuming," he asked, "that the more we train people in theater, the more that field will expand?"

"Theater constantly eats people up," Marjorie Dycke replied. "They continually need new faces." As director emeritus of New York City's High School of Performing Arts, she made no apologies for the fact that many of the theater majors did not go on in that field. "Theater training makes you a human being," she declared with the strong inference that what is learned in theater can be applied in any number of ways in any number of fields.

Maurice G. Eldridge, principal/director of the Duke Ellington School of the Arts in Washington, D.C. (begun in 1974), took another view: "Schools of the Arts have a responsibility to audience development," he said, "so the students who do not choose to go on become the educated audience that provides employment to other artists." He noted that "Many of the parents of these students also become more interested in the arts."

INTENSE PROGRAM

These schools provide talented students who have aspirations for careers in the arts with an intense program of professional training. Some of the high schools, like New York's, require auditions before students are selected for admittance. Dr. William Tribby, dean of general studies at the North Carolina School of the Arts in Winston-Salem (founded in 1965), explained that each art area has its own requirements for audition spelled out in the school's catalogue. "[Students] must show artistic talent, then, secondarily, academic ability and good behavior. We don't look for talent alone but for potential." Students are permitted to remain in the program as long as they show progress. Each music student has a jury at the end of every semester, after which some are dropped. But in drama, it takes the faculty two years to find out whether a student has potential. At that time, about fifty percent of the students are asked not to continue. The difference between music and theater is due to the stronger background of preparation in music students, particularly among those who have taken years of instrumental lessons.

David Simon, director of Baltimore's School of the Arts, felt that the selection process depended upon having a fine professional staff. "They will know what to look for," he said. In the case of ballet, he explained, the thirteen-year-old must have some preliminary training. But this is not the case for those who aspire to go into modern dance. In music, instrumental training is more critical than vocal background.

The audition process is handled differently at the Duke Ellington School. "Many students," Eldridge stated, "are not able to prepare for an audition. We try to discover artistic potential in spite of that. Even in music, we take some students who haven't had any training. After a year, we look for commitment. Many of our students cannot afford lessons, so we give them time to show their potential. They are subject to many demands once we take them."

PARENTAL DOUBTS

Eldridge lamented the fact that there are parents who don't see the arts as a way to make a living. He spoke of one student with real promise as a symphony musician who was persuaded by his parents not to continue in the school. They felt that the risk was just too great. All high schools of the arts have to understand that the commitment to a career in the arts may not be as set among high school students as it is for those at the college level.

When the arts school drains away the best talent from all the other high schools, what is the effect on those schools? Simon saw an immediate connection between this question and why these schools came into existence in the first place. "It goes back to the type of arts education high schools have been providing." The superintendent of schools in Baltimore answered the question by saying, "Those schools had a long time to do something about the kind of arts education they were offering to talented students; they never did anything."

Eldridge acknowledged that "people fight over the talented students." But eventually, he believes, every high school will have a special program. There will be magnet schools in every field. Dycke said that there are many students with fine artistic talent that do not choose to go into the arts or, therefore, to attend a high school of the arts. All of this talent is left in the other high schools.

CAREERS ACHIEVED

The real value of these arts schools can be measured in terms of what students do with their careers. Both the New York and Winston-Salem schools have well-established track records to show that large numbers of their graduates have gone on to be successful, established artists. The Baltimore and Washington schools are too young for that, but seventy-five to eighty percent of graduates from the Duke Ellington School go on to higher education, compared with fifty percent from the other high schools.

"Numbers of students have gone on to college who might not have, if they hadn't gone to Ellington," Eldridge claims. "At Ellington students gain a new self concept.

They discover that they have talent and that they can believe in themselves. They feel special just to have been admitted. Then they strive to live up to it. They have to earn staying in the school. They have to learn to produce." He recognizes that being a small school (435 students) helps. There is more individual attention, more caring. "Urban education itself," Eldridge says, "would be far more effective if schools were smaller."

Perhaps such schools, with their focused programs that permit students to delve in depth into an area that interests them, can serve as a model for the restructuring of all high school programs. North Carolina evidently thinks so. It has just opened a High School of Mathematics and Science in Durham.

The fact remains that, with sixty to seventy of these schools, already in existence in the United States, high schools of the arts are providing talented students with the opportunity to develop that talent with a career as a goal. Many school systems simply cannot afford to offer in-depth theater, dance, music, and visual arts programs in every high school, but they can manage, usually with the help of some outside funding, to provide them in one. In this sense, then, the high school of the arts represents an economic solution assuring that the talent of the younger generation of Americans is developed.

6

MUSICAL ACHIEVEMENT: GOOD NEWS & BAD

MUSICAL AMERICA 32 (May 1982)

In 1978–1979, the second National Assessment of Educational Progress was administered. While the *New York Times* did not present it as a rousing success, there was reason to be pleased with the results. More students mentioned valuing the arts, and understood better the role of music education in the schools. Another promising outcome was that students who participated in the arts showed better aptitude, and especially over a longer period of time. It was also reported that roughly 75 percent of high school students were involved in music classes of some sort. While there were still concerns about and struggles by some students relative to general understandings of music and performance, overall the results were stronger than they had been in 1972. One expert interviewed for the article mentioned that more offerings outside of traditional performance opportunities would be helpful for students. It seems this remains the case today—will we ever listen?

—CR

* * *

"STUDENTS' KNOWLEDGE of Arts Found to Decline" stated the headline in the *New York Times*. But that headline did not convey the substance of the second national music assessment of elementary and secondary school students conducted by the National Assessment of Education Progress, the Federal Government's program to monitor the nation's public schools. In truth, the news is neither as bad as one might fear nor as good as one might hope.

THE GOOD NEWS

Nearly three-fourths of students at each age level (nine, thirteen, and seventeen—age levels that mark the end of primary, intermediate, and secondary education) value music as an important realm of human experience. As the report states, "These results are indicative of a fairly high degree of awareness of and sensitivity to music and musical experiences by American youth."

The report also provides some proof that the nation's music educators are doing something right. Those thirteen- and seventeen-year-olds who had participated in school musical activities and classes performed better than students who had not. Moreover, longer participation produced greater achievement. For example: achievement results are twelve to thirteen percentage points different between students who had no band or orchestra and those who had at least three years of participation in this activity. The same holds true for students who participated in choir or glee club, although there are just six to nine percentage points difference between those who participated and those who did not.

Now you might say that these kinds of results are what might—should—be expected. But these tests measured not only how students value music and their ability to perform it, but also their ability to create music and to identify its elements and expressive controls (requiring them to demonstrate knowledge and understanding of such things as rhythm, pitch, and tone quality while hearing a musical selection), as well as their ability to identify and classify music historically and culturally. Evidently performance classes are teaching far more than just technique. That really is good news.

I was also pleased to see that the majority of American students have been exposed to music in school. Among nine-year-olds, eighty-four percent nationally report being taught music in school during the 1978–79 school year, the year the assessment was administered. Seventy-two percent of thirteen-year-olds and eighty-two percent of the seventeen-year-olds have taken a class in general music or music appreciation. In addition, about a third of the junior and senior high school students report that they have participated in a vocal or instrumental music group for at least a year.

THE BAD NEWS

A comparison of this assessment with the previous one conducted in 1971–72 revealed that nine- and seventeen-year-olds "declined significantly" in the interim, while thirteen-year-olds showed no significant change. In interpreting these changes in musical achievement, Dr. Diana V. Owen, an independent music education specialist from Denton, Texas, said, "I am disappointed, but not surprised, that there was a decline for the nine- and seventeen-year-olds. The formal music education experience for these two age groups is noticeably lacking. Thirteen-year-olds across the nation would have had the most opportunities for formal music education experience."

The decline can be explained not by what goes on in music classes but by the lack of such classes in many schools. The report shows that these two age groups suffered their greatest losses on the tests about musical elements. A comparison of thirteen- and seventeen-year olds in this area reveals little or no gain during the high school years. For example, the exercises measuring the understanding of a variety of musical terms and expression markings showed that slightly fewer seventeen-year-olds (forty-eight percent) than thirteen-year-olds (fifty percent) were successful in their answers. "One would hope to see more seventeen- than thirteen-year-olds with this kind of knowledge," observed Dr. Richard M. Graham of the University of Georgia, another interpreter of the results.

As Graham reasoned, "The fact that a greater number of thirteen-year-olds than seventeen-year-old demonstrated understanding of these musical concepts points out the clear need for additional music education opportunities in the nation's high schools—opportunities that are as attractive as our performing groups but which may not require extensive performing skills."

Older students also showed poor results in being able to identify and classify music historically and culturally. In one part of this test, for example, forty exercises required students to identify and describe the music and musical style of various stylistic periods in Western civilization.

Only twenty-six percent of thirteen-year-olds and thirty-two percent of seventeen-year-olds were successful. Although senior high school students did better than those in junior high, the interpreters were concerned that less than one-third of the seventeen-year-olds responded correctly. Again, these results show, as Dr. Owen points out, that "There are very few high schools across the nation that offer a course in music history where students could attain that type of specific knowledge of music history."

THE IMPLICATIONS

"It would be wonderful," Owen said, "if high school students could have their choice of music classes—music appreciation, music theory and history—in addition to the performing classes. Currently, students are offered only the performing experiences, and these are not at the beginning level. Very few high schools offer a beginning course in instrumental music."

Although they support a diversity of course offerings in music at the secondary level, the interpreters lamented the fact that instrumental music experiences are available to so few students generally, and to so few beginners on the high school level. The assessment shows that students in band and orchestra programs did better on all aspects of the test than students who had only general music, choir, or an introduction to <ill/> course.

It may be that some of the decline in scores during the seven years between the assessments is due to cutbacks in school music budgets which affect the number of required and elective courses in music that are offered, particularly at the school level. Roy H. Forbes, director of the National Assessment, commented, "I believe that the data and the statements of the interpretive panelists demonstrate a strong contradiction in our nation. As a society, we value art and music and place importance on them. Yet we provide very little opportunity for students to receive formal, structured education in either area—other than perhaps at the senior high school level. If we are serious about art and music being goals of our educational system, then we must create more opportunities for students to learn about them."

The report also shows the part that socioeconomic and background factors play. Students with at least one parent having some education beyond high school and those who attend schools in economically advantaged urban areas are above national levels. Conversely, students living in the Southeast, those attending schools in disadvantaged urban areas, and those whose parents have less than a high school education are below the nation. Girls outshine boys in music at all three age levels.

7

A LOOK INTO THE CRYSTAL BALL

MUSICAL AMERICA 34 (January 1984)

In July 1983, the Eastman School of Music sponsored a conference titled "The Future of Musical Education in America." The meeting was designed to look seriously at music teaching and learning in the United States, and to consider how to improve the future of the field. While Eastman and MENC both issued reports, Fowler here offers incisive and nuanced analysis based on his decades of experience in the profession, as both insider and outsider. Many important names were represented at the conference, including Charles Leonhard, Russell Getz, Robert Freeman, Christopher Lasch, Frank Hodsoll, and others. In short, major themes were the value of music, significance in education, looking inward and outward, connecting music better with curricular goals, the role of creativity, and the competing interests of performance and pedagogy, among others. If one wished for a good overview of music education advocacy and purpose in the early 1980s, this summary outlines it in thorough measure. In addition to the compelling discussion, separating out the names and topics would provide interested readers with plenty more research to keep them occupied.

—CR

* * *

"THE FUTURE of Musical Education in America" was the title of a provocative and broad-ranging national conference held at the Eastman School of Music in Rochester, New York in July 1983. Sponsored by Eastman's music education department along with the Music Educators National Conference and dedicated to the memory of Howard Hanson, founder and first director of the school, the conference called upon a diverse group of speakers and discussion group leaders to sort through the major issues facing music education today with the help of 120 participants attending from all over the United States.

The fortuitous timing of the meeting, coming as it did right after the release of four major national reports calling for radical educational reform [see this column in November and December 1983], added a special urgency and intensity to the deliberations.

Since both Eastman and MENC will issue reports on the conference, I have chosen here to offer some highlights together with my own impressions and interpretations. People did not drift in and out of this conference as is usually the case. Everyone attended each of the seven major presentations, then broke into small groups to discuss the issues that had been raised. Responses ranged across the width and breadth of music education and, deliberately, no attempt was made to reach a consensus.

However, through the myriad of words and ideas, certain issues emerged and re-emerged with enough frequency to call them to special attention. These, it seems to this observer, are the problem areas that most plague music education today.

TWO PURPOSES

It struck me in the aftermath of the conference that, though unspoken as such, there are really two fundamental purposes to which the music education profession addresses itself: to make music (1) a vital and valued art in American society, and (2) a significant force in American education. The obstacles to our achieving these purposes were well defined and documented by the major speakers and the possible solutions thoughtfully proposed and seriously discussed by both the speakers and conference participants.

In light of all the anguish unleashed at this meeting, it is apparent that the music field, at least at this juncture, is almost unanimous in looking to its own practice rather than to outside forces as the direct cause of most of its own failures in attaining these purposes. This has not always been the case, and I think such self analysis and professional soul-searching marks a new willingness on the part of music educators to consider the necessary personal and professional changes—some painful—that must be undertaken.

If the Tanglewood Symposium of 1967 was an assessment of the profession in view of the changing times, Eastman was an assessment arising from a sense of frustration. Tanglewood generally looked outward; Eastman, inward.

GETTING OUR ACT TOGETHER

Russell Getz, president of the MENC, pointed out that the root problem is factional bickering and the splintering of the profession, what Robert Freeman, director of the Eastman School, referred to as music's isolated "islands." The theme was reiterated by Charles Leonhard, professor of music education at the University of Illinois, who spoke of "the divisiveness and competition that divide us." In this regard, Leonhard called for a "common cause for the arts"—a phrase, I think, that sums up the emotional message, if not the intellectual content, of this conference.

And what of the role of music education in assuring that music is a vital and valued art in American society? Christopher Lasch, author of *The Culture of Narcissism*, asked the question: "How does it happen that the great tradition of Western music still remains so little understood and appreciated in this country?" His answer:

> "The crisis of high culture is not so much an American issue as a twentieth-century issue.... If we look at the situation of contemporary music as a whole, what strikes us most forcibly is not the vitality of European music as compared to American music; what strikes us is the hostility of audiences to modern music, in Europe just as in the United States; the self-conscious, self-referential, and academic quality of most of the music now being written; and the endless recycling of masterpieces composed in the eighteenth and nineteenth centuries. The musical tradition in Europe has become as custodial in its orientation as the American tradition."

BROADENING THE RANGE

That term "custodial" got bandied about a good bit. The idea that music education deals largely with relics was amplified by Leonhard:

> "The failure of public school and college music programs to initiate music students and general students into music other than the standard repertory has resulted in a level of conservatism in the preferences of the broad music audience that is not characteristic of audiences for the other arts."

The crisis of music education, Lasch believes, derives "from its attempt to disseminate a tradition that no longer has much life." If classical music has become a dead language, then music teachers, like their Latin counterparts, will have to "save it from academic extinction."

Along this same line of reasoning, Sydney Hodkinson, an Eastman composer and professor of conducting and ensembles, decried the lack of audience for twentieth-century music. But for him, maintaining the vitality of music in society is not just linked to enlarging the repertoire. "Although," he says, "we now have hundreds—probably thousands—of fine school bands, orchestras, and choruses in our land, are their members allowed any *real* insights into the workings of the creative imagination?"

CREATIVITY

For Hodkinson, the way to keep the language of music alive in our society is to make it more creative. He says, "In music, unlike sculpting, writing, and visual arts classes, our practice of performance—*re*-creating, not creating—does not enhance comprehension of the *imagination* one whit! We need to instill *creative* concepts, not only the *re*-creative skills."

But Hodkinson was not alone in calling for more creative emphasis. Willard L. Boyd, president of the Field Museum of Natural History, was on the same wave-length. He began his presentation by declaring: "Our future depends upon our creativity.... As our physical resources become less plentiful, we must rely more heavily on human resources—our creative selves." He called artistic creativity "the moving force in arts education." Pre-service training for arts specialists for the schools, he said, "should emphasize artistic creativity."

INTEGRATING ART AND LIFE

If creativity and broadening the repertoire are ways to bring greater life and meaning to music, Lasch felt that its value to society also depends upon achieving "a new integration between art and everyday life." He says:

> "The democratization of leisure has not democratized the consumption of high culture, and even if it had, the creation of a broader audience for the arts would not restore the connections between art and everyday life, on which the vitality of art depends. Works of art, as Dewey put it, 'idealize qualities found in common experience.' When they lose touch with common experience, they become hermetic and self-referential, obsessed with originality at the expense of communicability, increasingly indifferent to anything beyond the artist's private, subjective, and idiosyncratic perception of reality."

Personally, I don't see any conflict in all these modes of thinking—but rather their complementarity. To keep music vital and valued, music education must strive to make it a language of self—not selfish—expression, a language that once again communicates, and does so for people now, in our own time. The universities, as the twentieth-century benefactors of artists, have encouraged an ivory-tower world cut off from the mainstream civilization. As Freeman reminds us: "In the modern American university, the principal support of the 'serious' American composer, neither the *cognoscenti* nor the people are allowed to judge, but rather the composers themselves. This insular tendency may be good for academic governance, but I do not believe that it well serves the broader interests of music."

The protected, salaried, and status-guaranteed existence of university-subsidized artists assures an independence that allows them to be indifferent to reaching a more public market on which their livelihood would otherwise have to depend. But, then, when Italian opera became so stodgy a vehicle that even the English elite were repelled, a new form arose—exemplified by *The Beggar's Opera*—to replace and reform it. So, perhaps what we are witnessing now is the transition of music from an elitist to a more populist art, and music education has great stakes and responsibilities in that transition.

But this conference gave equal stress to the second fundamental purpose of music education—to make music a significant force in American education. The fact that most conference participants represented college and university music departments and public school music programs largely precluded discussions that ranged beyond those institutions to efforts outside—the work of private music teachers, independent schools of the arts, and the educational programs of opera companies and symphony orchestras. But the conferees were eager to take a hard and critical look at their own areas.

DEVELOPING AUDIENCES

In his opening address to the convention, Frank Hodsoll, Chairman of the National Endowment for the Arts, called the state of arts education "inadequate." He noted Andre Watts' Congressional testimony in which he declared that we are raising a generation of children to whom music is an elective, a frill. "As our conservatories produce better and better musicians, our schools produce more and more ignorant audiences," Hodsoll said.

Of course, for years, music educators have talked about reaching "the other eighty-five percent"—those high school students who receive little or no instruction in the arts. Here the rhetoric of "music for every child" far exceeds the actuality. While Getz acknowledged that serving the fifteen percent simply didn't answer the need for developing audiences, he expressed concern for how to involve the others and asked if, indeed, we can handle them. But there was no doubt expressed about the need to try. Nurturing an audience for music was urged by Hodkinson, who advised the field to "back off from developing electives for only those students who *already* have strong musical backgrounds; we can cease favoring the talented at the expense of the general school population." Leonhard, too, called for music departments in colleges and universities to assume "an essential role—the musical education of the general college student."

QUALITY

Hodkinson indicted music education programs in the schools for their use of trivial, banal, "educational" music rather than music "of all styles, forms, and cultures" as MENC has advocated. Getz agreed that "we must encourage a broader view by emphasizing the performance of both folk and composed music of our own and other countries." But he went much further, citing Ed Gordon's research, which found that the most important period for musical talent development is from birth to age nine. Greater individualized attention to this period, Getz reasons, would permit "all students to proceed far beyond present musical levels."

To attain higher quality programs, Getz also called for the profession:

- To scrutinize music programs based upon competition and take a position on this issue.
- To make music classes at the high school level comparable to the standards of the present Advanced Placement Program.
- To better design and plan general music classes for greater participation and learning.
- To make performing groups meet more demanding standards of a planned course of study.
- To de-emphasize music as entertainment, where school groups are utilized as public relations functionaries.
- To recognize that ninety-seven percent of those who graduate with music degrees eventually teach and, accordingly, to redesign a unified undergraduate degree program for everyone.

Boyd gave considerable attention to improving the training of arts specialists, artists ("all artists teach"), elementary school teachers ("so that they can bring aesthetic awareness to the general class"), and teachers and volunteers in cultural institutions ("educational institutions are cultural and cultural institutions are educational").

CIRCULARITY

But if anyone took the profession to task, it was Leonhard. I've heard a number of thoughtful presentations by him over the years, but his Eastman address was unique in pointing the finger at his own area—the collegiate institutions—as the main cause of the problems that beset music education today. He spoke of the "vicious circle" of programs that repeat each other at every level. "Any limitations in the preparation of music teachers," he said, "are inevitably passed on to the students of those teachers." He believes that this crippling cycle must be broken at the college level and that it is up to them to make the break and step out of the mold.

He spoke against the "homogeneity of college music programs" and attacked the National Association of Schools of Music, the sacred accrediting agency, for aiding and abetting every school and department of music "to assume the roles of music programs in the conservatory tradition, the liberal arts tradition, and the teachers college tradition regardless of the quality and extent of its resources." He observes:

> "Small departments emulate large ones; mediocre departments emulate distinguished ones. As a result, thousands of music students have been graduated with inferior undergraduate and graduate degrees in applied music and composition (the conservatory tradition), in music history and theory (the liberal arts tradition), and in music teacher education (the teachers college tradition).

And he asks: "How many mediocre pianists does the country really need?"

To end this "stultifying homegeneity," Leonhard recommends that "Institutions emphasizing the conservatory tradition [should] be limited to schools with musical resources comparable to those found at Eastman, Juilliard, and a few of the megauniversities. A few such programs of high quality," he says, "can prepare a sufficient number of concert artists, symphony players, opera singers, composers, and conductors to fulfill the needs of the country." In like manner, other institutions should "adopt roles in musical education consistent with their resources and the needs of their clienteles."

The Eastman conference, it seems, was a primal cry for an honest and direct appraisal of the present state of music education and an identification of the necessary changes that must be borne by all if the field is to effect the future vitality and value of music in American society and its significance in American education. That is the common cause that unites and, hopefully, moves us.

8

MUSIC: A BASIC INTELLIGENCE

MUSICAL AMERICA 34 (June 1984)

Those in education circles will likely know the work of Howard Gardner and his theory of multiple intelligences. In 1983, he put forth the notion that cognition comes from myriad ways of understanding the world: linguistic, mathematic, musical, spatial, kinesthetic, and personal. In his book *Frames of Mind: The Theory of Multiple Intelligences,* he outlines connections common in all peoples, and argues that these connections support the flourishing of abilities beyond what had been previously considered. Explored here are challenges to the traditional systems of education, implications for teachers and students, compelling ways to engage the minds of children, and understanding of the codes that we create to evaluate the learning world around us. A strong argument is made for the value of the theory and its inherent proposition of the value of music and arts learning from his research, and the possibilities presented by the theory for artistic and creative education. While Gardner has since updated his theory, the discussion has not stopped. Those interested might very well update their own knowledge of the theory by reading here from the beginning.

—CR

* * *

IT IS RARE that a book creates enough impact to change the face of education. Perhaps in this century only John Dewey's *Democracy and Education* and his *Experience and Education* could claim that distinction. Howard Gardner's new book, *Frames of Mind: The Theory of Multiple Intelligences* (New York: Basic Books, 1983, $23.50) has the potential for that kind of impact. Here is a wholly new and broader view of cognition that could radically alter prevailing educational practices and, almost unintentionally, elevate the arts in the process of schooling.

SIX INTELLIGENCES

Put quite simply, Gardner convincingly expands cognition—"the deployment of mind"—beyond linguistic and mathematical abilities, the staples of the basic curriculum, to include four other intelligences—musical intelligence, spatial skill, bodily-kinesthetic or movement intelligence, and the personal intelligences that enable us to understand ourselves and others. Significantly, the six major human intelligences that Gardner has so far identified—there may well be others—are deeply rooted in human beings of all cultures. They are imbedded in our nervous system and are part of our physiological and genetic being.

Each of these six major human intelligences functions independently. They are autonomous abilities or "frames of mind." Gardner's proof for this independence is extensive and is derived largely from studies of brain-damaged individuals. For example: he tells us that severe aphasic patients, persons who have totally lost the power to use or understand words, retain their abilities to be musicians and visual artists. Individuals with Gerstmann syndrome—persons who exhibit isolated impairment in learning arithmetic and in distinguishing left from right—speak normally. "That's how we know they are not generally retarded," Gardner says. In like manner, "Individuals who have completely lost their visual memories nonetheless remain capable of learning and remembering complex motor sequences and patterns of behavior."

IMPLICATIONS

Enough of the theory itself. The educational implications of Gardner's theory are provocative, to say the least. The idea of multiple intelligences challenges the whole educational system, IQ tests, and educational evaluation in general, since these focus on only a few of the intellectual abilities all children possess. As we know, the modern school places a premium on linguistic intelligence and on logical-mathematical ability. "The remaining intelligences," Gardner tells us, "are, for the most part, consigned to after school or recreational activities, if they are taken notice of at all."

But the nature of the intelligences that Gardner has identified is the real startler. Out of the six, three—just half—are directly related to major art forms. There is musical intelligence; then spatial intelligence, which clearly relates to the visual arts; and bodily-kinesthetic intelligence, which relates to dance. The arts, in other words, *are cognition.* They are forms of intelligence equivalent to language, math, and science.

ENGAGING THE MIND

Educationally, Gardner says, it doesn't make sense, "to put all your eggs in one intelligence basket." The schools should provide opportunities for children to develop all their intelligences—their entire mind. That is the strong implication of Gardner's work. As a psychologist at Harvard and, for years, co-director of Project Zero, a study of how children learn the arts, we know that he understands that the arts are not mere hands-on activity but that they engage the mind to the utmost. His theory shows that in denying children access to the arts—neglecting whole aspects of intellectual competence—the modern school has delimited learning and cut students off from developing their own intrinsic abilities. In this sense, schools have been guilty of constraining children from developing whole frames of their mind, intelligences that make them fully human.

Now, perhaps, I begin to understand what Vachel Lindsay meant when he wrote:

Let not young souls be smothered out before
They do quaint deeds and fully flaunt their pride.
It is the world's one crime its babes grow dull,
Its poor are ox-like, limp and leaden-eyed.

The success of the Suzuki method of teaching violin to Japanese toddlers proves that, in Gardner's words, "If you bathe kids in music you can make them at least decent musicians." In his way of thinking, "There is no environment where you couldn't do something similar." The accomplished singing of Hungarians due to the Kodaly method used in their schools and the high quality of instrumental performance among the Balinese gamelan players, Gardner says, "suggests that musical achievement is not strictly a reflection of inborn ability but is susceptible to cultural stimulation and training." In other words, normal children have enormous possibilities for development of all these intelligences if they are provided the opportunity. "Conversely, and perhaps more obviously," Gardner states, "even the most innately talented individual will founder without some positive supporting environment." Accordingly, he recommends that "every individual have available to him as many options as possible as well as the potential to achieve competence in whatever fields he and his society deem important."

CODES

But Gardner gives us other reasons to regret the restrictions of most school curricula. Each of these intelligences, he says, functions as both a means of acquiring knowledge and transmitting it. We code our understandings of the world spatially in visual arts, kinesthetically in dance, and with sounds in music. We have invented symbol systems to convey these intelligences. And with these systems we fashion symbolic products—stories, plays, poetry, mathematical problems, scientific formulas, photographs, graphs and maps—as a means to convey and preserve a set of meanings. This is the way we socialize our intelligences—share them. Gardner calls the introduction to and the mastering of these symbol systems "a major burden of childhood" and "the principal mission of modern educational systems."

Given the fact that as much as ninety percent of the human brain goes unused, Gardner's theory that there are multiple intellectual regions in which most human beings have the potential for solid advancement should reverberate throughout the educational establishment. He provides evidence to show that "except perhaps in the case of certain exceptional individuals, these intellectual competencies never develop in a vacuum." The onus, then, is clearly on the schools, which must come to realize "that individuals are not all alike in their cognitive potentials and their intellectual styles and that education can be more properly carried out if it is tailored to the abilities and the needs of the particular individuals involved." For some students, the visual (spatial intelligence), the manipulative (bodily-kinesthetic intelligence), or the world of sound (musical intelligence) may constitute a dominant avenue of learning.

Gardner believes that the schools should recognize each child's intellectual profile and match it to the material of instruction, certainly not a radical thought. In this way, he says, "the intelligences can function both as subject matters in themselves and as the preferred means for inculcating diverse subject matter." Perhaps as schools pay more attention to what human beings are like and adapt education to our growing knowledge of human minds, the powerful educational potential of the arts will finally be realized.

9

THE SHAMEFUL NEGLECT OF CREATIVITY

MUSICAL AMERICA 35 (September 1985)

If one is interested in improving music education, this piece deserves serious attention. It has often been said that music helps foster creativity in children and enhances how they look at the world. The reality in music classrooms can be far different, and often the only creative figure in the room is the teacher or director. The notion here is challenged head on, with convincing clarity, and was already an argument that had been under debate for more than twenty years when this was published in 1985. Fowler himself was a major proponent of true creativity infused into music education classrooms, from his dissertation in 1964, to his years as editor of *Music Educators Journal* (1965–1971), to his final writings in the mid-1990s. While this colloquy certainly will spark thinking in your own mind, ideas on implementation make for more than a mere diatribe on the merits of the idea. Most music teachers in the early twenty-first century are considering the merits of creative education, so when a strong argument is required, this article delivers the needed support.

—CR

* * *

OF ALL THE ARTS, music is taught in the least creative way. At every level, from kindergarten through graduate school, music is presented to students as, fundamentally, an already formed, preexisting body of literature to which the student must become enculturated. Acquaintance with and understanding of that enormous repertoire of musical "standards" is exacted slowly over many years, primarily through learning to listen, to sing, to play an instrument, to read musical symbols, and to analyze technical aspects and style. Seldom, if ever, are students invited to use the medium of sound to fashion their own totally original musical expressions. Incredibly, most doctoral programs in music do not require even one course in musical composition.

This slighting of creativity is debilitating to music education in three very critical ways: (1) it calls into question the credibility of music education programs; (2) it limits the importance and value of music in education; and (3) it fosters the view that music is a dead or dying art-of-the-past. Here are the problems as I see them, along with some possible solutions.

CREDIBILITY

One of the prominent goals of most music education programs is to develop the students' musical creativity. The study of music, we often hear, develops creative self-expression. This is a goal that most parents, educational administrators, and school boards find highly desirable.

Unfortunately, the rhetoric of music education doesn't live up to the practice. Many music teachers delude themselves into thinking that interpretation is the equivalent of creativity. True, there are some decisions in the process of interpreting a piece of music that do invite some creative choice. But, for the most part, these decisions are usurped by the conductor and presented to students as a fait accompli. Teachers rarely invite their students to try performing a piece in a number of different ways, to evaluate the various effects, and then to decide which approach is the most appropriate and affecting.

Nor is improvisation—the spontaneous creation of a melodic composition or variations on a theme—a basic and integral part of most music study. Almost invariably, students are taught to read the printed notes. Even in high school and college jazz bands, where one might expect that improvisation would be the rule, students are taught to adhere to the charts.

Granted, music series text books for elementary and junior high schools make a modest nod to creativity. Book 2 of the Silver Burdett Music Series, for example, asks students to create a collage of pictures (i.e., people walking, trees bending in the wind) that show beat and no beat,[1] and to create a "sound piece," using swoops of upward and downward sounds.[2] In the first case, creativity is used as a means of teaching a

[1] Elizabeth Crook, Bennett Reimer, and David S. Walker, *Book 2, Silver Burdett Music* (Morristown, New Jersey: Silver Burdett Company, 1981), pp. 14 and 15.
[2] *Ibid.*, pp. 20–21.

musical concept. In the second, children are engaged in actual creative musicmaking. The distinction here is important. Only the act of musical creation teaches students that music can be an art of total self-expression. Children are asked to create four other sound pieces and several simple rhythm accompaniments in Book 2, a minimal amount of musical creation, if we suppose that this book forms the basis for a year's work. In its treatment of musical creativity, the series is fairly typical.

In contrast to music, dance is generally taught as creative movement. The art of theater is developed through improvisational techniques. Creative writing is learned by writing original poems and stories. The visual arts are taught largely through the process of production. Music is the only art that is presented to youth as work already created, as something that, somehow, always preexists. By and large, music teachers, many of whom have had little creative music-making in their own education, think of their subject primarily as an art of re-creation. As far as students are concerned, composers are dead people, and music is a finished art.

Musical creativity is given basic emphasis in the method of teaching and learning music that was invented by the German composer Carl Orff. Where this method is in use in American schools, children are learning how to express themselves through their own musical inventiveness. But these schools are the exception rather than the rule. American education, for the most part, neglects musical creativity or ignores it altogether. In observing numbers of arts classes in American schools, John I. Goodlad noted that "They did not convey the picture of individual expression and artistic creativity toward which one is led by the rhetoric of forward-looking practice in the field."[3]

Music teachers who choose to promote the goal of creativity but do little to realize it, do a disservice. They deceive their clientele—students, parents, administrators, and schools boards. They appear to inflate the educational merits of their subject. After all, goals infer content (curriculum) and methodologies. Practice must match rhetoric, otherwise credibility is sacrificed. And that is a loss of inestimable proportion. In education, when you don't live up to your stated worth, you're devalued.

IMPORTANCE

Perhaps, then, the best approach is simply not to make any claims for creativity, or to disavow any goal that addresses the development of creative self-expression through music. This approach has the advantage of avoiding false expectations. But it has a very serious drawback as well: it limits the potential educational significance of music.

Just as any art is a means of expression and communication, music is one of humanity's *systems of meaning*. It follows, then, that learning to use music to convey meaning must be part of what an education in music is about. But isn't this accomplished through performance? Doesn't a student learn that music expresses meaning

---

[3] John I. Goodlad, *A Place Called School: Prospects for the Future* (New York: McGraw-Hill Book Company, 1984), p. 220.

by singing or playing, say, "The Battle Hymn of the Republic"? In the act of re-creation, students learn to communicate the meaning of the composer. Ideally, they adapt to that expression and convey it as if it were their own. They may have a good deal of empathy for the thought expressed, but such performance does not teach students that they can use sound to function as a medium for conveying their own personal inner impressions.

All symbolic systems invite people to form new representations of the world. That is one of their primary functions. We use our senses and our mind to analyze our world, to interact with it, and to understand it. And we record these impressions in a variety of symbolic systems that we have invented precisely for these purposes. We need all these systems because some forms of human experience are better expressed through one means than another. Science can explain a sunrise, but the arts can convey its emotional import. In the third part of the ballet *Daphnis and Chloe,* as the light of dawn gradually fills the stage and birdcalls are heard, Ravel's musical score evokes the exhilaration of daybreak. The expressive character of a sunrise is also an important aspect of its meaning, here captured and conveyed through music.

Learning the value of—and how to use—all of our various symbolic systems is the basic function of education. But to acquire real understanding, students must be able to use the systems to express their own meaning. It is not enough merely to learn to admire the way others have used music to express and convey *their* meaning, however universal. The real challenge in mastering an art is in employing its technique to our own ends, to be able to use it to convey our own personal observations and reactions and understandings of our world.

It is, then, precisely in the act of being creative with an art form that we come to exercise our real intelligence—to translate our observations symbolically in the process of formulating and conveying our understandings. The process of translating our intuitions, feelings, and spirit to musical constructs requires the exercise of judgment, of estimating possible outcomes, of weighing the result of particular choices, of deciding among unlimited options, and of taking action based upon such estimates. Creating one's own music is not a matter of merely following rules or of memorizing procedures. It is problem-solving of the most difficult order—a challenge that immediately gives rigor and substance to the study of music.

In music education, the choice of whether the students are invited to invent is a pedagogical one. Some teachers insist that the rules of musical notation be mastered before any attempts are made at personal musical expression. Such teachers emphasize music as re-creation, as a way of decoding what others have expressed musically. They reduce music to a second-hand art, forgetting that, historically, musical creation occurred first, and then notational systems for it were devised. Following that same original sequence, students can express their own original musical "thoughts," then create their own codes to record them. In this way, they come to see the need for musical notation. The act of musical creation can thus serve as the impetus for learning the means to record music in symbols, just as we learn to speak before we write. But, in any case, the act of creating music need not be constrained by the students' knowledge of notation, or their lack of it. Creation can be a totally aural process.

The ability to develop one's own musical constructs lies at the heart of musical intelligence and its development. It is basic to the understanding of music as an art. Musical literacy is not just the capacity to interpret or to master the technique of playing and singing what others have created. It is also the ability to create and to use sound as a means of self-expression and communication. Learning to use sound to represent one's own meaning allows students to use their musical intelligence to interpret themselves and their world musically. This use of music as a system to capture and record meaning permits students to see it as an ingenious human invention that is of fundamental importance.

AN ART OF THE PAST?

When an art form fails to invite practitioners to explore it creatively—to use it as a medium of contemporary expression and communication and as a vehicle for expressing the current times—that art tends to lose its vitality. How audiences and musicians are educated determines their musical values and expectations. When music is promulgated primarily as a maintenance of masterpieces, as the preservation of an art of the past, performance may become all important, but the art itself atrophies.

If music is to be a living art that communicates in our own time, students of the art must become involved in its creative aspects. They must learn to use sound as a medium for their own personal communication. Whether by exploiting the technique of improvisation, experimenting with the organization of sound with the help of computers and synthesizers, or simply inventing their own musical expressions, students can experience music as an art of *self*-creation rather than *re*-creation.

Involving students in the performance of one of their own original musical ideas can be instructive to all. They will begin to understand themselves as musically thinking beings at the same time that they grasp the nature of the art as a means of representing that thought. But more important, in coming to terms with how and what one can "say" with music, students will naturally come to value and to better understand the musical creations of others. And they will begin, quite naturally, to accept and relate to contemporary musical expressions. Music, as an art, will be reaching forward instead of looking back. The art will become enlivened. Audiences will be developed that relish sharing the musical expressions of their own time, a phenomenon too seldom achieved today.

Certainly music education programs that are content with simply passing on the classical and ethnic musical culture *as is* tend to be prosaic and staid. Maintaining the *status quo* isn't a particularly stimulating business. Without investing in its creative aspects, we consign music to history. By steeping our young talent and our audiences in the standard repertoire, we sap the vitality of our art. In contrast, theater does not restrict itself to Molière and Shakespeare, nor visual arts to Da Vinci and Rembrandt.

To attain its rightful value and importance, music must be presented as a living art that speaks urgently and vibrantly in our own time. Those who study music deserve to see it as a record and revelation of the human spirit, both yesterday and today. Creating their own musical expressions allows students to relate music directly to their own lives and times. It permits a precious inner aspect of their beings to speak and to be heard. It allows their musical intelligence to be explored and developed. That makes the study of music more personal, more vital, and more significant.

10

ACADEMIC EXCELLENCE IN TEACHING THE ARTS

MUSICAL AMERICA 36 (August 1986)

The College Entrance Examination Board produced a series of treatises on various disciplines around 1983–1984 designed to help secondary teachers better prepare their students for higher education. Several of these, named by color (red, green, and so on) were reviewed; the focus here is to look at the suggestions for music and arts education. The commentary is detailed and insightful, and tackles the long-controversial question about what *academic* means in arts classrooms. Although several suggestions are found in the report, the techniques are more or less useful to varying degrees. Abilities highlighted as important include knowledge of how to produce and perform, knowledge of analysis-interpretation-evaluation, and knowledge of music and art works from various periods and cultures. Teaching vignettes are offered, along with other ideas about how to increase the academic component of music teaching. I suspect the reader is not surprised that Fowler had a thing or two say on this topic, and his thoughts illuminate the definition of academic in music, and challenges what it really should mean. A poignant letter from a high-school music teacher drives home the point about how ideas in the report really influence practice. This topic is clearly central in the early twenty-first century, and those who need definitions and support for the academic in music should consider starting here.

—CR

* * *

THE EDUCATION REPORT of the College Entrance Examination Board, the so-called "Green Book" that was reviewed in this column in November 1983, has now been followed up with a series of six treatises on the various disciplines. *Academic Preparation in the Arts: Teaching for Transition from High School to College* (College Board Publications, New York, NY) is one of these, and it is intended to show how the outcomes for each art that were outlined in the Green Book might be translated into actual curricula and instructional practices.

The overall outlook is clearly in response to the general decline in the academic attainment of high school graduates as reported by the Green Book and other national studies. This Red Book is not aimed just at those students who are going on to college, as was the Green Book. Instead it offers "suggestions that will be useful in achieving academic excellence for *all* students." In aiming at the broad spectrum of high school students and not those currently in the "academic track," the College Board takes a stand against a tracking system that consigns a disproportionately large number of minority students to the low track, where very little is expected of them. The Board says:

> We are convinced that many more students can—and, in justice, should—profit from higher education and therefore from adequate academic preparation.

As its title suggests, this book is a guide to making high school courses in the arts more academic. And it presents a generally convincing case for why and how this might be accomplished, although I find myself taking issue with the latter. Since this volume is a sequel, it is important to remember that its precursor sketched learning outcomes that could serve as goals for high school curricula in six basic academic subjects, the arts being one. In the arts, three kinds of abilities were identified: (1) knowledge of how to produce and perform; (2) knowledge of how to analyze, interpret, and evaluate; and (3) knowledge of art works of other periods and cultures. Few would disagree with these purposes—the *whys* of art education.

But when it comes to the subtleties of the *what* and the *hows* of arts education, there may be less ready agreement. Given the bold attempt of this brief volume to suggest the means—even though the intent is not to be prescriptive—there are some things I really like about this presentation, and some which very much concern me.

What I really like here in terms of the approach are the examples of arts courses that are provided in each art form (Chapter 3) and the vignettes of how teachers of the arts actually work with students to achieve the skills through specific courses (Chapter 4). This is real information drawn from actual cases. Through these course descriptions and vignettes we get a glimpse of what arts teachers actually do in their classrooms. This is a rare treat in the literature of arts education not only because it is seldom done but also because much of what these arts teachers do is imaginative and thought provoking.

In music, learning such skills as the ability to identify and describe various musical forms from different historical periods, the ability to listen perceptively, the ability to read music and to evaluate a musical work or performance, and to know how to express oneself by playing, singing, or composing music pose particular challenges. We are told that many music teachers

> ... have developed excellent strategies for teaching performing skills—whether in choir, band, or orchestra. Yet, these same teachers may find it difficult to accomplish outcomes related to a knowledge of music history, style, theory, and criticism. The challenge is to achieve polished levels of performance—often in a very limited time period—and also to help students examine carefully and caringly the structure and historical background of the works they are performing.

For purposes of college preparation, we are told, "a balanced approach to music curriculum is essential; students need to be prepared as listeners as well as performers." The implication here is that too often musical performing groups stress skill development as an end in itself. Students learn to play the tune. That's it. Their skills are not used as a means to acquire broader understandings. And it is those broader—academic—understandings that are advocated here.

In the music vignette, an instrumental music teacher has taken his high school band and orchestral students downtown to hear the local symphony orchestra perform a movement from a Tchaikovsky symphony which they have studied in a simplified orchestration. These students have written papers about this work, sung all its themes, compared different recorded performances—"practically 'lived' it," we're told. After this experience, they will write a critical appraisal of the performance. "Their project book," we are informed, is "filled with reports, critiques, and musical analyses . . ."

One can presume that this example was carefully chosen to demonstrate an academic approach in music. But if there is any doubt, what the Red Book is advocating is fully expressed in the final chapters. Here the book points out and promotes the "relationship between a mastery of the arts and the development of the broad academic competencies that students will need in all college subjects—reading, writing, speaking and listening, mathematics, reasoning, studying, using computers, and observing." We're told that "It is important to study the arts for their own sake; it is also important to recognize that they provide additional opportunities to enhance these basic skills."

The last chapter urges teachers to move "beyond production and performance." It explains that "A major challenge for arts teachers is to widen, and consequently deepen, the traditional focus of arts instruction."

There is a serious issue underlying this whole outlook and approach that is barely alluded to in these pages and that bothers me. In a preface directed "To Our Fellow Teachers of the Arts," the Arts Advisory Committee that oversaw the preparation of this publication states:

> As arts teachers, we often occupy a special position with respect to our students. The art room, the auditorium, and the rehearsal studios are often regarded as "safe havens," places where school ends and enjoyment begins. With some

students, that enjoyment turns into an almost passionate commitment to working creatively. For other students, it may take a less constructive form—a time for relaxation and socializing. Another of our great challenges in teaching the arts is to convince all students that the arts demand the same kind of serious study that is required in their other subjects.

One of the phrases that causes me problems is "where school ends and enjoyment begins." Students do think of the arts differently. They don't see them as places to get out their notebooks and to listen to the teacher lecture. Nor do they see them as sullen places, serious to the extent of drudgery. They do get plenty of that in some of their other classes, and by companion the arts provide a respite if only because the activities are different.

I see no reason why arts teachers should apologize or be made to feel like second-class citizens because their subject is user-friendly. I'm not one of those who believes that education is only effective when it makes the learner miserable. Granted, it isn't enough to be social. The arts should teach; they should challenge the student to learn. But the fact that the arts are generally liked by students is not the issue.

The issue is how the term "academic" is defined. Does being classed as an academic subject mean that students in the arts have to suffer? Obviously, in the College Board's view, enjoyment turned into a passionate commitment to work creatively isn't quite enough. But how far must arts teachers go? Should they make students do research, listen to lectures, take notes, read books, write papers study at home, etc.? Should they make the arts like all the other subjects students take? This seems to be what this publication suggests.

I for one do not believe that being more academic means doing more lecturing. God knows, there is already enough of that in the arts, where you would least expect to find it. Nor do I believe that arts teachers need to give up their uniqueness to become broader about their subject matter. We can continue to teach the arts in ways not readily accessible to teachers of other subjects. We can use performance as the means and the motivation for teaching these other dimensions of the art.

The danger, I think, is that by following the examples and the advice here, many arts teachers might get off base. I think most arts teachers agree that their courses can be enriched by broadening them. But it's a matter of degree and kind. It is important that in the process of broadening, they don't forget that what they are teaching is essentially a performance class, if that's the case.

Not long ago I asked Christie Hubble, music director at Lakeland High School in Rathdrum, Idaho, to comment on how she was adjusting to that state's move to require the arts for high school graduation—in effect, to make the arts academic. Her letter in reply, printed here in part, is very revealing, particularly in regard to this discussion:

During the fall of 1984, my district decided that credit for band and choir would not be given more than once unless I could show different course content at the sophomore, junior, and senior levels. So, I designed a workable outline where I can show three different levels of learning going on at the same time in my band and chorus classes. . . .

My classes are about seventy percent performance oriented in order to meet the performance demands of this community. I will not drop below this percentage level because my students have elected to take my class because they like to play and sing. Too much "book learnin'" quickly turns them off.

The remaining thirty percent of their class time is devoted to the following: ten percent Theory; five percent History; five percent Listening (classical recordings, solo artists, and pop and concert sample recordings from major publishing companies), five percent Appreciation and Evaluation Skills. I also spend about five percent of their time presenting individualized performing skill practice sheets and playing exams.

My concern is not that we broaden curricula; that is long overdue. It's not even that we will throw out the baby with the bath water. Diligent music teachers like Christie Hubble, and we have many, won't let that happen. My concern is that we will misinterpret "academic" to mean all those insufferable things we had to endure in high school, and that we will lose the one edge that we have—that the arts are refreshingly different in the way they are taught and learned. I believe that we can be academic and experiential at the same time and that by no means do we give up one for the other. I agree with the Advisory Committee that all students should be convinced that the arts demand serious study, but not necessarily *the same kind* of serious study that is required in their other subjects.

The intention of the Red Book is to "spark more detailed discussion" among teachers who have the responsibility for ensuring that all students are prepared adequately for college. But the Red Book is also designed for guidance counselors and school administrators who must understand the work of these teachers in order to give them the kind of support they need. I hope they will understand that, during this very difficult period of transition, the content of arts curricula and the methodologies have not been set in stone but require much further study.

Wisely, the book advises that curriculum and instruction (the what and hows of art education) "should be a more prominent part of the nationwide discussion about improving secondary education." The classroom, it says, is "at the beginning as well as the end of improvement," and it acknowledges that "what teachers and students do in classrooms must be thoughtfully considered before many kinds of changes, even exterior changes, are made in the name of educational improvement." That may sound like just good common sense, but as is often the case, it is the obvious that is often overlooked, and the simplistic solution that becomes the hue and cry.

11

EVALUATION: PROS & CONS

MUSICAL AMERICA 36 (November 1986)

Discussing the challenges and opportunities of evaluation in school-music settings is most certainly a conversation happening in classrooms in the early twenty-first century. However, the arguments are not new, and looking at best practices for assessing our students has been a topic in music education circles for at least fifty years. Here, the pros and cons are discussed through the viewpoints of Charles Fowler, Patricia Shehan (Campbell), Robert Badal, Shirley Corey, Barbara Moody, and others. A general idea centers on the need for assessment, and the fact that music and arts teachers are engaged in it at almost every moment. However, is assessment being incorporated in the best ways? Are students benefiting from the best modes of evaluation? Are standardized tests driving curricular and assessment choices? What should music educators be doing to promote the most effective ways of measuring their students' performance? Other issues focus on subjectivity versus objectivity, best timing for evaluation, and purposes versus rationale, among others. I suspect many of the ideas presented here are as timely and relevant as ever.

—CR

* * *

Of all the areas in arts education, evaluation remains the most controversial and uncertain among arts practitioners. Many arts teachers feel that they know little about it. Yet most of the arts teachers I have observed are evaluating their students at every turn. Music teachers evaluate every note their students sing or play. But far from thinking of themselves as experts at evaluation, many feel threatened.

The application of science to the arts is feared by artists and arts educators, who tend to trust feelings and intuition and to suspect logic and objectivity. Then, too, a large part of the difficulty derives from the fact that evaluation is a relatively new discipline, and is still evolving. Much remains to be learned about the productive applications of evaluation to arts education.

Evaluation in education is a procedure for judging worth. It is a way of telling the quality of a particular approach, activity, or product in the teaching-learning process. As such, evaluation provides data necessary to making improvements in that process.

Measurement is one way of gathering information to be used in evaluation. It is a way of making a judgment quantitatively. A teacher can test students' ability to identify particular musical styles before, during, and at the end of a course of study. Such tests provide a concrete measure of one part of what has been learned. They might also provide some indication of the effectiveness of teaching materials and methodologies.

As a means of verification, evaluation can determine the differences between what is assumed to be happening and what is actually occurring in the classroom. Teachers often suppose that certain goals are being achieved. Unfortunately, such assumptions—guesses—are biased and unreliable. In contrast, evaluation assesses results on the basis of an objective interpretation of collected data. Because information is assembled from a broad data base, the result is more reliable.

Mary Barr Rhodes, art teacher at the Putnam County Gifted Art Program in West Virginia, has, like many teachers in the arts, invented her own assessment techniques that cover the broad range of the program. Unit reports, based upon written tests, are shared with parents bimonthly. Twice a year, a more general report addresses the question, "Does the student show progress in using the language of art?" But Rhodes acknowledges a need for standardized tests in the arts, tests that imply a well-organized, sequential curriculum.

A story-telling program at Seekman Elementary School in Imperial (MO) uses artist residencies to improve language skills. The program uses a number of objective instruments to evaluate its success: check lists, rating scales, observations, student work, descriptions, the numbers of books checked out of the library, and visual indications. Donald Corbin, principal of the school, says, "When you spend time and money, you need to evaluate. We must be able to show that we're reaching our objectives."

In these cases, evaluation is revealed as a systematic process of collecting information about a program from many sources. Many of the instruments for this process must be created specifically to fit the task. Once collected, the information is pooled and carefully analyzed. Based upon the careful interpretation of these data, decisions about the program are made. If the techniques of evaluation have been observed with care, those decisions will be sound and the program will improve accordingly.

As concerns for educational standards become more pressing and schools move to give greater stress to academic pursuits, arts proponents face more urgent demands to prove the educational credibility of the arts. Many who are familiar with evaluation believe that, when the arts are tested as seriously as other subjects, they will be perceived as more important by parents, school administrators, and other educators.

Evaluation is a means for proving the effectiveness of a particular program. But, if it can reveal what is strong, it can also point out what is weak or lacking. According to Ann Timberman, State Arts Consultant in Indiana, assessment of grants programs on the state level have forced them "to evaluate in areas where we might otherwise not have." She finds that "Numbers and hard data as well as descriptive information allow us to reach various audiences." Evaluation, Timberman says, "gives us commitment, clout, and credibility."

Robert Badal, dean of the Division of Arts and Humanities at Moorhead (MN) State University, says that "Without evaluation, we lack information to make a case for the arts." At a time when education itself is being reevaluated, he points out that "Persuading decision-makers requires statistical substantiation." Other subject areas are validated by testing; the arts should be no different.

"We are irresponsible if we don't show our worth," declares Richard Levy, executive director of the ArtsConnection in New York City. Dwaine Greer, professor of art at the University of Arizona in Tucson, asks pointedly, "How can we claim that the arts is the one area that is not accountable?"

What are the strengths of arts education programs? What are they contributing of value in the total educational process? Are students achieving an acceptable level of literacy in the various arts? What methods and materials are the best for teaching the arts successfully? The answers depend upon evaluation.

When it comes to evaluation, there are a number of problems that continue to plague arts teachers:

Subjectivity vs. Objectivity. One of the consequences of an artistic orientation is a set of aesthetic goals. Such goals are rarely specific and are generally too amorphous to test, yet they are often preciously regarded by teachers of the arts. For example, a choral teacher might strive to teach aesthetic sensitivity in the way students approach the rise and fall of a phrase. To the teacher, this is a very legitimate goal. But how can such sensitivity be evaluated?

What arts educators fear is that the indigenous goals of arts education will be altered to favor lesser, but more specific and more readily testable goals—that the cognitive aspects of their subject will be emphasized at the expense of the affective. In this view, the whole process of evaluation begins to invade not only the process of teaching, but also the philosophical underpinnings of arts education itself.

Patricia K. Shehan (Campbell), assistant professor of music at Washington University in St. Louis (now at University of Washington), notes that arts specialists find the measurement of the affective areas—sensitivity, emotions, and awareness of self—both "tough and controversial." She points out:

> While the more objective and quantitative aspects of evaluation have received considerable attention in music education research and practice, the more subjective, personal, and qualitative aspects need considerable development if a balanced and holistic approach is to be achieved.... It is true that there are some outcomes of a good arts program that are at present impossible to evaluate, but this does not excuse the specialist from scrutinizing those areas that *do* lend themselves to evaluation. Though the tools are limited, better decisions are made when they are used than when they are not.

Shehan reminds educators that "We *can* measure skills, knowledge about, and attitudes toward the arts." And she points out that, for this purpose, standardized tests in music and in other arts are already available. But if a program is new and no pertinent tests are available, she suggests using teacher-constructed tests.

Barbara Nicholson, a member of the College Entrance Examination Board, acknowledges that the arts are unique *because* they are romantic. But she goes on to say that "There is a body of knowledge that is measurable. We must evaluate where we can." Nicholson believes that it is not persuasive to claim that the arts are important because they make us better human beings. She says that arts educators must be able to show that they are in the knowledge business just like the teachers of any other subject matter.

Standardized Tests. In American public schools, standardized tests are a major determinate of curriculum. College entrance examinations tells high schools what to emphasize. Administrators and parents tend to attach special value to areas that are tested. The tested areas are what schools and teachers tend to teach.

But, if arts education is going to achieve a new rigor, standardized tests in the arts will not be simple to construct, nor will they find easy acceptance. Given the fact that such tests generally assess only the cognitive areas, arts teachers fear that such tests will sway the curriculum. Teachers may begin to stress only what is tested and ignore the affective areas, which many people believe are the most important and unique aspects of arts education.

Even when testers have deliberately tried to treat the affective areas, there is resistance to such tests. The art and music tests that are part of the National Assessment of Educational Progress are a good example. They have not been widely used, nor are they looked upon with particular favor by many arts educators or, for that matter, by school administrators. Arts teachers are generally paranoid about the evaluation of progress. Then, too, arts programs are not standardized. Few states have established mandated curricula in the arts. Curricular programs in the arts not only vary considerably from state to state, but also from school district to school district, even from school to school.

According to Michael George, coordinator of fine arts for the Madison (WI) Metropolitan Schools, standardized tests such as the National Assessment of Education Progress in art and music are most effective on the local level as a way for teachers to compare their work. "They are not impressive," he says, "to state education departments, governors, and state legislators." Connecticut, Minnesota, and Michigan have used these quantitative assessments, he says, but "there still has not been a great impact on what goes on day to day in schools in the fine arts."

If standardized tests of educational progress in the arts appear to be problematic at present, so, too, are tests for evaluating teaching methodology and techniques in the arts. There are no available instruments. Again, standards would be diffcult to establish. But the accountability of arts teachers is as valid an issue as it is for teachers of other subjects.

The difficulty that arts educators face with standardization is the need to know what to test in each art at all levels. This means that there must be a dialogue between all the levels of education. It implies a sequential, perhaps national, curriculum. Evaluation thus necessitates a whole approach to curriculum planning and development. It is not simply a device that is tacked on at the end.

When and How? There is confusion about when to use evaluation and how it should be used. Richard Levy observes that "We don't evaluate science to justify science in the schools." Arts educators must know what they should assess and why. If the reason is to persuade the decision-makers, then evaluation might not be the best means. On this point, Shirley Trusty Corey, supervisor of arts and education for the New Orleans Public Schools, is emphatic:

> Maybe we shouldn't be talking about evaluation at all. We are trying to set ourselves up like everyone else. What are the other ways we can use to get people to perceive the value of the arts? Maybe this is the important question. The arts may have a different role to play.

Sometimes neither information or evaluation is the correct route to persuading the decision-makers, sustaining programs, and assuring budgetary support. Wisconsin's Arts World Program is a case in point. This program serves 75 talented high school students in the summer and is financed by funds from the state education agency. After the state superintendent of public instruction saw the program in operation and was notably impressed, he advised the directors to "Do a good evaluation so we have evidence to support the program in the future." The evaluation was done, but at the same time, the students who participated were encouraged to write letters to their state legislators. The letters were all that was needed. George says, "The evaluation is still in a cardboard box, but there is $300,000 for Arts World."

According to George, school boards would like to know what the cost of the arts program is compared to other programs, how many students are involved, what the impact of the program is on the school environment and image. None of these areas is measured by the evaluation of achievement. "We must," says George, "gather the information we need."

For What Purpose? Evaluation in the arts stands at the heart of every philosophical, programmatic, and methodological dispute in arts education. For example, at Booker Arts Magnet School in Little Rock (AR), quantitative evaluation is used to measure the effect of the arts on student achievement. The program uses the Torrence Test of Creativity. These measures, which have been used to test fourth, fifth, and sixth graders, have shown that moving the arts into the curriculum has improved academic achievement.

Shirley Trusty Corey has had similar results using the Scott Foresman Reading Inventory Test. This test showed that students in the arts made twice the gains in reading skills over those without them. She acknowledges that "We must learn how to use that research to best advantage. We should use it as a lever." Corey relates how such tests have resulted in parents wanting to bring the drama specialists back once they realized how that program was a key factor in reading improvement.

Like numbers of arts practitioners, Barbara Moody, coordinator of cultural arts resources in the Little Rock School District, believes that this kind of evaluation is a means of assuring the survival of arts programs. And she adds, "If we can show that we can encourage creativity, we have won the day." Many educators believe that quantitative measures that would assess such matters as the effect of the arts on the education of the whole child or how the arts can affect improvement in reading and other subject areas could prove to be of great value in winning support for the arts as an essential part of basic education.

But establishing the educational value of the arts on the basis of their affect upon other areas in the curriculum seems to be a matter in considerable dispute. Greer, for example, reminds us of the non-productivity of certain evaluative approaches—what he refers to as the "paradox of advocacy." He says that "The more we attempt to prove the value of the arts on the basis of their contribution to other areas of the curriculum, the more we give evidence to hard-headed administrators that the arts can be eliminated." He believes that evaluation in the arts must be put on the same basis as all other subjects.

But this, too, remains an area of contention. In one discussion I heard, a teacher wanted to know "if there are ways to address the uniqueness of the arts in evaluation rather than their similarities to other subjects." Some arts teachers resist the notion that the arts can—or should—be treated the same as science or mathematics. They insist that the arts are unique precisely because there are no "right" answers, and they believe that evaluation takes away that dimension.

The problem of evaluation in the arts is not going to go away. Warren B. Newman, now superintendent of the South Pasadena (CA) Unified School District, says that evaluation is "... like castor oil. It may be disconcerting, but it's good for you." And Lonna Jones, consultant, Rockefeller Brothers Fund, observes, "Just because you don't want judgments doesn't mean they won't be made. Arts programs are inevitably evaluated."

Arts education suffers a lack of credibility when it cannot answer questions with facts. The field would profit from being able to measure progress and document its impact on students. Without such measurements, arts education's potential self-esteem is diminished and the general progress of arts programs is impeded.

Evaluation is a tool. In the intensified race to claim the minds of American youth, it could serve as one means to make sure that the arts command an equable share. As a tool, evaluation can convince. More than mere rhetoric, it promises to provide the hard data needed to persuade the skeptics as to the value, role, and educational significance of the arts in American education.

12

MUSIC IN OUR SCHOOLS: THE FIRST 150 YEARS

MUSICAL AMERICA 108 (November 1988)

The establishment of public-school music education in the United States is generally attributed to Lowell Mason in Boston in 1838. The history of the profession of music education is certainly a rich one, and one that has spanned many years, movements, reforms, and accomplishments. In 1988, MENC celebrated the 150th anniversary of the founding of music education with a special segment held at its national conference in Indianapolis (along with several prior publications and events). Numerous sessions were devoted to the role of music education in the schools, curricular and pedagogical reforms, general music, instrumental, and choral music, issues of race-ethnicity-culture-sociology, Western and non-Western repertoire, and related critical and compelling topics. Many influential music educators participated, including Donald Corbett (MENC President), Timothy Gerber (Ohio State University), Hortense Kerr (Howard University), James Mumford (Indiana University), Michael Gordon (Indiana University), and Barbara Lundquist (University of Washington), among many others. While some conferences could have done a better job of invigorating participants, it seems that this one was closer to the mark.

—CR

* * *

IN 1838, Boston's Mayor Samuel A. Eliot, former president of the Boston Academy of Music, led the fight to win public support for music instruction in the city's schools. He called the school committee's approving vote that year "the Magna Carta of music education." Behind the action was the persuasive work of Lowell Mason, who might well be thought of as the country's first music educator. It was Mason who applied the principles of Swiss educational reformer Johann Pestalozzi to music and convinced the public that children can learn music. Through Mason's publications and effective efforts in educating teachers, Boston became the first school system to include music instruction by a special teacher in the regular curriculum of every grammar school.[1] From there, the idea spread across the country.

This year, the Music Educators National Conference (MENC) marked the sesquicentennial celebration of music in US. schools with a series of events and publications that culminated with its national convention in Indianapolis in April. MENC's 55,000 music educators bring music to the lives of nearly 20 million children and young adults in schools and universities across the nation. According to MENC President Donald L. Corbett, the celebration was a reminder that "without music in the schools, many children would be deprived of the lifelong benefits of music study."

This national conference gave one a sense of where the profession is after 150 years of effort. There was an up-beat feeling at this meeting that was decidedly different from the gloom and doom that have pervaded some recent national meetings. Perhaps music teachers feel that they have weathered the current educational-reform movement, which began in 1983 with the publication of *A Nation at Risk,* and that they will survive after all.[2] For a while, the situation looked grim. Music programs in many places, notably in some of the larger cities, had already been suffering curtailments for a decade, particularly at the elementary level. Although the reform movement did not exclude music altogether, the more intensified concentration on study of the basics tended to further erode its educational status.

But then there were some positive developments. Several of the subsequent educational reports included the arts in their definition of the basics. Some state departments of education took action. Rather than see the arts squeezed out of the curriculum by demands for more credits in history, English, mathematics, and science, a number of states mandated credit in the arts for high school graduation. Then the state university systems in California and Ohio began to require high school credit in the arts for college entrance, a very promising breakthrough. The signals from Washington gave hope as well. For an administration that has not been particularly hospitable to the arts, Education Secretary William Bennett, in a major report on elementary education, said that the arts in the elementary schools "are an essential element of education, just like reading, writing, and arithmetic." This year, in its report on

---

[1] For a lively account of the 150-year history of music education in American schools, see the special February 1988 commemorative issue of *Music Educators Journal.*

[2] The National Commission on Excellence in Education, *A Nation At Risk: The Imperative for Educational Reform* (Washington, DC: U.S. Government Printing Office, 1983).

arts education, the National Endowment for the Arts called for two years of arts study to be required of all students for high school graduation.

Granted, everything in the world of music education is not satisfactory or promising, but the crumbling of music programs and the threats of further cuts that were very real for more than a decade appear to have been curbed and contained. The field can now turn its attention to matters other than survival. It can afford to plan ahead, reach, and do a bit of building for the future, now that a future seems secure. And that is exactly what seemed to be taking place at this convention.

The best news is that a vibrant interest in general education is afoot at all levels. More and more music educators seem eager to learn how to reach all the students, not just the talented who happen to sing or play instruments. Perhaps this long low period has taught them something: either music is in the schools for everybody, or it may not be there for anybody. It is refreshing to see high school band and choral directors attending sessions to learn how to teach general music at that level. No doubt the profession is accepting the responsibility that goes with the recognition that arts are basic studies like math or English. These teachers appear intent to learn how to provide music instruction for all students to meet the new graduation requirements. MENC's Society of General Music put on a stunning series of sessions at this conference, emerging as a major new force in the organization.

Change, however, does not happen without some prodding. If music teachers in the future are going to be expected to teach general music, their college education should prepare them for it. At a panel discussion on the subject of preparing teachers for general music, Timothy Gerber, professor of music education at Ohio State University, noted that few prospective music teachers aspire to teach general music. They see their own high school band, chorus, and orchestra directors as models. They aspire to the glamour of the podium. Gerber pointed out that only a surprising 50 percent of new teachers remain in the profession after the sixth year. Unfortunately, says Gerber, "These prospective teachers don't want to teach general music because, as band or choral members, they were exempt from it and don't know anything about it." As John Langfield of Northwestern University pointed out, general music requires "a hand without a baton in it."

There is an apparent conflict between much of what music education students learn in most of their music classes and what they need to know to teach general music. For example, if they study voice, they inevitably and exclusively learn bel canto, certainly not folk-song style or vocal improvisation in the scat tradition. Yet general music teachers need to command more than the ability to sing in the best operatic style. General music encompasses a far larger scenario than just Western European music. Yet on many campuses students are expected to become familiar with this larger musical world in the one "methods" course they are required to take as preparation for teaching general music. The question arises, can general-music teachers be adequately prepared without invading the whole college music curriculum?

At a session called "Music Miseducation: The Absence of Black Music in the Schools and Black Students in Music," the National Black Music Caucus expressed indignation at the lack of black music in the curriculum of American schools. Here again, the problem goes right back to the college curriculum. Hortense R. Kerr of Howard University said, "White teachers do not know about black composers or think they are of no consequence." And she complained that "black students are being robbed of music in the elementary grades." James Mumford of Indiana University noted that "some blacks don't want to sing anything but gospel." Yet he noted that others "are uncomfortable about anything other than European music." He spoke of the ethnic directives that emerged from the 1967 Tanglewood Symposium[3] and asked, "But is it happening? Lip service has been given. The less exposure to black music, the more negative the attitudes toward it. My principal would have a fit if he heard me do gospel."

At this same meeting, Michael Gordon, also of Indiana University, said that he grew up in an all-black environment and didn't know he was supposed to be inferior. "We did Thompson's 'Alleluia' and Dello Joio's 'Jubilant Song' in high school. Now black people aren't interested in that." At state festivals, he said, "You don't hear black music. Why?" Gordon called for a national symposium on the subject of black music. Among all these voices, there is a common message of frustration that needs to be vented and heeded.

Solutions to the problem hinge on learning how to deal with our multicultural musical heritage, a subject given considerable attention at this conference. Barbara Lundquist of the University of Washington noted that the emphasis in music study is on the elements of music and on the development of skills. "Little attention is given to society and culture," she says. "We must recognize what universals actually exists [sic] across cultures, similarities in process if not in product." She recommends that all music teachers be required to have expertise in more that [sic] one musical culture.

As with all change, however, there is the danger of people going off the deep end. A prime example is the music teacher who stood up at one of these sessions and said, "I'm tired of yet another performance of the *Missa Solemnis*." (The College-Conservatory of Music of the University of Cincinnati had performed the Beethoven masterpiece the evening before.) For the sake of accuracy, it should be noted that the many performances during this conference spanned music of just about every kind, from classical to jazz to folk and ethnic, from Josquin des Prez to Duke Ellington, from solo and small ensemble to band, chorus, and orchestra.

The range of topics explored was just as varied, giving some idea of the diversity and complexity of the field: administration and supervision, audiovisual resources, barbershop quartet, buildings and equipment, computers and electronic music, guitar, keyboard, special learners, and research. In addition, there were numbers of miscellaneous sessions on such subjects as evaluation, learning theory, teaching musical composition, teaching jazz techniques to young string players, music for the young

---

[3] Among many other major pronouncements, music educators at Tanglewood agreed that "music of all periods, styles, forms, and cultures belongs in the curriculum. The musical repertory should be expanded to involve music of our time in its rich variety, including currently popular teenage music and avant-garde music, American folk music, and the music of other cultures."

trombonist, and so on. But the big themes were the emphases on general music and multicultural education.

This conference was far better attended than meetings during the past decade, another sign that music teachers are pulling themselves out of the doldrums and responding to the beat of a new drummer. In many ways, these educators are like the monks of the Dark Ages. They are attempting to preserve our cultural heritage in the face of hostile social forces—today, specifically, the overriding stress on science and technology in our schools, at the expense of other values. They believe in a value system beyond materialism, beyond pop culture, beyond crass commercialism. They maintain that music and the other arts generate the mechanisms of human perception and understanding, of creativity and communication, and of thought and feeling that are essential to the conduct of life and society.

It is reassuring to realize that, in spite of everything, the music education tradition that started in Boston 150 years ago is still very much alive. That is just short of a miracle, given the fragile state of human and cultural values in many of today's schools. Music educators are trying to make certain that the future will be better. By recognizing that music is an essential means of confirming the wonders of our multicultural heritage and by determining to make music instruction of basic value to every student, they are reaffirming their claim on the curriculum. And in that process, they are also assuring that they will be around in 2038 to celebrate the bicentennial of music in American schools.

II

Advocacy and Arts Education Policy

13

EDUCATION IN THE ARTS: GETTING IT ALL TOGETHER

MUSICAL AMERICA 25 (February 1975)

In October 1974, an historic gathering of state-level arts education leaders gathered at the Kennedy Center in Washington, DC. The National Council of State Supervisors of Music and Art sponsored the meeting, with some 165 in attendance representing 42 state departments of education. A major purpose was to outline plans to incorporate music and the arts into education curricula nationally, and considerable progress was made toward that goal. Topics included inclusion, collaboration, competitiveness, curriculum, administration, humanities, academics, logistics, and politics, among others. Many of the challenges and possibilities are outlined, along with a sample of successful state integration, and further calls for action. Perhaps more shared work today would create similar enthusiasm for the value of music and arts education in schools.

—CR

* * *

IN A HISTORY-MAKING meeting of arts education leaders from forty-two state departments of education, held at the John F. Kennedy Center for the Performing Arts in Washington, D.C., October 17–20, 1974, art, dance, drama, film, and language arts educators set a new course for arts education in the United States. The meeting, sponsored by the National Council of State Supervisors of Music and Art and funded by the National Endowment for the Arts with assistance from the John D. Rockefeller 3rd Fund, brought together 165 arts educators, artists, community arts leaders, state arts council leaders, college and university arts teachers, local and state level school administrators, officials from the U.S. Office of Education, and leaders of the major arts education organizations to focus each state's attention on "comprehensive arts planning and development." Organized under the direction of Dr. James L. Fisher of Maryland's State Department of Education, the meeting was a huge success.

After four days, the consensus of the state plans that were drawn up during this conference provided a clear picture of the future thrust of arts programs in public education. State arts leaders are determined to incorporate the arts as a humanizing dimension in the education of every student. They recognize that value-centered education is as important as idea- and information-oriented learning. They assert that man is essentially an aesthetic being, reacting with his feelings and his senses as strongly as with his rational mind. To harness the emotional as well as the intellectual self is to recognize that there are other, often neglected, parameters of each human being that must be exercised in the educational process.

The plans assert that we cannot afford another generation of computerized people who are unaware of their inner creative resources and their ability to respond with their whole humanness. Education for leisure is a necessary complement to education for work.

The arts, these leaders believe, afford a way to personalize education in every subject matter, to reengage the affective and cognitive functions of people for the reinforcement of the total being, and to motivate the student in all learning through the joy of individual arts involvement.

Arts educators recognize the enormous responsibility they have taken upon themselves. In a long-overdue move, if this meeting is indicative, they have joined forces to achieve their purposes. These educators are saying that the arts, like the sciences and mathematics, constitute a major area of educational concentration. Visual, performing, and literary arts educators are now beginning to view their arts, not simply as independent special subjects for special students, but as allied areas that provide unique and valuable experiences for every human being. Relationships between the several arts and between the arts and other subject matters can be mutually reinforcing. Given this new outlook, the arts, for the first time, stand the chance of emerging nationally as a major united force in American education.

COMPETITIVENESS

Traditions, however, do not die easily. The various arts have operated independently for a long time. They are often protective and competitive about their own realms.

To achieve unity is to reinterpret the notion of autonomy. Independence, after all, is really inner-directed. But the various arts disciplines have operated defensively. Unlike the language arts, mathematics, and science, they have always been forced to fight for their usually meager slice of the annual budget. They have had continually to defend their place in the curriculum. They have struggled against schedules that often prevented them from reaching the students who needed them most. They have expended endless energies trying to impress the power structure that their subject matters are worthy of being counted equal to the more acceptable, "legitimate" fare. Arts educators have probably written more articles justifying their existence than all the other educators combined. No one ever seems to question the worth of algebra, even though few students ever use it the rest of their lives. It's simply "good for the mind."

Unfortunately for the arts educators, true autonomy is not won by efforts that are motivated and controlled from outside. What they serve or compete with, they tend to end up being driven by. Arts educators are seldom their own masters, certainly not in the same sense as teachers of history, mathematics, or science. Arts educators are always trying to prove something, while all the other teachers are free to concentrate on the work at hand: teaching.

The insularity of the various arts disciplines was one of the basic problems alluded to in the discussions at this meeting. To view the arts comprehensively causes some apprehension among arts teachers because they fear the loss of their private domains; yet, in essence, they never really had much autonomy. To band together, to work as a conglomerate, to join forces, is to gain the power that could release this vast dimension of refreshment upon the students and upon the educational system itself. Perhaps this new alliance will wash away some of the educational disillusionment presently felt by students, teachers, and administrators alike.

As arts educators begin to work cooperatively, one other outcome could be even more significant. This joining of forces brings a whole new attitude of *inclusion*. The joining of hands precludes whole programs that exclude and, instead, begins to make a place for every student in the arts. When arts educators are able to relax into less protectiveness, they will open themselves more willingly to others.

The new approach, of course, does not mean that these various subject matters— the visual, performing, and literary arts—will no longer be taught as discrete disciplines, for in that sense they would be no different from biology, chemistry, and physics. But the unity of the latter subjects is that they constitute the sciences, a major area of valued human thought and endeavor. That the arts find areas where they can interact, reinforce—and, yes, contrast—yet still attain that status as one of the primary focuses of man's achievement was the fundamental impetus and triumph of this four-day meeting.

PENNSYLVANIA'S LEADERSHIP

Among all the state teams present, the Pennsylvania State Department of Education has asserted special leadership in advancing the allied arts concept. For the better part of a decade their arts personnel, under the leadership of Dr. Russell Getz, have been working toward a unified approach. Their success in achieving this union is exemplified by the commitment of John C. Pittenger, Secretary of Education for the Commonwealth, who called his own Conference on the Arts in Basic Education to express the need for arts experiences as a central component of education: "One of the roles of the arts in education is to give people the capacity to imagine beyond the scope of their own daily experience.... Equally important is the need to give every young person a chance to develop along the lines in which he or she has shown the greatest talent. I am more and more impressed by the importance of having young people come out of schools with some sense of confidence, some sense of their own worth. This sense is an absolutely indispensable foundation for their doing anything else in life.

"For some young people," Pittenger observes, "this sense of worth and confidence can come from mathematics or it can can come from history. For others it can come from football or squash. There are many young people for whom the arts are the natural avenue toward the skill and confidence that comes from being able to do something at least moderately well. For both of those reasons, the capacity to imagine and the development of a sense of worth, I would strongly urge upon you, particularly those of you who are superintendents and principals who shape educational policy, the notion that the arts are central and not peripheral."

It seems evident that the tides are changing and that the educational establishment is willing to take a fresh look at its priorities. The comprehensive view of the arts as a major area for study is attracting attention nationwide. One can begin to see the music, arts, and drama departments being replaced by one arts department that also encompasses dance and film-making, as well as creative writing. It has happened on the state level in places like New York and Pennsylvania and there are strong indications from other states that this is the direction for the future. College and university arts departments have also amalgamated and the trend will filter through the public schools.

A CALL FOR ACTION

This meeting made it clear that state arts supervisors are casting off their traditional support role and opting for true leadership. They are asserting action for change in the whole structure and content of arts programs in their states. These state arts leaders are searching intensely for every means to bring the arts experience into a central position in the school curriculum. They are cataloging community arts resources, garnering broad community support, enlisting the aid of administrators, boards of education, and others in the educational power structure, reeducating arts teachers as well as classroom teachers, and looking to community and state arts councils and other arts groups and agencies to assist them in what they believe could be a significant turn in the general education of every child. What was officially launched in Washington is a massive educational campaign aimed at the public and private sectors to prove—once and for all—the value of the arts in the general education of every American.

The state teams who met in the nation's capital represent a vast, determined, and potentially powerful group armed with a sensible and captivating idea that should win wide support. Collaborative programing involving the visual, performing, and literary arts has proved enormously successful through such projects as Arts IMPACT, the Cemrel Aesthetic Education Program, and the Arts in General Education Program of the JDR 3rd Fund. With the impetus of this meeting it seems inevitable that school districts will begin to incorporate the arts in new ways, viewing this vast area of study as an essential and significant component of education. An infusion of arts in education as experiences that are a complement and equivalent to science, mathematics, and language studios may bring to the American people, in the not too distant future, some restored sense of the goodness, beauty, and true worth of life.

14

THE ROLE OF THE NATIONAL ENDOWMENT (FOR THE ARTS)

MUSICAL AMERICA 27 (March 1977)

The National Endowment for the Arts (NEA) was established by the US Congress in 1965. One of its mandates was to support and expand the cultural resources of the nation, along with related duties. A gray area, however, was the role that the NEA should play in educational endeavors, such as music and arts education. In order to clarify this issue, the NEA met in November 1976 to present and consider the results of the *Arts in Education Study Project*. There was some debate on the purpose and mission of the NEA, and whether or not it should be engaged in support of education over artist assistance and similar tasks. Music educators were expressing some concern that their requests for funding seemed to be passed around rather than handled quickly and directly, and that the NEA was less interested in, or felt other offices should handle, their projects and grants. The study recommended that the NEA should pursue more research on the value of arts education; strengthen communication with those in the arts; receive more support from other government agencies; and discuss the need for comprehensive arts education, and the role of the NEA to bring together stakeholders involved in the debate to help improve overall music education in the United States. Lofty goals to be sure, but who better to address them than the national body designated to provide funding, advocacy, and backing for major arts initiatives in America?

—CR

* * *

THE NATIONAL COUNCIL on the Arts, the star-studded group of twenty-six Americans-in-the-arts who guide the programs and policies of the National Endowment for the Arts, recently commissioned a study of the Endowment's own educational programs. At a meeting of the Council in Washington, D.C. on November 19, 1976 they heard the results of that study. A.B. Spellman, the black poet recently of Harvard who has spent the past few years in activities committed to bettering the state of arts education, was asked to direct the Arts in Education Study Project.

CONGRESSIONAL MANDATE

Spellman's report to the Council attempts to clarify the role of the NEA in educational programing. There has been considerable confusion regarding the posture of the Endowment in this area. The U.S. Congress explicitly mandated the NEA, when it established it in 1965, to encourage and assist the nation's cultural resources, a mandate that does not by any means eliminate education. The Endowment receives and allocates private as well as government funds to individuals, public agencies, nonprofit tax-exempt groups, and state arts agencies.

In the view of many arts educators it appears that most of the Endowment's funds have gone to arts organizations and artists, with little left over to offer any aid to programs in the field of education. Arts educators with worthy proposals have been continually turned down or sent to the U.S. Office of Education (which also has scant funds to expend on arts education), even though the Endowment boasts of having an Education Program.

The director of that program, John Hoare Kerr, speaking at the same meeting, distinguished the difference between the work of artists and arts educators: "By concentrating on the arts and the artists transmitting the arts essence, by not removing it to be interpreted by someone less well prepared, as it were one generation removed, one achieves a higher reality or understanding of the arts and of the creative process itself." Kerr also made no apology for what the Endowment has accomplished in education in comparison to the U.S. Office of Education: "While other agencies more directly in line to the Congressional mandate for Education have been virtually ignoring the need for substantial Federal dollar commitment to artists and arts in education, while others have been criticizing the lack of quality in arts education today, the lack of a unified policy, the lack of adequate evaluation of 'learner outcomes,' and so forth, the Council and the Endowment have *acted and funded*." (Italics added.)

A CLEARER POLICY

Spellman has tried to set this record straight at the same time that he has attempted to formulate a clearer educational policy. His report notes that "the Arts Endowment has been involved deeply in the schools since its inception." The pattern of support takes four forms, according to the report: provision for artists to perform, create and display their work in schools; provision for cultural organizations to offer their resources and services to schools; support for research, demonstration projects, planning and developmental projects and other activities designed to have far-reaching impact upon the status of the arts in schools; and informational dissemination, staff outreach, and other forms of active advocacy for the cause of arts in the lives of American youth.

The report notes the general hiatus of Federal support for arts education. It suggests that the Council hoped "that there would be a concommitant growth of arts programing in other Federal agencies which address the needs of the schools . . ." and it acknowledges the pressure "from those active in the field of arts education" to rectify the situation.

The Endowment's Education Program has two main funding categories: Artists-in-Schools (see November 1975 issue of MA) and Learning Thru the Arts (formerly titled Alternative Education). The latter provides support to make artists available to communities to perform educational functions or complement and enhance educational activities. All of the other Endowment Program areas—Expansion Arts, Music, Dance, Theatre, Museums, Architecture and Environmental Arts, and Public Media and Literature—also support educational endeavors, although, again, largely through the work of artists.

In spite of this activity Spellman points out that the Arts Endowment has not operated as an educational agency. The Endowment, he says, is not intent upon having a major impact upon education, but rather to continue in its advocacy role. NEA will collaborate to the extent to which other agencies want to use artists in school situations. That distinction is critical in understanding the programs of the NEA in education.

A MORE CONSISTENT PRESENCE

The policy is clearly set forth in the main recommendation of the Arts-in-Education Study Project: "As the National Endowment for the Arts sees artists and cultural organizations as its primary clientele, support for their involvement must remain the central thrust of Endowment programing. However, the Council remains sensitive to the need for a more consistent presence of art in all aspects of education, and will continue to recommend funding planning efforts, studies and developmental projects on an ad hoc or pilot basis. Also, the Council and Endowment will continue to act as an advocate for excellence in arts education and all its aspects, even though it cannot attempt to be a principal funding source for the field." Clearly, the U.S. Office of Education must assume the major responsibility for the support and development of the arts in education.

Among the other recommendations of the study: that the Endowment should continue to support research which would enhance the situation of the arts in the schools, particularly research that reveals what is actually taking place in school arts programing; that communications with organizations that deal with the arts in education should be strengthened and that the Endowment should offer guidance and information in educational programing; that informational materials that address various aspects of the arts in education ought to be prepared and disseminated; that the Endowment should continue to encourage other federal agencies to strengthen their commitment to arts education; that the Federal Council on the Arts and the Humanities should address itself to the question of the need for comprehensive planning for arts education; that where legally possible the Endowment will accept as matching funds for in-school arts projects monies from the U.S. Office of Education and other federal agencies in order to encourage such support from other sources; and that the Endowment should provide new leadership in bringing together artists, educators, and cultural institutions in a major effort to improve substantially the quality of arts education in the United States.

15

A NEW RATIONALE FOR THE ARTS IN EDUCATION

MUSICAL AMERICA 27 (September 1977)

An important report on the state of the arts in education was released in 1977. Titled *Coming to Our Senses: The Significance of the Arts for American Education*, this was a work with a strong contribution from Fowler himself: he was involved as a consultant, with David Rockefeller and his panel, which produced the report. The contributors represent important figures in the artistic community, including James Michener, Lorin Hollander, Glenn Seaborg, Melissa Hayden, and others. They not only engaged in contributing to the report through expertise and interest, but also testified about the results before the US Congress (including Rockefeller). In addition to concerns presented, other positives are noted in the book, such as model programs, recommendations for moving forward (ninety-eight of them!), and other insights that capture a snapshot in time on the state of arts education in America. The timing of the book was compelling, as it arrived ten years after The Tanglewood Symposium (1967), which was the most significant reform movement in music education to date. Guess who connects the dots? Yes, you are right: Charles Fowler was directly involved in both important events. To see the entire picture, read *The Tanglewood Report* and *Coming to Our Senses*.

—CR

* * *

Mr. Fowler wishes readers to be informed that although he has endeavored to remain objective, his report on the Rockefeller Panel study is not disinterested. He himself represented the study as Organizational Liaison, and interviewed some seventy leaders representing forty organizations in the arts, education, and arts education fields. He has also worked to disseminate information. He does not classify himself, therefore, as a totally uninvolved reporter in dealing with this subject. Let the reader beware, if he wishes! (Editor, Musical America)

WITH THE PUBLICATION last May of the Rockefeller panel report, *Coming to Our Senses: The Significance of the Arts for American Education* (330 pages, McGraw-Hill), a new and stronger case in support of the arts in education was presented to the American people. The twenty-five-member panel, which included such luminaries as author James A. Michener, pianist Lorin Hollander, newspaper publisher Barry Bingham, Sr., dancer Melissa Hayden, and Nobel Prizewinning physicist Glenn T. Seaborg, said that the arts, far from being frills, can perform a function in American public education as essential as the three R's.

PROTESTING SEGREGATION

The report emerges as a rallying call to the nation to reverse the historic segregation of the arts from American education. It traces the separation of the arts from formal learning back to the first schools in this country, which were dominated by the pragmatism and asceticism of Puritan settlers. It was here that the arts were labeled as idle pleasures more akin to the Devil than to the ideals of the Protestant work ethic. This division of the arts from education, the panel argues, is at the heart of claims by supporters of a "back-to-basics" movement that regards the arts as expendable in the face of budget stringency.

David Rockefeller, Jr., chairman of the panel study, says that it is the group's central thesis that the arts must "be seen as one of the basics, not merely as a subject distinct from the three R's, but as a tool for teaching the fundamentals and almost anything else we want our children to learn."

As part of its affirmation of "basic education," the panel maintains that "the arts, properly taught, are basic to individual development since they, more than any other subject, awaken all the senses—the learning pores." The report contends that arts education must extend beyond looking at art or listening to music to "making art, knowing artists, and using art as a general tool of learning." The panel calls the process "learning in, through, and about the arts."

ROCKEFELLER TESTIFIES

At a joint hearing of the House subcommittee on Select Education and the Senate Subcommittee on Education on May 25, 1977, Rockefeller and several members of the panel and other witnesses conveyed to the Congressmen the essence of the report.

"Our panel asserts that American education exaggerates the importance of words as transmitters of information," Rockefeller stated. "The fact is we send and receive a torrent of other information through our eyes, our ears, our skin, and our palate. We use all our senses to interpret and convey the complexities of daily life. Is a job interview settled on a written resume alone? What of the handshake, the style of dress, the mannerisms of speech and gesture?

"Verbal and written language is essential, but all our sensory languages need to be developed as well if words are to fulfill their deeper function and deliver both subtle and vivid messages."

In effect, Rockefeller then spelled out to the Congressmen a new rationale for the arts in education. "Perception and communication—both fundamental learning skills—require much more than verbal training. And since the arts (painting, dancing, singing, acting, and so forth) can send important nonverbal messages from a creator or performer to an observer, they are ideal vehicles for training our senses, for enriching our emotional selves, and for organizing our environment."

Perhaps his most convincing argument is the last. "Our environment is what we make it," he said. "And how we shape it depends upon how we perceive it. Through the arts we can learn to see our environment more clearly; to sense its color, song, and dance; and to preserve its life and quality."

OUR "SENSELESSNESS"

The fact that many of our schools have become fearful, gray fortresses and our cities and towns a gridwork of dismal frontage and automotive clamor, bear testimony, Rockefeller said, "to our general 'senselessness.'" The implication is that our lifestyle is influenced by aesthetic considerations which, once perceived and developed, can make it less harsh and jarring. In other words, if we want to improve the quality of our lifestyle, we must come to our senses.

"We endorse a curriculum which puts 'basics' first," Rockefeller said, "because the arts are basic, right at the heart of the matter. And we suggest not that reading be replaced by art but that the concept of literacy be expanded beyond word skills."

Barry Bingham, Sr., in his testimony, gave other reasons why the arts are basic. "Art," he said, "determines how we furnish our homes, the music we play in our leisure hours, the shows we watch on television, the kind of public housing we approve, the type of shopping centers we build, and the amount of urban space we demand. Ray Pierotti of the American Crafts Council informed the panel that the American people 'must come to see the importance of design in the development of the American culture, design meaning all the visual aspects of our communities, from the objects we eat out of to the trash cans on the street corners.'"

The object, of course, is to make the arts part of everyday living in the United States and a legitimate part of education for all citizens. These goals are not new. They have been part of the ten-year-old arts-in-education movement begun by the JDR 3rd Fund, and they are the basis of CEMREL's Aesthetic Education Program as well. That the rationale for this approach has been given a thorough statement and that the case has been brought to the attention of the American people, *is* new.

"The arts provide unique ways of knowing about the world and should be central to learning for this reason alone," Rockefeller maintains. "But it is also significant that arts education can influence two elements of human behavior which concern every teacher: discipline and motivation.

"Artists are often accused of being undisciplined, but quite the reverse is true. Art requires tremendous discipline—the dancer at the exercise barre, the pianist playing endless finger exercises, the meticulous editing of the filmmaker, the centering of the potter. Learning an art is learning to care passionately about tiny details as well as over-all excellence.

"On the other hand, the arts can bring enormous pleasure, and all of us are motivated to do what brings us pleasure. Think of schoolchildren completing a mural on the playground wall, producing a musical in the gymnasium, or videotaping a parade: these are arts experiences which can energize an entire school population, and which can teach principles of design, geometry, speech, carpentry, political science, electricity, and more. A successful art experience motivates the child to look further and deeper."

MODEL PROGRAMS

The report highlights upwards of one hundred model school arts programs which exemplify in one way or another the panel's conviction that strong arts programs that reach every child, far from deterring learning, enhance it. The panel found that the finest arts programs are often those that offer the broadest alternatives. The report states, "The traditional curriculum consisting only of courses in visual art and music is no longer sufficient." The panel recommends that the curriculum be expanded to include the disciplines of dance, film, drama, poetry, design, and so forth.

James Michener, in his testimony, noted that "These other arts are poorly represented in American schools at the present time. Only one quarter of our high schools, for example, present what could be called strong programs in theater. Of all arts forms, dance undoubtedly fares the worst in the schools. Although dance performances have become more popular than ever, and though small dance companies are springing up all over the country, dance teachers at the secondary level represent less than one percent of all teachers."

In light of the great potential of the arts to help people live fuller and better lives and to add new dimensions that would make education more thorough and effective, it is ironic and unfortunate that the arts are fighting for survival in many school systems. In New York City, for example, forty percent of the music teachers were fired last year. The report points out that "In most schools the arts tend to receive limited time and limited resources."

At the same time, the arts appear to be flourishing as never before in America. According to estimates by the National Endowment for the Arts, during the period 1965 to 1975 the number of professional orchestras doubled; resident professional theaters quadrupled; arts councils quintupled; and resident professional dance companies increased sevenfold.

"A CLEAR CASE OF SCHIZOPHRENIA"

Barry Bingham, Sr. said, "The American people appear to believe the arts are important, but simultaneously they are hard put to reconcile that view with their conviction that the schools should concentrate on reading, writing, and arithmetic. The disparity between what goes on in American society in the arts and what goes on in American schools points to a clear case of schizophrenia. There is a lack of synchronization between American schools and American culture."

The report's ninety-eight recommendations attempt to rectify this situation. They speak to every level of government, to teachers, arts specialists, school administrators, and parents. To make certain that the report has maximum impact, Rockefeller has established a new private agency, "Arts, Education and Americans, Inc.," to see that the report's recommendations are implemented.

This study, which has been three years in the making, has already accomplished one important objective. It has brought to the attention of federal officials the plight and the potential of the arts in education. Even though only four of the twenty-one members of the House and Senate Committees were present at the hearing, the findings of the panel were read into the record. Considering the amount of apathy surrounding the issues that the panel has raised, Rockefeller has stated that "We cannot pretend that the changes we recommend will take place quickly." He has promised to return to the Congress in a year to bring formal recommendations for action.

The new wave of energy in American education could well come from the arts. As Rockefeller asserts, "In the Fifties, with a nudge from Sputnik, America recognized the central importance of science education. In the Sixties, with a lateral pass from the Kennedy clan, the nation reaffirmed that physical education was essential. Now, in the Seventies, it is time to acknowledge the power and urgency of arts education."

(Forthcoming articles will deal with the significance of the recommendations and other aspects of the report.)

16

WHAT'S WRONG WITH MUSIC EDUCATION?

MUSICAL AMERICA 28 (April 1978)

Challenges to music education in the schools are unfortunately not a new phenomenon. While the profession generally is not happy to hear about its own problems, often an open discussion is just the needed spark to move toward meaningful change. Here, after some interesting data on student music enrollment, several insightful suggestions are offered. These include understanding music as a creative art; the need for music in schools to become less print bound; music as practical study; music for everyone, rather than merely the talented or fortunate; music as inclusive curricular and academic subject; music as part of the school mainstream; and music educators serving as their own best advocates. A reader of contemporary music education literature will not be surprised at these ideas; indeed, why do we still encounter these problems if they were highlighted over thirty-five years ago?

—CR

* * *

THE LATEST statistics from the U.S. Office of Education show that the percentage of pupils enrolled in music courses in 1972–73 declined from the percentage in 1960–61, while enrollments in art courses increased from 20.3 to 27.6 percent of total pupils. (In absolute numbers, music showed a modest increase of from approximately 5 to 6 million, while art increased from 2.4 to 5.1 million, a striking rise.)[1]

As if this statistic isn't bad enough, music, particularly in the big cities, is in serious trouble. Especially at the elementary level, many programs are being curtailed or excised altogether. In Philadelphia, for example, recent cuts are crippling what used to be one of the country's finest music education programs. In September 1977, Philadelphia dismissed fourteen instrumental specialists and closed eight Saturday Morning Music Centers. The latter program alone affects over two thousand students. The loss of the centers means that Philadelphia will no longer have district orchestras, bands, or choirs. The future of the all-Philadelphia performing groups is also in question.

School boards have been steadily whittling away at urban music programs for the past five years. Washington D.C. lost seventeen elementary music specialists in 1977. New York City has all but eliminated music in the elementary schools. Other cities have made similar cuts. What's wrong? While many reasons can be given (slackening enrollments, inflation, bankruptcy, parental demands to go "back to basics," etc.), some of the problem lies right at the feet of music educators themselves. If music is going to deserve or attain a higher priority in American education, some basic changes are called for.

(1) Music must be taught as a creative art. The greatest failure of American music education is that music, by and large, has not been taught as a self-contained expressive system. Expression is restricted, for the most part, to reinterpretation. In delimiting musical expression to the re-creative, music becomes a second-hand art. (How can colleges grant degrees in music without requiring a single course in musical composition?)

The re-creative emphasis stresses performance by imitation. The result of this emphasis is that music is heavily laden with tradition and burdened by history to the point of neglect for the present and future. This imbalance could be corrected by the injection of an equal emphasis on creativity. If music is to be important to all students, it must be taught as a personally expressive medium.

(2) Music must become less print-bound. Most musicians tend to be slaves to the printed page. In high school and college programs that have finally added jazz after all the years of resistance, what is the approach? Students are taught to read the charts! Yet this music originated as a primarily aural and improvisory art, where the inner need to express was fulfilled through the invention of sounds without the intervention of someone else's notations.

Improvisation should be given greater emphasis to the point where it becomes a deliberate and important part of what every student learns in the music classroom. As

---

[1] Logan Osterndorf, *Summary of Offerings and Enrollments in Public Secondary Schools*, 1972–73 (Washington, D.C.: National Center for Educational Statistics, 1975), pp. 4 and 17.

the gate through which students gain access to music as a self-expressive art, improvisation is central to what music education is all about. It is interesting to note that both the Orff and Dalcroze methodologies place emphasis on improvisation and creativity, yet they have not won over the vast majority of music teachers, who tend to go on teaching in the way in which they themselves were taught.

(3) Music must be approached as a practical study and not as an esoteric, ethereal art. If music is thought of as a frill, it is because, for the most part, it has been taught as one. When entertainment gets to be more important than edification, music education debases itself. Particularly in the early years, sharing is more important than showing. The process should always be as important as the product.

Too often, music is viewed as an ornament or accessory to life rather than as a fundamental means to reinforce, express, and understand human lifestyle. Music is not a mere embellishment of the environment, although it is frequently taught as such. On the contrary, it gets at the heart of what cultures and peoples are about. Above all, it has *meaning*. In reaching into the depths of human feeling, it reveals the spirit and hope of mankind, giving significant counterbalance to cruelty, hypocrisy, crime, war, and other foibles of humankind. Music education should reconstitute its efforts to make certain that the fundamental nature of the art is conveyed through every lesson.

(4) Music must be seen as for everybody and not just the talented. While music educators have given lip service to this notion for years, they have not found the curricular solutions to implement their belief. Granted, they have added electives in some schools in guitar, electronic music, popular music, etc., which are designed to attract and reach a larger number of students, but the focus of most music programs remains on the selective and restrictive performing groups.

In music, many people are eliminated early from the main events. They get the message, and they remember it. Instead, all students should be given opportunities to play with sound in the same way they play with paint. They must be continually invited to express themselves musically until they discover the possibilities this art form provides for personal expression and communication. Students are not the mere recipients of a rigid and finished musical commentary on the world as it was; they are participants in a malleable and evolving symbolic system that permits them to express their world as it is.

In assuming a completely democratic stance, music educators will shed any remaining vestiges of elitism and open the art to every student. They will cease making distinctions between "high" and "low" art or between the "fine" and "applied" arts, so that the study of music can encompass all its forms and styles. Musical taste is not refined through confinement to specific styles, but through coming to terms, personally, with the appeal, appropriateness, and accomplishment of a wide variety of musical works.

(5) Music education must consciously and conscientiously drop its isolation and join the main business of schooling. Compartmentalization and specialism should be traded for infusion and commonality. Music should enter the bloodstream of the school instead of being willing and even content to exist on the periphery. This means

that music education must involve itself with the primary purposes of education. Too many music educators serve their own purposes and make their courses supernumerary to the primary goals of education.

(6) Music educators should take the lead in promoting the arts as a curriculum area comparable to the sciences. As representatives of the oldest art in public education and the most established, music educators could form the strongest and largest advocacy group for the arts in the nation's schools. By broadening their focus to promote aesthetic, instead of just musical, sensitivity and understanding, the case for music and all the arts would be strengthened.

Students need more options in the arts, if each person is to find a rewarding and compatible realm of expression. When this happens, the arts most assuredly will be valued in education. The arts and sciences will be seen as complementary fields, the arts being, as Herbert Read observed, "the representation, [as] science [is] the explanation—of the same reality."

The agenda for music education is challenging and fraught with promise. In meeting their own problems head on, music educators will better their prospects for the future. In fulfilling its own promise, music education will improve its status in the schools and begin to solve many of the problems that now plague it throughout the nation.

17

FUNDING FOR ARTS PROGRAMS: THE TOTAL IS NOT SO BLEAK

MUSICAL AMERICA 30 (February 1980)

One of the exhausting problems of music and arts education is the constant lack of funding and support. While the news is usually bad, here we have a glimpse of an example when the bigger picture seemed to be on track. One of the benefits that Fowler brought to the profession (among many) was his ability to collect and evaluate large bodies of data related to serious problems, and then bring them down to a manageable size. Add this to his clear and direct style of writing, and often the issues at hand seem less bleak. This is a review of a collection of funding projects that were underway from about 1977 to 1980, which offers a comprehensive snapshot of federal, state, and local support at the time. Organizations include the US Office of Education, the National Endowment for the Arts, National Endowment for the Humanities, National Institute of Education, and others. Groups that received funding were boards of education, large public-school systems, theater arts cooperatives, community education organizations, numerous magnet schools, and programs for those with special needs. While someone today would need to do a bit of digging to find more recent data, the template is here to find the right places to seek the information. Another compelling use for this information currently would be comparisons to see where we have been, and where we need to go.

—CR

* * *

AN EXHAUSTIVE inventory of all of the U.S. Office of Education's programs reveals that more than three hundred arts-related projects were funded in 1978-79 under agency programs specifically concerned with other educational purposes and not arts education. The extent of arts education support within these non-categorical areas is estimated in excess of $13 million.

Out of the 120 programs in the Office of Education, thirty programs, or one quarter, gave some funding to arts education. Under Title IV-C of the Elementary and Secondary Act (Improvement in Local Educational Practices), for example, some 160 projects were funded in arts education totaling almost $4.5 million. In addition, under other provisions of IV-C (Strengthening State Departments of Education), twenty-six arts positions were supported in sixteen state departments of education. In this case, monetary figures were not available.

This list of funded projects and activities reveals that arts educators left few, if any, possibilities unexplored in seeking support for their programs. The Clark County Board of Education in Athens, Georgia received $30,000 in Adult Education funds for the Development of Enrichment Units in the Areas of Art, Music and Literature. The Boston Public Schools received approximately $200,000 from OE's Bilingual Education Program for a Bilingual Theatre Arts Program. Under Career Education, New York City's Children's Art Carnival received $150,000 for Career Training Through the Arts for Children Ages 8–18. Some seventeen magnet schools for the arts were funded under OE's Emergency School Aid Act, Magnet Schools. Other arts projects were funded in Environmental Education, Gifted and Talented, Indian Education, Instructional and Equipment Grants, Public Library Services, Alcohol and Drug Abuse, Community Education, Vocation Education, and Women's Education.

A survey by OE's National Center for Educational Statistics released in August 1979 reveals that during the 1977–78 school year every state except one used at least one of eleven such federal programs to support arts projects. The national average was about four per state.

The following is a list of eleven federal programs and the number of states using them for arts projects:

Title IV-C, ESEA: Education Innovation and Support   38
Special Projects Act: Gifted and Talented   30
Education of the Handicapped Act   26
Title IV-B, ESEA: Library and Learning Resources   25
Emergency School Aid Act   18
Title I, ESEA: Educational Disadvantaged   16
Special Projects Act: Career Education   14
Special Projects Act: Community Education   11
Title VII, ESEA: Bilingual Education   7
Adult Education Act   3
Vocational Education Act   3

State level support for arts education is clearly on the increase. The survey revealed that thirty-one state boards of education have adopted resolutions or policy statements supporting arts in education. Eleven of the resolutions were adopted in the past two years. Three more states plan to adopt similar resolutions within a year.

State funds often reinforce these policy statements. The survey indicated that in the 1977–78 school year twenty states supported in-service training programs in the arts; fifteen backed various types of demonstration projects; and thirteen funded arts education advisory councils to lend leadership in the implementation of their school arts programs.

IN-SERVICE TRAINING

The survey also collected state views on needs for improving arts education. Nearly all respondents reported that, if new funds were made available for improving arts education, they would use them for in-service training and integrating arts into the curriculum. Forty-eight states would support workshops and conferences; forty-four would underwrite demonstration projects; and thirty-one favored funding preservice training of arts educators.

All this federal and state support is in addition to OE's categorical support for arts education. This includes $750,000 for the Alliance for Arts Education, a program at the John F. Kennedy Center that supports a state network of AAE committees that promote comprehensive elementary and secondary arts education programs and supports the American College Theatre Festival and Children's Programs at the Center; $1 million for the National Committee, Arts for the Handicapped; and another $750,000 for state and local education agencies. In 1977–78, this program made grants to forty-one state and thirty-eight local education agencies for arts programs in elementary and secondary schools. During the current school year, an additional $500,000 was awarded on a contract basis.

But a true picture of the totality of federal support for the arts in education must take into account the programs of other federal agencies, not just the U.S. Office of Education. The Artists-in-Schools Program of the National Endowment for the Arts, for example, has a budget of $4.6 million a year. The states' match for these federal dollars has risen from $6 million in 1977 to $11 million in 1979. The program now supports five thousand artists in as many schools who reach two million students in all states and territories. (As a footnote to the success of this program, the United Kingdom, Australia, Denmark, Japan, Okinawa, the Philippines, and Korea are all starting artists-in-schools programs modeled after the Endowment's.)

NEH & NIE

The National Endowment for the Humanities and the National Institute of Education (OE's research arm) also support arts education projects to the tune of several million dollars each year. The point cannot be missed: support for arts education has increased dramatically in the past decade.

These increases are no doubt due to the efforts of arts educators to gain greater political influence at the state and federal levels. By working together during the past several years, they have won wider support among state and federal legislators, school administrators, and the public at large. They have also benefited from the steady and persuasive national advocacy efforts of Joan Mondale and David Rockefeller, Jr. Outreach endeavors at every level have captured wide attention and attracted a broader and more committed constituency.

This is not to say that arts education has arrived or that local, state, and federal levels of support—philosophical and financial—are sufficient to meet the needs. But the current data do substantiate the fact that vast strides have been made which are a credit to the field.

18

ARTS EDUCATION: DOES THE LEFT HAND KNOW?

MUSICAL AMERICA 30 (June 1980)

The well-known saying alluded to in the title (*does the left hand know what the right hand is doing?*) is here applied to music and arts education. Often, arts programs in schools operate in isolation, and there is little collaboration between them. This is certainly the case in many music programs, between band, orchestra, chorus, and general music—so imagine where art, dance, theater and others fit in. A strong argument is made for teachers becoming more involved in their own understanding and collaboration with other arts disciplines, especially since they know the scene on the ground and in the field. To help in this endeavor, a report was produced in 1979 that was sponsored by the National Endowment for the Arts, National Endowment for the Humanities, and US Office of Education. Titled *Arts Education Technical Assistance: An Interim Strategy for Collaborative Federal Support,* a number of suggestions are offered to bring more groups together and encourage a stronger collaborative approach. After all, more people advocating means a louder message getting through to those who need to hear it. A practicing music teacher, administrator, parent group, or school board could certainly take these ideas to heart today.

—CR

* * *

IN THE FIELD of arts education in the United States, the left hand often doesn't know what the right hand is doing. One school system's curriculum in the arts consists of general music, band, chorus, and some broad courses in the visual arts. Another's encompasses not only music and art, but also dance, theater, creative writing, photography, filmmaking, television, design, and architecture.

In some schools, arts courses are reserved primarily for the talented. In others, the courses are broadly constituted and are open to all. While the arts are taught only by arts specialists in many systems, in others they are taught by a cadre of classroom teachers, artists, community volunteers, personnel from various local arts institutions, as well as specialists. The arts in many schools are treated as discrete disciplines; in others there is a deliberate attempt to relate them to the total educational enterprise.

In a sense, these wide variances in approach can be viewed as positive and healthy—an example of the flexibility and interpretation that result from local control of the schools. In another sense, however, they can be viewed as manifestations of a schizophrenic field. At the very least, they signify that arts education is in a critical period of redefinition.

OVERCOMING INSULARITY

One of the great hurdles the arts face, if they are to solidify into an educational curriculum the equivalent of the sciences, is to overcome the traditional insularity of the various arts disciplines. The necessary collaboration this implies would require new means of communication between the various singular arts fields and a far broader sharing of information and expertise between school systems.

The lack of sufficient and regular channels of communication has been a sore point with arts educators for a number of years. During the past decade, a variety of national projects, studies, task forces, and conferences concerned with arts education at all levels have identified the lack of adequate communication and assistance mechanisms as a major problem of the field—a problem that results in ignorance about ongoing programs and services, under-utilization of available resources, and duplication of efforts.

Recently, the National Endowment for the Arts, the National Endowment for the Humanities, and the U.S. Office of Education took the problem to heart. Acting jointly, they funded a study to determine what role the federal government could and should play in providing the needed technical support for arts education. Underlying the study is the notion that collaboration on the federal level can serve as a model for collaborative efforts on the state and local levels.

During the summer of 1979 a contract for the study was awarded to Applied Management Sciences, an independent research group in Silver Spring, Maryland, to conduct a four-month inquiry to determine what actions might be feasible on the federal level. Their report, *Arts Education Technical Assistance: An Interim Strategy for Collaborative Federal Support,* was published in January of this year.

Deliberately, the report proposes an interim strategy rather than a permanent long-term solution, the aim being, as the report states, that "a solution be found that enables practitioners in the schools and communities to receive the support they need now without the delay that would be inevitable if the plan required wholly new governmental structures and legislation."

RECOMMENDATIONS

The report, which is directed to the federal agencies, recommends that they "should provide for the establishment, training, and support of a resource facilitation and linkage function [read: someone in charge of communication and technical assistance] in each of the major federal arts education related agencies; and the encouragement, training, and support of a similar function in state arts, education, and humanities agencies.

"The federal agencies should provide an *operating structure* at the federal level for the implementation of this strategy that: (a) facilitates the more effective focusing of federal resources on the goals of arts education; (b) supports the development of state internal and external arts education networks; and (c) provides a visible, national model of the advantages of collaboration for arts education."

The report further recommends that "The initial service activities of the arts education technical assistance process should concentrate on the development of mechanisms, and networks for: (a) the generation, collection, and exchange of experiential information among arts education practitioners in the states; (b) the collection of information about available relevant human and material resources; and (c) the provision of timely responses to specific requests."

Lest these recommendations appear simplistic, the study was carefully based upon the kind of communication and technical assistance successful arts education programs have actually used. The study found that "The information of most use to practitioners comes mainly from other practitioners addressing similar problems." Rather than suggest that the federal government set up a national clearing house in arts education—a mechanism other fields have used but found inadequate to meet the real informational needs of their practitioners—this study opts for "Shared Experience Banks." The difference is significant.

A PRACTICAL APPROACH

Above all, this is a practical approach. It permits practitioners—those who have learned what works in the schools—to feed information back into the system, and, just as important, it encourages a free exchange of ideas and information among peers. The approach suggested by the report is sensible in another dimension: it wouldn't cost enormous sums of new funds to implement.

With the report in hand, it is important that these government agencies take action without further delay. Responsibility for undertaking the recommendations might well fall under the province of the Special Counsel for arts and education, a position that was created in 1979 to provide a mutually supported bridge between the U.S. Office of Education and the National Endowment.

The report itself, developed under the direction of Lewis A. Rhodes, suggests the kind of delivery system that will guarantee accessibility to information and materials heretofore not easily available—a sharing of accumulated wisdom that is crucial to the improvement of arts education programs.

19

CONGRESS AND THE ARTS: GETTING WITH IT

MUSICAL AMERICA 34 (May 1984)

It seems that the federal government has a difficult time making up its mind. While the general trend in the 1970s was to defund most music- and arts-education initiatives, there was some positive progress in 1978 with the passage of an update to the Elementary and Secondary Education Act, among other legislative priorities. This, coupled with intense lobbying and advocacy efforts, put the US Congress in the position of actually showing support for music and related education. Then in 1981, the funding structure was changed, and programs were once again struggling. In 1983 a congressional report, *The Interrelationship of Funding for the Arts at the Federal, State, and Local Levels*, was released and provided some revealing information. In short, the government now seemed back in the business of supporting arts education. Some insightful comments are offered, as usual, along with details about how central organizations were involved, such as the NEA, NEH, and others. For many educators, following politics may be not a favorite activity, but keeping up with legislative actions and the shifting winds of governmental opinion empowers us to be better stewards of our profession. Add to this more understanding of the history behind current trends, and our advocacy and practice can be even stronger.

—CR

* * *

INSTEAD OF VIEWING arts education as an expendable "frill," a congressional report released in December 1983 urges that the arts promptly be returned to the public school curriculum for the country's 39.1 million students. The report also emphasizes the importance of the arts for the adult population because of their impact on the economy, employment, and audience development.

In the report, *The Interrelationship of Funding for the Arts at the Federal, State, and Local Levels* (House Report No. 98–547 of the 98th Congress, 1st Session, dated November 15, 1983), the House Government Operations Committee points out that in 1978 Congress first stipulated that "The arts should be an essential and vital component for *every student's education.*" (Italics mine.) This Elementary and Secondary Education Act (ESEA) reauthorization bill (Public Law 95–561, Nov. 1, 1978) also states that "The arts should provide students with useful insights to all other areas of learning," and that "A federal program is necessary to foster and to maintain the interrelationship of arts and education."

"ENCOURAGE & ASSIST . . ."

The report reminds us that the bill's declared intent was to initiate, as the bill states, "a program of grants and contracts to encourage and assist state and local educational agencies and other public and private agencies, organizations, and institutions to establish and conduct programs in which the arts are an integral part of elementary and secondary school curricula."

However, the report declares, "In reality, the federal mandate for arts education was dropped in 1981 when twenty-nine separate programs were folded into a basic block grants program. States were given full discretion on how the funding should be reallocated. An investigator for the House Intergovernmental Relations Subcommittee of the Committee on Government Operations said they had discovered that educational block grant monies were now being spent primarily on purchasing computers and library books. The twenty-nine separate programs, including the arts, were no longer considered a priority by state or local school districts, the investigator said."

A LOWER PRIORITY

The report goes on to admit that "The federal government is assigning a lower priority to overall spending for education, in general, and the arts, in particular." And to counter the notion that federal education initiatives threaten local autonomy—a belief widely touted in Washington these days—the report gives reassurance to the partnership idea: "States can develop their own educational programs for the arts in partnership with the federal government. Such programs can allow each school and school district a degree of autonomy as well as the individual teacher who supervises the classroom instruction. The local level can provide the innovations while the federal level offers a degree of national consistency in quality, content, and evaluation."

The report further acknowledges that "Some observers reject the arts as worthy of inclusion in the school curriculum, opting only for 'the basics' of math, science, and computers, without the 'frills' of plays, music, poetry, or painting. Still others see arts education as a pay-as-you-go process, ignoring the fact that admission fees eliminate many from such enjoyment."

Then the report defines the value of arts education: "Appreciation of the arts—both as an individual and as a part of a larger audience—does not necessarily mean knowing the differences between a Rembrandt, a Renoir, or a Rothko painting. It is, in essence, the opportunity for exposure to new and varied experiences which stimulate creativity and an awareness of the unique visions of the surrounding world portrayed by each artist and witnessed differently by each listener/viewer/participant in the artistic process."

THE FED'S ROLE

The role of the federal government and the schools in arts education is clearly stated: "Without the vital encouragement of the arts at the federal level, the arts in the schools have quickly disappeared as a necessary part of the educational process at the state and local levels. For many children, the schools constitute their only exposure to the arts, since their families lack the financial, educational, and physical resources to provide such opportunities."

These are the strongest statements of support for arts education to come out of the federal government in years.

The Subcommittee, which has jurisdiction over the National Endowment for the Arts and the Humanities, the Institute for Museum Services, the Smithsonian Institution, and the President's Committee for the Arts and the Humanities, also recommended that the purpose of the NEA be reaffirmed "as part of our national arts policy." The report quotes the NEA's guidelines to show that their goals—set forth in the original legislative mandate—are, at least in part, educational. As the mandate, states, the goal of the NEA is:

> To insure that all Americans have a true opportunity to make an informed, educated choice to have the arts of high quality touch their lives so that no person is deprived of access to the arts by reason of geography, inadequate income, inadequate education, physical or mental handicaps, or social or cultural patterns unresponsive to diverse ethnic needs.

"This NEA purpose," the report states, "should be affirmed in national budgeting considerations by the Office of Management and Budget [David Stockman] so that this goal can be carried out."

And the report makes it clear that "The President's Committee for the Arts and the Humanities should be viewed as a mechanism to stimulate and to encourage private sector giving to the arts, not as a means to replace all public sector funding. Neither sector can fund the arts alone."

It is significant that this bipartisan Committee reiterated that the private sector alone cannot be the mainstay for funding the arts. It also recognized the federal government's own weak response to supporting the arts in recent years with Administration proposals in fiscal year 1982 to cut the budgets of the NEA and NEH by fifty-one percent and to totally eliminate the IMS.

AUDIENCE DEVELOPMENT

To encourage audience development, the report recommends that "The National Foundation for the Arts and the Humanities (through the Endowments and the Institute for Museum Services) should seek ways to provide cultural programming to mass audiences." And it calls for the NEA to "expand touring programs in order to bring the arts to a broader geographical and social spectrum." And it further recommends that "NEA, NEH, and IMS should carefully weigh future program cutbacks that affect their grants for audiences of school children, the elderly, the handicapped, the poor, and those who benefit from large-scale public offerings such as subsidies for television broadcasts, plays, and mass audience events."

Recommendations in education and the arts are equally strong and reassuring: "The 1978 Elementary and Secondary Education Act provision that declared that the 'arts should be an essential and vital component for every student's education' should be reenacted as part of federal arts policy," the report states.

The Committee also recommends that the Cooperative Resources Act, first funded in 1957 and subsequently incorporated into Title III and Title IV amendments to the ESEA, "be reenacted on a matchingfund basis for state and local school districts." This act supported student exposure to live theater and musical performances, supplemented by classroom instruction and discussion by teachers and professional actors and musicians. Federal funding was merely the catalyst, with the state or local government picking up the cost of the art education program.

The report says much more about the economic impact of the arts, about tax incentives, placement assistance for workers in cultural fields who are unemployed and underemployed, and other topics.

20

ARTS IN BASIC EDUCATION: A FIGHT FOR LIFE?

MUSICAL AMERICA 34 (August 1984)

As many know, the 1980s were a time marked by reform movements in education nationally. From major appraisals such as *A Nation at Risk* to multiple federal and congressional reports, to books and conferences, this was a time of fluid and rapid change for classrooms in the United States. Perhaps it is good news that the body politic of the nation was focused on the critical goal of educating our children. The issue, however, is that winners and losers are ultimately chosen, and in this case, music and arts education were in a struggle for their life. Another contribution of *Musical America* was its in-depth reporting on these matters, and Fowler was just the man to do it. In his usual meticulous and well-researched fashion, he brought the complex and dense reports down to clear and manageable size. Here he lays out the issues, then takes us through several major states and their initiatives, challenges, and innovative ideas. The states highlighted here include Colorado, Utah, Montana, Arkansas, Maryland, Michigan, Texas, and Tennessee. For those considering efforts in their own states, they may just find a model that has precedent and success on its side.

—CR

* * *

SOMETIMES IT SEEMS as if a huge wave washes over the nation. This appears to be the case at present with the ubiquitous and deeply rooted concern of the American people about the state of public education. Growing out of that concern has been a variety of studies and reports documenting the problems, confirming the crisis, and offering numerous recommendations for improvement. (See analyses of six of these reports in this column in the November and December 1983 and the March 1984 issues.)

In response, some forty-five states now have educational task forces studying ways to strengthen public school education. These task forces are giving serious attention to the recommendations contained in the recent reports. No wonder arts educators and arts supporters are worried—and working. Considering the fact that some of the reports see the arts as basic while others almost, or wholly, ignore them, it is not surprising to find arts groups in the states mobilizing to assert the importance of the arts in education.

Depending upon which report a particular task force finds compelling and which state voices are most persuasive, curricula in the arts could be increased, sustained, reduced, or, in some cases, eliminated. Subjects like English, social studies, history, science, and mathematics are not threatened by reduction or elimination—they are all considered to be "basics," safe and honored components of general education. But only three out of six major education studies consider the arts basic. So, once more, the arts must fight to justify their right to be considered basic and essential education for all students.

As a basic, a subject area is accorded educational status and, with it, priority access to resources—time in the curriculum, adequate numbers of teachers, and a fair share of the school budget. The distinction is critical—the difference between being considered truly important or merely peripheral. And what is peripheral in education can be eliminated.

ORGANIZED EFFORTS

Lest the arts be threatened by a new onslaught of curtailments—this round borne of misguided efforts to achieve educational excellence at the expense of the arts—supporters are organizing efforts on the arts' behalf. Some examples:

In response to the reports of the National Commission on Excellence in Education and the College Board, the Colorado Council on Arts and Humanities adopted a resolution on arts and education. The state agency declared that it "emphatically supports the inclusion of the arts as an integral part of education, kindergarten through college," and it urged the Colorado Department of Education "to disseminate to school districts and to accountability committees statewide information on the critical and demonstrable role that the arts play in education." It further urged them "to encourage and to facilitate the inclusion of the arts into school district curricula statewide" and "to take a substantial role in encouraging the inclusion of the arts in local school district curricula."

- The Utah Arts Council's response to the report of the National Commission states that "more attention should have been directed toward the major contribution arts education and a knowledge of the fundamentals of aesthetics provide in the achievement of these goals."

- The Montana Arts Council issued a resolution in response to this same report that calls upon "all Montanans to begin a dialogue for public policy on the role of the arts at all levels of education." Council chairperson Jessica Stickney said, "We feel it is essential that the arts and training of human aesthetic spirit finally take their proper place at the core of this new national education dialogue, and not at its fringes," [*sic*] Copies of the resolution have been sent to the governor, the state superintendent of schools, the commissioner of higher education, the Board of Regents, the Board of Public Education, the presidents of all professional education associations, the presidents of the various university system branches, and leaders in the Montana legislature.

These initiatives on the part of state arts councils are significant. While they are but three examples—there are undoubtedly many more—they represent a new priority for educational concerns within the National Endowment for the Arts. Also on the state level:

- Governor Bill Clinton of Arkansas lobbied the state legislature and succeeded in getting it to ratify new standards for education in the state and to pass tax increases to pay for them. Heretofore many students were never offered art or music, but the new standards require such courses. You can bet that arts educators and other supporters of the arts were involved in achieving this new status for the arts.
- In April, Maryland's state superintendent of schools, David. W. Hornbeck, recommended tough new graduation requirements for high school students, including additional mandatory courses. The recommendations, which were similar to those made last fall by the state's blue-ribbon commission on secondary education, include adding another year of mathematics and a year of fine arts to the current core of required subjects. The year of fine arts, Hornbeck said, can be in music, dance, visual arts, or drama. This initiative probably would not have come about had it not been for the lobbying efforts and letter writing campaign organized by arts educators, particularly music teachers under the guidance of R. Bruce Horner, State Chairman of Government Relations for the Maryland Music Educators Association. The state board of education will hold public hearings before deciding which recommendations to adopt.
- In Michigan, a new statewide arts advocacy organization has been formed: Concerned Citizens for the Arts. Supported by Governor Blanchard, the group is governed by a board of directors representing major economic, political, educational, and arts forces throughout the state. There is a small executive committee to manage daily affairs and a 200-member advisory committee. Their slogan is "Help us keep Michigan a State of the Arts."

One stimulus for forming this organization was the failure of the Michigan Commission on High Schools to make the arts a required course of study. The commission did recommend that "local boards of education should review the important areas of foreign language, fine arts, physical education, and vocational education to assure that a wide range of educational opportunities are available." Arts teachers and administrators in the state admonished them for not taking a firmer stand and making the arts required study. And they organized Concerned Citizens for the Arts.

- In Texas, the Governor's Select Committee on Education released a report calling for $4 billion to improve education and charging the State School Board to make the necessary changes. House Bill 246 was a result, but arts teachers were not happy with its provisions. The music teachers formed a network throughout the state and gathered the support of other arts educators and teachers. The result: many changes have been adopted that now favor the arts.
- In Tennessee, Governor Alexander's Ten Point Better Schools Program will go into effect in 1984–85. Through the efforts of the Tennessee Music Educators Association, the General Assembly has, for the first time, ear-marked funds for music in the state's elementary schools.

HOPEFUL SIGNS

These diverse actions by arts supporters at the state level demonstrate that the arts community is wary and alert. They show a determination to ensure that the arts maintain their own and perhaps even improve their status through the educational dialogues now going on across the country.

Arts educators know that the current debates are crucial, and they appear to be taking the necessary steps to make an effective case for the arts in education. The true test will be what happens on the local level, in school districts and individual school buildings. State mandated educational improvements will have a great bearing on this. Much effort and wisdom will be needed to make certain that national and state waves generated for arts education don't become a mere trickle in the classroom.

21

ARTS POLICY IN THE U.S.—DO WE HAVE ONE?

MUSICAL AMERICA 34 (December 1984)

Despite the state of music and the arts in schools and throughout the United States, the good news is that at least plenty of important people have gathered regularly to talk about it. These meetings, conferences, seminars, summits, and other gatherings, have served not only to keep the conversation going, but also to focus on important issues of policy and how to keep the arts alive and thriving in practical terms. In May 1984, the American Assembly gathered in New York State to discuss "The Arts and Public Policy in the United States." The American Assembly, a national nonpartisan educational institution, was affiliated with Columbia University and focused on issues of schooling, policy, and related matters. This meeting focused on arts policy, and a number of influential professionals gathered to discuss numerous issues related to the topic. Those in attendance included W. McNeil Lowry (Ford Foundation), Stanley Katz (Princeton University), Howard Johnson (MIT), Schuyler Chapin (Columbia University), Roger Stevens (Kennedy Center), Veronica Tyler (Metropolitan Opera), Paul DiMaggio (Yale University), Philip Johnson (Famed Architect), and representatives from business, the NEA, and the Rockefeller Foundation, among other institutions and organizations. I suspect a look at the report produced from the meeting would address many of the same challenges we face today in music and arts education and policy, and offer evidence to strengthen contemporary arguments.

—CR

* * *

FOR FOUR DAYS, last May 31 to June 3, leaders in the arts—artists, artistic directors and administrators, and representatives of foundations, the government, universities, and corporations—met at Arden House in Harriman, New York to discuss "The Arts and Public Policy in the United States." This was the sixty-seventh meeting of the American Assembly, a national nonpartisan educational institution affiliated with Columbia University and founded in 1950 by Dwight D. Eisenhower. W. McNeil Lowry, formerly vice president for the humanities and the arts at the Ford Foundation, served as director of this Assembly, which was financed by a number of foundations and the New York Community Trust.

In a sixteen-page final report, the participants agreed on a general statement of beliefs, findings, and recommendations. While they declared that people in the United States "need a more clearly understood public policy" in the arts, they found to their satisfaction that "our country's policies in the arts reflect the pluralism and diversity in which our society evolved." They resisted any movement toward establishing an official national policy—federal or otherwise.

A MIX OF INFLUENCES

Oddly, no one at this Assembly offered to define the term "policy," so I tender the following: policy consists of the principles that govern action—in this case, the way the arts are managed and conducted in this country. Perhaps Lowry came closest to a definition when he defined public policy as "strictly speaking, a set of influences."

In one of the background papers prepared for this Assembly, papers that will be published in book form this fall by Prentice-Hall, Stanley N. Katz, professor of Public and International Affairs at the Woodrow Wilson School of Princeton University, states that "America's pluralism and regionalism create a constant pressure for the decentralization of cultural public policy," and he concludes that "to have no policy is actually to have a policy."

As the saying goes, "money talks." The mix of monetary support from individual donors, foundations, corporations, and the government at the federal, state, and local levels means that all these entities combine to influence arts policy. Howard W. Johnson, chairman emeritus, Massachusetts Institute of Technology, in an address to the Assembly, said that "if the fine arts are felt to be in the national interest . . . the component of federal support in the mix is going to be necessary." The Assembly agreed that diverse sources of patronage in the arts are "the best protection from the possibility of outside interference or control." And it found that the record of the

National Endowment for the Arts and of the state arts agencies in avoiding political interference "has been good."

UNIVERSAL ACCESS

But the participants did agree that the United States does have policies governing the arts, even if broad and tacitly accepted. "The goal of universal access to and availability of the arts," they stated, "is an essential component of a public policy in the arts." To this end, they recommended "lower admission prices, more even distribution of arts facilities, and greater recognition of minority art forms."

The policy of universal access is tied closely to their belief that "Clear public understanding of the central place of the arts is more important than any official national policy." Access, after all, is the door to understanding and valuing. It was a point that Schuyler Chapin, present dean of the School of the Arts at Columbia University and former manager of the Metropolitan Opera, made early on, in one of the three continuing discussion groups. Chapin said, "The underlying basic problem is recognition of the arts as important in our society. We still do not take the arts seriously. Any policy in the arts must address this problem."

MEDIA, GOOD AND BAD

Address it they did, and from a number of different perspectives. For example, they called attention to the cavalier manner in which the press—"particularly the large urban newspapers widely syndicated across the country"—deal with the arts, and they decried "the growing tendency for even the most noted of these to treat the arts predominantly as 'entertainment,' 'leisure,' or 'style.'" Roger Stevens, chairman of the John F. Kennedy Center for the Performing Arts, in an angry outburst at one of the evening discussions, assailed the *New York Times* as "a dictator in the arts." He said it wields the power in cultural affairs in this country, and everyone is afraid of it. "They broke up the Standard Oil Company," Stevens said, "why not the *New York Times?*"

But media, specifically public television and radio, were also recognized as "prime sources of dissemination of the arts." The report recommends "speedy restoration of federal funding for the Corporation for Public Broadcasting and Public Broadcasting Service." The participants agreed that the need to support the primacy of direct access to live performing and exhibiting spaces is "of equal importance."

EDUCATION

The report also recognizes the essential role of education in developing greater understanding of the importance of the arts. "Appreciation of the arts is by and large developed through the educational system," the report states. "We cannot hope to establish the centrality of the arts to this society or their value to the individual without a clear recognition of this fact. More support for the arts in education is needed, especially at the local level."

Metropolitan Opera singer Veronica Tyler, a participant, believes "We have a responsibility to educate the public to the human need for the arts. Parents need to understand this." She feels that "Artists are like lepers. The public needs to know that we don't do art for selfish purposes but to uplift the human spirit. From this standpoint, the arts are vital to human survival." On this matter, the report states that "The arts function in the national interest as a recorder of history and experience and as a force illuminating the human condition." They constitute "one of America's great underused and vital resources."

RESPECT FOR ARTISTS

If one of the broad themes of policy concerned the means of asserting the value of the arts in American society, another dealt with winning a higher status for the artist. "We have recognized," the report states, "that the artist must be more central in the formulation of public policy in the arts." And further on: "The efficient management of the nonprofit organization must not divert its artistic objective, which must remain the province of the artistic director."

Much discussion in the small groups centered on the belief, as one participant expressed, that "artists are not respected. Museum boards do not have artists on them. Artists are not a part of many deliberations and administrative policy decisions that affect their lives." Artists don't see themselves as the makers of their own destiny perhaps because the power in many arts organizations is in the hands of dilettantes. Artists feel powerless, and the report reflects this sentiment:

> An understanding of the fiduciary responsibilities of the trustees is essential for
> the director and artistic personnel, while genuine sensitivity to the creative goals
> of the artists on the part of the trustees is absolutely vital. It is urgent that each
> element of the organization guard against the erosion of high quality of perfor-
> mance and the integrity of the artistic process.

One person also had some advice for trustees: "Give, get, or get off."

NONPROFIT PROTECTION

Another of the broad themes addressed by this Assembly concerned the financial stability of artists and artistic institutions and the role of foundations, corporations, and the federal government in providing support. Surprisingly, the artists in attendance did not dwell on the usual financial plight of the arts. It would have appeared somewhat ludicrous in these surroundings—the palatial mountaintop home of Edward Henry Harriman which his son, W. Averell, gave to Columbia University. Instead, one acknowledged that, if the NEA budget was doubled, "this won't succeed in making the arts a part of everyday life in this country." Apparently the artists were more interested in protecting what they already have.

As Paul J. DiMaggio, associate professor at Yale University's Institution for Social and Policy Studies, points out in his background paper, nearly all our performing arts organizations and sixty-six percent of our art museums are not-for-profit institutions. Fear of the loss of this nonprofit status prompted the participants to state in the report that "The mechanism of the nonprofit corporation remains today, as it has for seven decades, inseparable from the institutional life of the arts in this country. It is grounded in the recognition by federal and state governments that art as an exercise in esthetic inquiry, performance, and exhibition is inherently deserving of tax exemption."

INFLUENCE OF THE MARKET

But nonprofit associations have an obligation to run their affairs for the public, and this can cause problems. Participants showed, perhaps, their greatest concern over the possible compromise of artistic excellence. One of the problems, as DiMaggio points out, is that smaller government subsidies in the United States mean that our arts organizations must place greater reliance upon earned income. "For this reason," DiMaggio says, "the extent to which American artists and artistic institutions are subject to the influence of the marketplace is virtually unparalleled." This causes performing arts organizations to make a greater number of artistic compromises. Repertoires, for example, become more conservative. Museums look for the "blockbuster" art shows that will attract a huge public and a corporate sponsor. Some participants even expressed concern that ballet companies perform the popular *Nutcracker* each Christmas, viewing it as a play for boxoffice rather than artistic achievement.

The NEA's five-year plan, introduced last year, summarizes the situation this way: "There is deep concern that financial stability is being achieved at the expense of the art form. This includes popularizing to increase earned income, insufficient numbers of performers to perform the full range of repertory, less rehearsal time in relation to performance. Artistic deficits may have been deliberately planned by producers to make ends meet."

DiMaggio elaborates on the last point. He sees the existence of a budget gap in nonprofit institutions as a necessity of existence. He says, "Net income is apt to make potential patrons—private and public—question the depth of need relative to that of other petitioners. Consequently, national arts managers will be not profit maximizers but deficit optimizers, ensuring deficits sufficiently large to attract grants and donors but not so great as to call into question their competence or the organization's survival. . . . If the budget gap did not exist, arts organizations would have to invent it."

Katz places the issue in further perspective: "While most citizens are appreciative of the growing governmental funds available to American artists, they must also recognize that the price for this swelling demand for 'public' support is public accountability, An inevitable tension exists between high culture and democracy, and, as cultural policy moves from the domain of the private to that of the public and popular taste, there almost certainly will be impacts upon the artistic process itself." We see a certain amount of this yielding to commercial pressures when boards of arts organizations bring marketing directors into their inner councils and when financial managers begin to make artistic decisions. According to some, NEA's support of programs for social rather than for artistic reasons is also a symptom.

DEMOCRATIZATION

In a paper submitted to the Assembly, Congressman Sidney R. Yates, chairman of the Congressional committee that oversees the NEA, asks, pointedly, "Are the arts suffering because of too much democratization?" And he answers: "It must be remembered that [the NEA] is a national program for the arts, a program for the whole country," and he quotes the Rockefeller Panel Report of 1965, which served as impetus to establishing the NEA:

> Effective development of the arts is, then, a complex matter. It becomes, in our time and country, a matter of creating new organizational arrangements—for teaching, for performing, for supporting the artist. . . . It becomes a matter of developing an audience as much as it does of training the artist. . . . It is also, of course, an unprecedented challenge for democracy. For we are seeking to create cultural institutions that will serve huge numbers of people—more than any cultural establishment of any other time or place has tried to serve. We are seeking to demonstrate that there is no incompatibility between democracy and high artistic standards.

Yates agrees with the goal of artistic excellence, but he says programs of art for the aged, the handicapped, children, and others "do not negate that purpose." (By the way, if you feel that dealing with the subject of U.S. policy in the arts is a sometimes murky affair, you can take reassurance from Yates's own reaction to reading the background papers prepared for this Assembly. He said, "I am like the man attending a lecture given by Professor Albert Einstein on his theory of relativity. When asked what he has learned, he replies, 'Well, I am still confused, but on a much higher level.'")

According to DiMaggio, the nonprofit organization is a self-protective device. "It is employed to buffer certain areas of human activity from the discipline of the marketplace. Recognizing this, cultural policy must regard the market as a tool—not a standard." DiMaggio advises: "Use the market only when it serves the purposes of the arts." In this sense, the influence of the marketplace need not necessarily lead to a negation of principles or a compromise of artistic standards. Programming, for example, may become more innovative in order to reach and serve new audiences.

FOUNDATION SUPPORT

Among the many questions discussed by the participants was the question of whether the authorization of the NEA should be made permanent. They thought not. At present, the NEA must return to Congress every five years for reauthorization. Without reauthorization next year, the NEA will cease to exist. Permanency was feared because the agency itself would no longer be subject to evaluation and adjustment.

Still, the corporate and foundation sectors represented at the meeting want the assurance of continuing government support for the arts. They felt, as one expressed it, that "The amount of funding is a reflection of the value the Congress puts on the arts. Money doesn't solve all the problems, but money well spent can help. Money is muscle; it solidifies policy." The NEA gives legitimacy that encourages others. But, Roger Stevens reminded the participants, "All the money in the world doesn't help creativity."

One foundation representative admitted that "All the things you really need—funds for operational costs, maintenance, rent, salaries, and endowment—we don't fund." Why? "Because foundations don't want to get locked in for the long term, and their funds are too scant to provide general operating support." And why are they reluctant to aid endowments? "Endowments are boring," one foundation representative admitted forthrightly, "you lose the sense of something you can see."

While the report recognizes that sources of funding "inevitably exert considerable influence in the formation of a public policy on the arts," it states that "The most important of all influences on policy begins with the artistic impulse itself.... The participants of this Sixty-seventh Assembly give conscious weight to the social, political, and economic uses of the arts, but we find the greatest priority in the intrinsic value of art itself."

PARTICIPANTS

Presiding at the Assembly was William H. Sullivan, U.S. ambassador to Iran during the Carter administration, who used all his consummate diplomatic skills in the sometimes difficult consensus-making process. Other participants included Phyllis Curtin, dean, School for the Arts, Boston University; Elizabeth Swados, composer and playwright; Phillip Johnson, architect; Michelle Lucci, principal dancer, Milwaukee Ballet; Deborah Remington and Esteban Vicente, painters; and Jon Jory, director of the Actors Theatre of Louisville. There were representatives of the Coca Cola, Ford, Hallmark, and Rockefeller Foundations as well as the NEA, and numerous arts organizations, associations, and institutions.

22

MUSIC FOR EVERY CHILD, EVERY CHILD FOR MUSIC

MUSICAL AMERICA 36 (May 1986)

The slogan in the title of this article is one that has been bandied about for decades among those of us in music education. There has also been some debate about whether or not we really mean it, as it still seems that the select few are the ones receiving the best music instruction, if any at all. A strong statement challenging this notion starts this article, although it seems the profession still has not taken much heed. While a number of states at the time were finally suggesting arts instruction as mandatory for graduation, the requirements were fairly thin, and minimal in reach. In addition to a full chart that categorizes the standards at the time, a number of individual states are highlighted and evaluated. A report like this must have been quite impressive at the time—a way to see what the competition is doing, and all collected in the same place. I suspect advocates and leaders today would find this detail—a way to understand historically the trends of requirements by way of comparison in current context—compelling. More importantly, will this encourage administrators and teachers to use the power of data to make a stronger argument for arts education, and perhaps really mean what the title suggests?

—CR

* * *

FOR DECADES, amid slogans such as "Music for every child, every child for music" and "All the arts for all the children," many arts teachers have been content to reach just the talented, the gifted, and the already interested. Hypocrisy not-withstanding, music teachers who agree philosophically that music programs should serve all students have often in practice focused primarily on developing new generations of musicians and music teachers, leaving the education of the masses largely to chance. Music education, particularly at the secondary level, has been elitist. By and large, music teachers have not reached the general high school student nor have they wanted to.

That picture appears to be changing. As a music teacher in Texas recently stated, "If we say 'music is basic,' we must also say 'for everyone.' It's just like math." Arts educators know that if the arts are to survive the present educational reform movement, they must be considered basic. Only the basics are accorded the full educational resources of planning, development, staffing, materials, and, most important, *time* within the school day. Only the basics are considered legitimate and necessary curricula. Only the basics flourish. But there is a catch. The basics, by definition, are areas of study that are important for *every* student. If music is basic, it must be essential for all.

We now have a number of states that consider the arts basic and require local school districts to act accordingly. States exercise control over arts instruction in public schools in a number of ways. Some require that a certain amount of instruction in the arts be offered in elementary and secondary schools. At present, forty-two states mandate such instruction, though mainly in visual arts and music. Only twelve states require that dance and/or theater be offered at the secondary level. Minnesota, for example, requires that all high schools in the state provide a minimum of two credit hours in visual arts with a minimum of 240 hours in each. This kind of requirement guarantees that schools provide a minimum number of arts courses, not that students must take them.

The accompanying table shows three other ways that states mandate the arts in public schooling. All twenty-two states shown now have graduation requirements in the arts. While Missouri has required one unit (one year) in fine arts (defined as either and *only* art or music) for graduation since 1960, most of these states have adopted these requirements during the past five years. Yet the requirements differ considerably in the demands they make on the individual high school student.

Two states require study of the fine arts for just those students who are college-bound or who are in the advanced academic program. Rhode Island requires these students to take half a unit of study in dance, drama, music or visual arts; Texas requires them to complete one unit of study in drama, music, or visual arts. These states have not established requirements in the arts for students in the general academic or vocational programs, those not intent on going to college.

Nonetheless, there is a good deal of interest, particularly in Texas, in creating new high school courses in music to meet this new requirement for advanced academic students. These students are not necessarily performers, so that they cannot or would not choose a performing group to earn this credit. Without other options in music, these students would be forced to earn the credit in drama or visual arts.

STATES WITH GRADUATION REQUIREMENTS IN THE ARTS

State	Number	Subject
*Arkansas	½, eff. 1987	Drama, Music, Visual Arts
California	1	Fine Arts (Creative Writing, Dance, Drama, Music, Visual Arts) or Foreign Language
Connecticut	1	Arts (Dance, Drama, Music, Visual Arts) or Vocational Education
*Florida	½	Fine Arts (Dance, Drama, Music, Visual Arts)
Georgia	1	Fine Arts (Dance, Drama, Music, Visual Arts), Vocational Education or Computer Technology
Idaho	2, eff. 1987 4, eff. 1988	Fine Arts (Creative Writing, Dance, Drama, Music, Visual Arts), Foreign Language, or Humanities
Illinois	1	Art, Music, Foreign Language or Vocational Education
Maine	1, eff. 1988	Fine Arts (Visual Arts, Music, Drama) or Forensics
*Maryland	1, eff. 1988	Fine Arts (Dance, Drama, Music, Visual Arts)
*Missouri	1	Music or Visual Arts
*New Hampshire	½	Arts Education (Art, Music, Visual Arts, Dance, Drama)
New Mexico	½	Fine Arts (Visual Arts, Music, Dance, Drama), Practical Arts or Vocational Education
New Jersey	1	Fine Arts, Practical Arts or Performing Arts
*New York	1, eff. 1989	Dance, Drama, Music or Visual Arts
Oregon	1	Music, Visual Arts, Foreign Language or Vocational Education
Pennsylvania	2	Arts (Dance, Drama, Music, Visual Arts) or Humanities
Rhode Island	½	For college-bound students only. Dance, Drama, Music or Visual Arts
*South Dakota	½	Fine Arts (Dance, Drama, Music, Visual Arts)
Texas	1	For advanced academic program students only. Drama, Music or Visual Arts
*Utah	1½	Dance, Drama, Music or Visual Arts
*Vermont	1	General Arts, Dance, Drama, Music or Visual Arts
West Virginia	1	Music, Visual Arts or Applied Arts

*States that require some study of the fine arts by every high school student.

This table is reproduced by permission from Arts, Education and the States: A Survey of State Education Policies (Washington, D.C.: Council of Chief State School Officers, 1985), p. 23.

Deceptively, eleven of the states in the table require a specific number of credits in the fine arts or other subjects for high school graduation. These other subjects range from foreign languages and the humanities, to computer technology, forensics, and practical or applied arts (shop and home economics). Such requirements may have little or no effect on the arts. In Connecticut, for example, any music course may be used to fulfill the one-unit requirement. But so may any vocational course, which can include almost any course so designated by the local districts. Accordingly, few students are actually affected by the legislation, and no special arts offerings have been deemed necessary. Acting optimistically, the Connecticut State Department of Education has suggested curriculum development in the areas of related arts, American studies, humanities, and other disciplines, particularly social studies, that could encompass the arts.

In Idaho, a humanities requirement of two units (effective in 1987) and four units (effective in 1988) embraces the arts. The requirement states that the credits "may be from any of the following: fine arts (including performing classes), foreign language, or humanities." Study in humanities, the accrediting legislation states, "is to be considered as an integrated program of studies which will incorporate the interrelationship of art, music, world religions, architecture, science, philosophy, and literature." But the ruling permits a student to substitute two credits in practical arts (vocational, prevocational, or consumer homemaking) for humanities. Such a student could then conceivably complete the requirements by taking two credits in foreign language, avoiding the arts altogether. Perhaps it is for this reason that the Idaho State Department of Education is not recommending a new course in general music, but rather broadening the curriculum in the performance classes to include significant components in language and structure of music; skills in performing, creating, and listening; understanding music history; appreciation and evaluation of music. These classes satisfy the graduation requirement for humanities.

Similarly, Pennsylvania requires two credits in the arts or humanities, or both. In response, the Pennsylvania Department of Education has issued guidelines for local districts that suggest possible linkages between the arts and humanities. "A course in the arts has a humanities component when works in the arts are considered from the standpoint of philosophy, history, or values." And, conversely, "A course in the humanities has an arts component when works in the arts are studied, performed, and/or created in order to understand their concepts and principles." Guidelines suggest that existing arts or humanities courses can be given the other dimension; they also suggest a number of new courses. It's too early to see what effect these new regulations will have on the district level.

When you get down to it, there are only nine states (those that are starred) that now require every high school student to complete some study of the arts in order to graduate. Four of these states require a half unit and four require one unit, while Utah requires one-and-a-half units. But this is only the beginning of the differences.

Seven of nine states permit—encourage—students to fulfill the requirement through a comprehensive program of dance, drama, music, and/or visual arts. One state, Missouri, requires students to complete one credit in art and/or music; and one state, Arkansas, gives students the option of taking a half credit in one of three arts—drama, music, or visual arts. The effect of these requirements on the music program varies considerably from state to state.

In Florida, June Hinckley of the State Department of Education reports that many students are opting to take the requirement in chorus. Schools are offering students other performance options such as guitar and, in some high schools, beginning band classes. About half the schools in the state have opted to lengthen the school day from six to seven periods in order for students to incorporate all the additional academic requirements and still have time for electives. In schools that have retained the six-period day, students no longer have the time to participate in performing groups, which has traditionally permitted a perfection of performance skills. Bands and choruses in these schools are suffering.

New Hampshire's Department of Education is advocating a new general music course geared to the average, non-performing student, although students can meet the requirement by taking vocal and instrumental music, music appreciation, theory, and other courses.

In New York State, which has instituted a one-unit requirement in fine arts effective in 1989, the State Education Department has published a syllabus for a new course for high school students, "Music In Our Lives," that requires experiences in five areas: listening, performing, composing, using basic tool skills (reading, following a score, conducting, etc.), and developing a special-interest, independent project (approved topics include computer music, synthesizers, new technology, the relation between music and its sister arts, utilitarian uses of music, a musical career, film music, music and dance in history, a musical composition, etc.). Students graduating in 1989 will have the option of three-and five-unit sequences in music in order to qualify for a Regents' diploma with a musical emphasis. One requirement of these sequences is that they include knowledge development along with the option of skill development or participation in a major performing group.

Utah's State Board of Education requires twenty-four units for high school graduation, including one-and-a-half units in dance, drama, music, or visual arts. A core arts curriculum with components in all four arts is mandated in the schools, K-12. High school students must pass a competency test in the arts to qualify for graduation. Core options in music at the high school level are music appreciation, music theory, chorus, band, and orchestra.

Effective in 1988, Maryland will require high school students to complete one credit of work in fine arts. Local school districts must offer high school courses that conform to the state curricular framework. While the music framework is in draft form at present and subject to change, it specifies four major goals: to develop the ability to perceive and respond to music; to develop the ability to creatively organize musical ideas and sounds; to develop an understanding of music as an essential aspect of history and human experience; and to develop the ability to make aesthetic judgments. The local school districts are responsible for developing music curricula that incorporate these goals.

As in most states, Maryland's goals permit school systems to determine their own courses, to use their own ingenuity and local resources in complying with the new graduation requirements. Proposed course outlines must be presented to the state for approval before such courses are eligible to count toward the credit requirement. Each school board in the state determines the core of mandated courses for graduation and those necessary to complete a sequence to qualify for special diplomas in certain academic areas, one of which is the arts. Courses must be made available in each high school to permit students to achieve an arts diploma if they choose to do so. But if no students sign up for these courses, they do not need to be offered.

Both Anne Arundel County Schools (Annapolis, MD) and Baltimore County Public Schools (Towson, MD) are meeting these new state requirements in music by broadening and modifying courses already offered and by adding other courses. Still, their differences show the latitude given to local districts.

Anne Arundel County high schools now offer band, chorus, guitar, and keyboard as well as a course called Current Music in Perspective, I and II (each a semester in length). Performance classes have been broadened to encompass the dimensions of creativity, history, culture, and the valuing of music. The proposed music sequence encompasses five courses: Music History, Music Theory, Music Theater, and Current Music in Perspective, I and II. The latter course is designed specifically for students who do not have a performance background. As currently planned, it will have units covering a wide range: words and music, Romanticism, Classicism, technology, innovations in music creation and performance, careers, various cultural influences on music, the creative process, music and related arts, etc.

Baltimore County high schools also offer a general high school music course designed for students who are not performance oriented. Called "Music Perspectives," the course takes a Great Books approach to the study of music. It develops an understanding of music concepts through the study of eleven examples of music style and content. The concepts are derived from studying masterworks by Bach, Mozart, Beethoven, Debussy, Stravinsky, Ives, Copland, and others, and by studying the background of the composer and the relevance of the composition to the listener. Resource tapes permit teachers to supplement this study with a broad range of musics, including popular and ethnic forms.

Performance classes in Baltimore County high schools have been injected with a general education component. Incorporated into these classes are two units from the Music Perspectives course. Since most of these same teachers are teaching this course, they know this material well and are growing to accept as a fact of life this new approach to teaching ensembles. These high schools also offer a music sequence, but it consists of four performance credits and one credit in music theory. Obviously, the state's new requirement can be met in a variety of ways.

Viewed collectively, these developments reveal a trend in a small but growing number of states to provide study opportunities in music to all students at the high school level. This trend represents a fundamental change in philosophy—a move from a highly specialized, performance-oriented music program focused on the few toward a broadened, more academic program serving the many. It balances the emphasis given to skill development with acquisition of knowledge. As music education becomes more broadly based and more egalitarian, so too does it establish its basic import. Singlehandedly, these changes elevate music to a new and higher status in American schooling. Educationally, the arts are simply more significant when they are presented as substantive studies for all.

23

ARTS EDUCATION TRIPLE JEOPARDY

MUSICAL AMERICA 109 (March 1989)

In 1988, the National Endowment for the Arts released what has come to be regarded as a seminal publication on the value of music and arts education in the schools. The report, "Toward Civilization: A Report on Arts Education," was mostly prepared by then NEA Chairman, Frank Hodsoll. Here a review is presented of the work, which was perhaps the most substantial federal government publication on the importance of arts education in American schools to that time. Aspects include a general state of affairs, recommendations for curricula, suggestions for years of study, statements on educational and artistic bias, hopes to include more children in arts study, debates about aesthetic as opposed to praxial instruction, and more. The main thrust, however, is that the government (albeit through the NEA) was taking a stand and putting forth the idea that music and arts education was actually important, after all. Anyone seriously interested in advocating for music education should consider obtaining a copy of this report. Not only will you receive a good deal of context, historical or otherwise, but it will add rigorous information and philosophical perspective to your arsenal of advocacy ammunition.

—CR

* * *

FOR THE first time in this century, the federal government has issued a major report on the state of arts education in the United States. In compliance with a 1985 amendment to its reauthorization legislation requiring such a study, the National Endowment for the Arts (NEA) has issued the 182-page document *Toward Civilization*. Unquestionably, if the recommendations in this report are heeded, arts education in the United States will be vastly improved.

The report is commendable for bringing public and legislative attention to the potential educational value of arts education for all students and for pointing out its present plight. The report calls for basic arts education for all students, meaning that students should become familiar with the several arts disciplines through sequential study. It recommends that two years of study be required of all high school students.

The report declares that "arts education is essential for *all* students, not just the gifted and talented," and it gives four reasons why every student should study the arts: "to understand civilization, to develop creativity, to learn the tools of communication, and to develop the capacity for making wise choices among the products of the arts."

What is the state of arts education? *Toward Civilization* finds that "the arts are in triple jeopardy: they are not viewed as serious; knowledge itself is not viewed as a prime educational objective; and those who determine school curricula do not agree on what arts education is." The problem, the report says, is that "basic arts education does not exist in the United States today." The report characterizes general arts education as suffering from imbalance, inconsistency, and inaccessibility: "There is curricular *imbalance* in the relationship between the study of art and performance and creation of art. There is *inconsistency* in the arts education that students receive in various parts of the country, in different school districts within states, in different schools within school systems, and even in classrooms within schools. Because of the pressures on the school day, a comprehensive and sequential arts education is *inaccessible* except to a very few and often only to those with talent or a special interest (p. 67)."

The report points out "a major gap between the stated commitment and resources available to arts education and the actual practice of arts education in schools." In the areas of curriculum, testing and evaluation, preparation of teachers of the arts, and research and leadership, the arts are found inadequate and improvements are called for.

Based upon months of culling the existing literature and sending drafts to an advisory committee on arts education, the finished report nonetheless reflects the views of NEA Chairman Frank Hodsoll, who personally wrote a good part of it. Lawyer that he is, Hodsoll has clearly tried to approach the issues fairly, but his own biases occasionally creep through. In emphasizing the acquisition of knowledge, the standardization of arts curricula, and national assessment, he tends to cast arts education in largely academic garb. Instead of basing the study on new data about what is and is not happening in the arts in public schools and colleges, it sets forth a doctrine of more disciplined practice.

It is in the areas of curricular emphasis and evaluation that the report strikes a controversial chord. Making a broad application of the visual arts' discipline-based curriculum promulgated by the Getty Center for Education in the Arts, the report calls for arts curricula to encompass "the history, critical theory and ideas of the arts as well as creation, production and performance." In music, the report expresses concern that "the performance bias, central to most high school music programs, contributed to the perception that arts education is, or should be, entertainment rather than serious learning." But how far should we go? One gets the feeling from this report that students in band and chorus should be taking notes, reading, doing research, and writing papers, particularly critiques.

In its discussion of testing and evaluation, the report maintains, quite reasonably, that "knowledge of, and skills in, the arts must be tested." But the report goes on to ask that the National Assessment of Educational Progress in visual arts, music, and literature, last given in 1979, be restored, and that methods for assessing theater, dance, and the design and media arts on a national level be developed. National testing, of course, would require—or result in—standardization of arts curricula, a move that many arts teachers resist as being a straitjacket. According to this report, standardized testing is necessary if the arts are to be considered legitimate basic school subjects, but will it have that effect? Will parents really get upset when they find their children cannot sing "America" or identify Velasquez? Will they believe that low scores in the arts are as serious a concern as low scores in math?

Beneath all the rhetoric, a questionable ideology is being foisted upon the field. In calling for standardized curricula in all the arts, in emphasizing the acquisition of knowledge, and in advocating enforced standards, *Toward Civilization* follows the perennialist philosophy that has been continuously promulgated by the Department of Education under the leadership of Secretary William Bennett. Perennialists believe that to acquire knowledge is the essence of education. Robert Hutchins gave the perennialist philosophy its most concise definition in his celebrated syllogism:

> Education implies teaching. Teaching implies knowledge. Knowledge is truth. The truth is everywhere the same. Hence, education should be everywhere the same.[1]

These are the educators who believe that every student should know "the great books." This is basic education in its purest form. Ironically, it is the same back-to-basics philosophy that undermined the arts to begin with. Now we are told, in effect, if you can't beat them, join them. *Toward Civilization* advocates a concentration on "the great works of art from all times and cultures." The report asks: "Which works of art and what artists should be known and understood by every elementary, middle, and high school student?"

This "aristocracy of intellect," as it has been called, demands the same sort of rigorous academic training for all, despite the fact that such book learning may retard the growth of attributes that are equally valuable. One gets the distinct feeling that it is

---

[1] Robert Maynard Hutchins, *The Higher Learning in America* (Yale University Press, 1936), p. 66.

the academic qualities of the arts that are prized here, not the creative and performing abilities that have been central to the arts for decades. That academic emphasis may have the effect of moving these other very basic attributes to the sidelines, making the arts look like every other subject in the curriculum. Instead of offering students some relief from the unrelenting acquisition of facts and knowledge that is demanded in other subjects, the arts will be more of the same. Moreover, book learning ignores the uniqueness of the arts as subjects that command the development of different mental and physical capacities.

It is as though the natural emphasis in the arts on "learning by doing" smacks too much of John Dewey to be acceptable to these educational arch-conservatives. *The Washington Post* expressed reservations about this academic thrust in an editorial on May 6, 1988: "This approach can be overdone; no curriculum plan will inculcate love of the arts by turning them into a purely academic, testable pursuit." *The New York Times* pointed out what it termed "a potentially controversial plan to steer arts education away from performance and exhibition and toward more disciplined study."[2]

I am reminded of Virgil Thomson's response to Aaron Copland's book *What to Listen for in Music,* in which Copland asks listeners to develop the ability to analyze music aurally. Thomson wrote Copland:

Supposing you do believe that analytic listening is advantageous for the musical layman, it is still quite possible and not at all rare to believe the contrary. It even remains to be proved that analytic listening is possible. God knows professional musicians find it difficult enough. I suspect that persons of weak auditive memory do just as well to let themselves follow the emotional line of a piece, which they can do easily, and which they certainly can't do very well while trying to analyze a piece tonally.[3]

Few would question the suggestion that curricula in the arts need to be broadened. But the emphasis remains an open question.

It strikes me as a bit odd that the NEA, of all institutions, should move away from an educational model based upon the artist and the making of art toward a model based upon the art historian, theorist, and critic. Such a stance seems far more like what we might expect from the National Endowment for the Humanities. If we want to reach all students with the arts—and this report makes great strides in that direction—we are not going to do it by making the arts a tough intellectual pursuit. It is one thing to recognize that the arts have their own history, theory, and aesthetic philosophy, quite another to make these central to study of the arts in public schools. Arts curricula need to be broadening in scope, but not at the expense of making art. The hands-on

---

[2] William H. Honan, "American Teaching of the Arts Is Assailed," *The New York Times,* Education Section, May 4, 1988, p. 2.

[3] From a review by Richard Freed, "Fanfares and Grace Notes," *The Washington Post Book World,* July 24, 1988, p. 6.

experience of music is still the best entrée to understanding it, as well as the best justification for learning something about the composer, the style, the form, and the expressive content.

One part of this document is both inaccurate and self-defeating. In the Overview, the report states: "The amount of time allocated to arts instruction in grades 1 through 6 averages 12 percent of classroom time for the majority of students. This goes up to 17 percent for the majority of students in grades 7 and 8 (p. 19)." Later, the report recommends: "Elementary schools should consider providing arts instruction, exclusive of English studies, for approximately 15 percent of the school week [and] junior high and middle schools (grades 6 through 8) should require *all* students to take arts instruction, exclusive of English studies, for at least 15 percent of the school year." Compared to what the report claims is already happening, these recommendations are extremely meager. They ask for too little.

In fact, the statistics about how much arts instruction is taking place in elementary and junior high schools are inaccurate. We know that there are school systems in which little or no arts instruction is being offered at the elementary level and substantially less than 17 percent is being given at the junior high level. Were the report's statistics derived from state education guidelines for the arts? If so, since these figures represent minimal standards *recommended* by the states, they are not indicative of what is actually being offered in the schools. This mistake strips the report of its possible impact on the problem of time-on-task in the arts.

Toward Civilization calls for balance between the three branches of learning: the arts, humanities, and sciences. Even so, the report does not recommend giving equal attention to each. If we leave 10 percent for electives, this would mean that fine arts, including literature, would comprise 30 percent of the curriculum. That would be my recommendation. And it includes creative writing, which, in the long run, will be a highly beneficial adjunct for the other arts.

It is important that these reservations about the report, however serious, not be allowed to detract from its fundamental importance. This report and the NEA's new thrust in arts education stand to provide a great service to the field. In September, the NEA sent its major findings and recommendations to every school principal and most school superintendents in the United States—over 100,000. The full report has been sent to key arts and education leaders across the country. Efforts will be made to bring the report to the attention of the House and Senate, which, it is hoped, will respond with increased funding. Chairman Hodsoll and Warren Newman, director of NEA's Arts in Education Program, are attending major conferences and symposia around the country to generate interest and stimulate dialogue at the local level.

This ongoing public information program is intent upon persuading states to redefine and solve the problems of arts education in the public schools—an unprecedented federal effort of incalculable value. One does not have to agree with every detail of what is in this report to champion the action that is being taken. The NEA deserves all the help and support it can get in these efforts. Given that support, the report could result in establishing a new legitimacy for the arts in American public schools.

III

Arts, Culture, and Community

24

THE SMITHSONIAN: TEACHING OUR MUSICAL HERITAGE

MUSICAL AMERICA 26 (January 1976)

Museums often supplement their visual and object offerings with lectures, tours, shows, and other interactive programming for patrons. Therefore, it is no surprise that this is the case at the Smithsonian, arguably the most famous and significant museum in the United States. In fact, in the context of the twenty-first century, this approach has been expanded even further, with restaurants, concert series, social gatherings, and other means of engaging people with artistic culture. In the mid-1970s, the Smithsonian was at the forefront of moving beyond the mere preservation of musical heritage, by making it more live and accessible to those outside its walls. As a living museum, programs, recording collections, concerts, and other events were on offer. Genres and areas included jazz traditions, popular song, dance and early music, folk musics, African and Native American music traditions, and several others.

—CR

* * *

AMERICANS, practical as they are, have never lavished the public schools with the arts. If you want a fine music education for your children, you might find it in the schools, but chances are, you will want to supplement what is offered there with opportunities available outside. One can study music at community schools of the arts, participate in classes and productions of community amateur and professional performing groups, enroll in preparatory departments in conservatories and colleges, study with a private teacher, or attend special programs sponsored by community organizations and institutions. Among the latter are arts education activities that are offered by museums.

Museum programs have expanded greatly during the past five years as museum directors have become increasingly aware of serving the broad interests of their growing audiences. Perhaps the Smithsonian Institution in Washington, D.C., one of mankind's great storehouses of history, science, technology, and art, best exemplifies what museums can and are doing in out-of-school education in the arts. The museum's music programs, in particular, provide unique educational opportunities for people of all ages.

A "LIVING" MUSEUM

S. Dillon Ripley, Secretary of the Smithsonian, views the museum not as a repository of static objects but as a "living" record of culture that breathes life into the past and educates people's perceptions in the present. While the Smithsonian's collection of musical instruments is one of the world's largest, it took Ripley to make them sing. His idea of a museum is to restore the instruments to operating condition and play concerts with them. Each year, the Division of Musical Instruments produces concerts, demonstrations, and recordings of restored instruments that show how differently music sounds when it is played on the original instruments. During October 1975, for example, a Haydn Festival featured thirteen concerts performed on instruments of Haydn's time. In one of these Lili Kraus played the late sonatas on the Dulcken fortepiano (c. 1780). Through this approach, people participate rather than simply look in scholarly silence. The difference engages. And educates.

The Institution's Division of Performing Arts, operating with a mandate for cultural conservation, gives recognition to and preserves living cultural traditions. James R. Morris, Director of the Division, explains the approach this way: "Museums cannot tell the tale of America's cultural history using artifacts alone. To complete the record, living performances of creative human expression are necessary. It is that role we are dedicated to filling."

PRESERVING JAZZ TRADITIONS

One way the Division attempts to accomplish this is through a series of concerts and demonstrations. The Jazz Heritage concerts, funded in part by the National Endowment for the Arts, bring to the public those artists who have been definitive leaders in various styles of jazz. This year's program includes an evening of jazz tap dancing, solo piano with Teddy Wilson, John Lewis, Hank Jones, and the music of Bix Beiderbecke performed by members of the New York Jazz Repertory Company. Another series, devoted to the Jazz Connoisseur, features The Countsmen (Basie alumni), the Heath Brothers (Jimmy, Percy, and Albert), and Sam Rivers. The concept behind these concerts is to bring to audiences a true picture of the importance of jazz in the American musical heritage.

According to Martin Williams, Jazz Program Director, "When you talk about Ellington, you're not speaking simply about a 'jazz' composer, or bandleader, or songwriter, you're talking about a man who is among the greatest composers America has produced. Jazz should not be thought of as an isolated form of music, but rather as part of the musical mainstream."

To help preserve jazz traditions, many of which are improvisatory, the Smithsonian in 1973 issued a Collection of Classic Jazz recordings. This collection of six LPs includes eighty-four original recordings from the archives of seventeen record companies. Included is a forty-eight-page booklet of jazz history, photographs, and a discography by Martin Williams. The music ranges from Scott Joplin's own rendition of his *Maple Leaf Rag*, through the work of John Coltrane and Ornette Coleman. Fall 1975 releases included the King Oliver Jazz Band (Louis Armstrong and his second wife were members), Louis Armstrong and Earl "fatha" Hines, and Classic Rags and Ragtime Songs conducted by T.J. Anderson. Through recordings, the concept of the jazz series is extended to the public at large.

MABEL MERCER & OTHERS

Mabel Mercer, that grande dame of song styling, will headline the 1975–6 American Popular Song series. Whenever possible, the settings for these programs, like the jazz series, are informal and the artists are invited to share anecdotes, give demonstrations, provide explanations, and otherwise converse with the audience.

People and Their Culture, another concert series, is designed to bring to life, through music and dance, the folk instrument collections at the Museum of Natural History. This year there will be groups from Tibet, Japan, Czechoslovakia, and Burma. Other series are devoted to chamber music and music from Marlboro.

In addition to these concerts there is a concert of American Band Music from 1876, programs of American banjo music, and an evening of Music and Dance from the Age of Jefferson. The latter program has been carefully researched—the musical aspect by James Weaver, Associate Curator, Division of Musical Instruments, the dance by Shirley Wynne, Director of the Baroque Dance Ensemble, and member of the faculty at the University of California at Santa Cruz. They found that Jefferson and his daughters took dancing lessons, and that his music collection contained minuets, country dances, reels, the Duke of York's march, waltzes, the Spanish Fandango, an "Almaine," a "Corant," and a quick step. This program of authentic music and dances of this period, with costumes, scenery, and lighting, was premiered in Washington on November 14 and then toured to four states. Again, the music is available on recording.

FESTIVAL OF AMERICAN FOLK LIFE

Undoubtedly the most educational of the Smithsonian's arts activities will be the 1976 Festival of American Folk Life. This tenth annual festival will be held on the fifty-acre Mall between the Lincoln Memorial and the Washington Monument from June 16 through September 7. Extended from two to twelve weeks on behalf of the Bicentennial, the festival will constitute the largest free public event in the United States and the major Bicentennial event in Washington. Over five thousand performers will appear on the ten stages. Thirty countries will be represented in addition to folk artists and artisans from throughout the United States.

The festival will present the music, dances, crafts, foods, and other folkways of ethnic populations in the United States in direct comparison to these folkways in the country of origin. The plurality of American culture is represented by the festival themes: Old Ways in the New World, Native Americans, Working Americans, African Diaspora, and Regional America. Through lullabies, songs of work and celebration, and other folkways, the public is invited to leaf through the many fabrics of American life to gain an understanding and appreciation of the multiple roots of American culture. For those who cannot attend any of the events in Washington, the foreign folk groups will tour to ninety cities throughout the country.

In perpetuating national and family folkways, the festival also gives recognition to them and thus helps to preserve these traditions. There is no question that the festival is, above all, educational. As James Morris states: "The living art that the American people make of their own experience is not taught in our educational institutions, performed in our concert halls or housed in our museums. Folk songs and dances may be taught in schools and interpreted by professionals in concerts; material culture appears in museum exhibitions and collections, but living folkways are drenched with rich, vital style which only the living tradition-bearers themselves can impart to the performance of a song, to the execution of a complex craft technique, to the telling of a tale. The Festival celebrates folk cultures as they persist in thousands of styles among millions of people who inherited folkways as part of their life styles." Museums—and the Smithsonian is by no means alone in this kind of effort—are supplementing and extending the arts education available in schools.

25

VALUING OUR CULTURAL TREASURY

MUSICAL AMERICA 26 (November 1976)

Cultural history is often overlooked in schools and communities. It seems especially interesting that those outside of a society may sometimes know more about regional artistic cultures than those living within that society. The Smithsonian Festival of American Folklife (today the Smithsonian Folklife Festival) explored various aspects of music, art, culture, education, and other formal and informal methods of music-making and creativity. Areas in this offering included American fiddle music, sacred harp singing, Appalachian clogging, gospel singing, Cajun music, and African and related musics, among others. This particular offering was especially broad, and is representative of the diverse musical cultures in practice and available in the United States (then and now).

—CR

* * *

JAMES MORRIS, director of performing arts at the Smithsonian Institution, tells a story about two plumbers installing the marble sinks at the John F. Kennedy Center. When asked if they would attend performances there, they replied, "Oh no, this is not for us."

While it may not be a conscious thing, Morris believes that "somehow we have communicated something about this monolithic cultural establishment. If you are educated, well-spoken, and have attained some status in your job, you are welcome. If you're not part of this mainstream, you're not welcome." The problem, as Morris sees it, is that people do not understand their basic aesthetic nature. "All humans," he says, "seek to be expressive in the way they dress, decorate their houses, prepare their food, and choose their entertainment. This is the same urge that creates all art—one stream produces Beethoven, another folk music."

FESTIVAL OF AMERICAN FOLKLIFE

The 1976 Festival of American Folklife, a cooperative endeavor of the Smithsonian Institution and the National Park Service, the tenth such festival to be staged on the Mall in Washington, was designed to provide Americans with the means to come in touch with their own aesthetic roots. Upwards of five thousand participants representing African, Asian, European, and New World cultures, as well as the various regional cultures of America, shared their folk ways in a summer-long festival that attracted several million visitors. The festival demonstrated the many human variations in the aesthetic process. As Morris explains, "The festival is about exploring alternatives in the arts."

To hear in close juxtaposition the vocal production of the Moving Star Hall (Gospel) Singers, Ko Nimo and Group from Ghana, Flora MacNeil, a Gaelic singer, and Alma and Eloi Barthelemy, Cajun ballad singers from Louisiana, is to realize the wide range and quality of human vocal expressiveness—all requiring integrity, technique, and emotive control. Ola Bell Reed, who sings for the sheer enjoyment of it, displays a rhythmic security and turn of phrase that would be the envy of any fine musician. The art of vocal ornamentation and improvisation mastered by many of these "amateurs" is the equivalent of musical style and practice in the Baroque. Here are alternatives of musical communication that are broader than the *bel canto* vocal tradition, yet as convincing and powerful in different ways. "We are not getting this in music education," Morris says. "It is rigidness that is so counterproductive in our educational system."

MUSICAL MYOPIA?

"In the so-called 'high' art," Ralph Rinzler, director of the festival, states, "everything is prescribed—bowing, dynamics, tempos, the notes, etc. The amount of innovation on the part of the performer is very limited. In folk music the only limitations are due to the parameters of the tradition the performer has grown up in, and the extent of his own innovative genius. The range of creativity in folk performance is far greater than the range permitted in the classical tradition. As a student I never heard as interesting a range of music in school as at home where we had the Library of Congress' *Archives of Folk Song* recordings." Tom Vennum, the Smithsonian's staff ethnomusicologist, says, "The attitude of classical musicians is myopic. They have boxed themselves into a corner."

That shortsightedness manifests itself in numerous ways. When Queen Elizabeth visited the Lincoln Memorial in July, members of the British Headington Quarry Morris Dancers, who were appearing at the festival nearby, performed for her. A member of the troup later remarked that, although they live just fifty miles from London, they had to come to the United States to perform for the Queen. America's folk performers haven't performed at the White House, either. The political and social establishments would rather be represented by symphonic, operatic, or ballet groups, not the indigenous music of the people.

If folk music teaches us the wide variety of expressive alternatives, it also makes us aware of our cultural roots. Folk style or folklore encompasses the customs, habits, and traditions that provide the homogeneous human group with its sense of identity, continuity, and coherence. "Every culture has a selective range of cultural characteristics that mirrors its identity," explains Bess Lomax Hawes, an anthropologist who is the festival's deputy director for presentation. "We begin to learn our musical language in the cradle. Certain musical styles concentrate on particular features and elaborate upon them. These may not coincide with the European modes. The really wicked thing we do," Hawes declares, "is to tell people we are teaching them music, when we do not include anything from their own ethnic heritage. When the black or Mexican-American child does not hear his own music, there is a disjunction. In effect, these children are taught that their own sounds are something other than music. The out-of-school sounds are not tied up with what is given to them in school."

CELEBRATION OF SELF

Ethnic differences and similarities can be rapidly assimilated by a simple comparison of folk styles. Folk music is one way that humans have invented to celebrate themselves. Compare, for example, the following two versions of this children's ring game:

England, 1898
   Little Sally Walker, sitting on the sand
   Crying and weeping for a young man.
   Rise, Sally, rise,
   Sally, wipe away your tears.
   Try for the East and try for the West,
   Try for the very one you love best.

Washington, D.C., 1974

Little Sally Walker, sitting in a saucer
Weeping and crying over all she have done.
Rise, Sally, rise,
Sally, wipe your dirty eyes.
Put your hands on your hips,
And let your backbone slip.
Oh, shake it to the East, Oh, shake it to the West,
Oh, shake it to the very one that you love best.

Like the adults they imitate, children's folklore also bears the flavor of their culture.

"Education," Hawes says, "should enlarge the horizons. The fault is to leave out the child's own culture or to provide poor examples of it. To give American Indians MacDowell is not to be ethnic or intercultural." Hawes, who has been a college professor, claims that the problem lies with the way teachers are educated. She suggests a required course in world music designed to teach people "that there are all these various systems for making sound."

Another lesson that can be learned from the experience of folk traditions, Hawes explains, is the crucial necessity of good models in learning any style. This is routine in classical music. Pianists, for example, listen to Rubinstein and other concert artists to perfect their art. "They are encouraged to attain the highest goals by example." The same thing occurs in traditional music which is transmitted aurally and by imitation. The problem, Hawes reasons, is that people are led to believe folk music is simple. "We don't encourage children to listen to the best models, but rather let them go off on their own and experiment. They want to sing like themselves, not Bessie Smith. The idea is not to end up performing exactly like the models, but rather to understand the broad range of possibilities."

THE ROLE OF THE CHURCH

Bernice Reagon, folklorist for the African Diaspora area of the festival agrees. "The training of traditional black artists like the Drake Family Singers begins when they start to go to church." At Mt. Early Baptist Church in Albany, Georgia, which both Reagon and the Drakes attended, they were taught to listen at first, not to sing. "We learned the songs at home. We played church. You don't sing until you actually become a member, then you follow. It takes three to five years before you try leading. Meanwhile you are developing your ear, voice, and repertoire."

In the crude, rural black church constructed on the festival site, whites join blacks in a revelation of their culture. When the singer fervently proclaims, "I'm a Christian. If you believe in God, take my hand," the people cross boundaries of cultures to reach out in order to understand by doing, regardless of their personal belief.

"Public schools do not use the resources of their communities," Reagon states. "Western education is highly structured and book-oriented. Teachers do not use the local sources, the carriers of the traditional culture." To learn sea chanteys from an actual chanteyman is to see immediately the relationship of the work to the structure, tempo, and length of the song. On the Mall the men hoisted a 2,500-pound weight rigged on a twenty-five-foot-high tripod to simulate the rhythmic coordination of song and work. The range of emotion can also be more clearly delineated by hearing actual examples, from the tear-filled mining songs and the joyous outpouring of Portuguese folk music to the plaintive wail of the Gaelic ballad.

TRADITION FADES

Unless something is done soon, much of the traditional culture of the world may be lost. Cultural pollution is causing the human race to become rootless. Cross-cultural influencing induced by international modes of communication and commerce, along with increased migration and mobility hastened by swifter means of transportation have begun to erode the purity of human life-styles, tending to amalgamate and homogenize them. The vast human tapestry, once rich with the variations of tribal lore, is in danger of going bland. Sameness is overtaking individuality. Cultural pluralism is being sacrificed for social centrism. Unfortunately, for many people, it seems that diversity is viewed as the antithesis of unity, when, in reality, it is lack of compassion and understanding that does not tolerate cultural and ethnic differences.

In a world that seems to grow smaller by the hour, how can human modes of life rub elbows but still maintain their separate personalities? The dulcimer player from West Virginia, the gospel singers from Georgia, the blues band from Mississippi, and the Chippewa Indian dancer from the Great Lakes all share the same macro-culture perpetuated by the schools and other social institutions, and by television, movies, newspapers, books, and magazines. Their micro-cultures—the particular character they bring to their own individual life-styles as expressed in their music, dances, celebrations, crafts, cooking, and other folk ways—deserve recognition, if only because, collectively, they represent the rich and varied creative energies that nourish the human spirit. Each folk style lends an idiosyncratic coloration to human existence. It represents the particular means people choose to express their inner aesthetic being. The extraordinary diversity of our inheritance as Americans should give us cause to celebrate. The Smithsonian Institution, by giving visibility to this inheritance, is helping to preserve the living aesthetic traditions of the past that so uniquely sustain the human spirit in the present.

26

THE COMMUNITY SCHOOL MOVEMENT

MUSICAL AMERICA 27 (July 1977)

Community music is rapidly becoming a hot topic in music education research circles. The idea of looking outside traditional modes of teaching and public schools programs is on the minds of many who work to provide quality music opportunities for everyone, and not just the elite few. In the 1970s, while many community schools existed, they still primarily served as local centers for music lessons, and much less so as national and international sites. Along with an interesting description and some historical context about community music schools, several programs and cities are highlighted. These centers include the East Bay Center for the Performing Arts (Richmond, CA), Settlement Music School (Philadelphia), Cleveland Music Settlement (Cleveland, OH), Harlem School of the Arts (New York), School of Fine Arts (Willoughby, OH), and Lighthouse Music School (New York), along with others. Note that these schools not only offer instruction to those who may rarely get it, but that some also work to support disenfranchised groups such as prisoners, the economically deprived, and those with special needs. Here is yet another program that can serve as a model for interesting and alternative ways of music teaching and learning in current settings.

—CR

* * *

THE PUBLIC SCHOOLS are only one means of obtaining a musical education. Private teachers of voice, piano, and other instruments abound throughout the United States, affording students concentrated study that the public schools often cannot provide. These teachers sometimes work independently, but they may also work in clusters, forming their own community schools of music and the arts.

No one seems to know how many community art schools exist in the United States, but they undoubtedly number in the hundreds. They are located in large cities and small, and many states can boast of several. Since they are community oriented, their programs are highly diversified and geared to local interests and needs. These non-profit institutions often offer instruction in music, dance, drama, and the visual arts, as well as highly specialized programs that are a social service to their communities. A synopsis of the programs in a few of these schools will illustrate.

- The East Bay Center for the Performing Arts in Richmond, California provides instruction in the music and dance styles of Africa, Asia, and Europe, reflecting the heritage of the ethnic makeup of this community. A number of Chinese musical instruments are taught, as well as Chinese vocal style. The study of Indonesian music includes the instruments of both the Javanese and Sudanese Gamelan (orchestra). Western folk music traditions can be studied through the autoharp, banjo, dulcimer, fiddle, guitar, and voice. In addition there are courses in jazz and rock, the music of Spanish-speaking peoples, electronic music, and Western classical music. The dance program is just as diversified. Courses in theater and visual media round out the offerings.
- Newark Community Center of the Arts in Newark, New Jersey has developed a pre-school music program in conjunction with twenty area day-care centers. Some four hundred pre-school children are enrolled. There is also an after-school program for older students that includes opera and drama workshops, dance classes, music theory, and instruction on most instruments. The programs are state supported with help from federal funds. Student fees account for only fifteen percent of the operating budget.
- The Settlement Music School in Philadelphia currently enrolls six hundred male and female inmates of the Philadelphia Prisons complex. Instruction in saxophone, flute, clarinet, trumpet, trombone, guitar, group piano, theory, piano tuning and maintenance, and dance are offered. The Resident Performing Ensemble, whose members are all inmates, performs both inside the prison and outside in the community.
- The Cleveland Music School Settlement works with mentally and physically handicapped children and adults in its extensive music therapy program, the first such program to be based in a community school of the arts. The program doesn't seek to develop performing musicians, but rather to use music to learn socially valuable skills such as interaction and communication. In conjunction with area colleges and universities, the school's music therapy

program is now a constituent element of a "Consortium" Bachelor Degree Program in Music Therapy.

- The Harlem School of the Arts in New York City was founded in 1964 in the wake of severe racial tensions in the community. The program offers an array of traditional music, dance, drama, and visual arts courses geared to the special needs and interests of the largely black and poor urban children it serves. As Dorothy Maynor, the executive director and renowned soprano recitalist says, "The launching of artistic careers is at best a secondary mission for us. We exist instead as a counterforce to the social cancers of Harlem, substituting pride and accomplishment for hopelessness, beauty and approbation for squalor, self-expression and personal fulfillment for the self-defeating escapes of drugs and delinquency."

- The School of Fine Arts in Willoughby, Ohio provides a full complement of music, dance, drama, and visual arts offerings to the non-urban population it services. The school has performance and exhibition facilities of all types that permit it to offer over a hundred public performances—exhibits, lectures, recitals, and the like—each year. A community outreach program brings arts events to over twenty-five thousand public school children yearly.

- At The Lighthouse Music School in New York City, a faculty of both blind and sighted musicians offers a traditional curriculum of instrumental instruction, voice, ensembles, music theory, and music history. The program, which is free of charge, is open to blind and visually impaired persons of all ages. The school's opera workshop presents fully staged opera performances with blind singers.

THE SETTLEMENT SCHOOL TRADITION

These few examples show the wide range of artistic enterprise that is carried on in community schools of the arts. The tradition arises from the settlement houses at the beginning of the twentieth century that sprang into being to deal with problems of literacy, citizenship training, unemployment, and other social concerns. Settlement schools were designed to assimilate urban immigrant populations into the mainstream of American culture. These schools served the neighborhood needs of the immigrant children in the urban settlements, where German, Irish, Italian, Jewish, and other ethnic groups attempted to acquaint themselves with the best of European culture, the "high" art of the day.

While their original intent was to supplement the public schools, over the years they have had an influence on reforming public education. Lillian Wald of New York City's Henry Street Settlement, for example, was instrumental in making the school nurse a fixture in the public schools. She was critical of the practice of removing sick children from the school without attempting to give them corrective medical attention.

While their role today has changed, many of these institutions still exist to meliorate the conditions of the urban slums. The Third Street Music School Settlement in New York City, founded in 1898, is a good example, as is Washington, D.C.'s Community School of Music. In offering alternative arts programs that are especially tailored to their clientele, the community schools of the arts provide a program that few public schools can match. They are attempting to respond to the real needs of the people they serve. In most cases their faculty are professionals in their field, and scholarship programs ensure that no student is denied instruction due to financial need.

The well-known story of Benny Goodman's fifty-cent lessons at Chicago's Hull House, an institution that helped children from poor families, is being replicated today by young, talented students all across the United States. Fifty of these schools are members of the National Guild of Community Schools of the Arts, Inc. They need support and assistance.

27

SENIOR CITIZENS' SYMPHONY BRINGS MUSIC TO CHILDREN

MUSICAL AMERICA 29 (October 1979)

Community and professional music groups often provide concerts of various sorts for school children. Some of these are formal and regular affairs, others a residency, and still others special opportunities that are unique and remarkable. One such example of the latter is the Wachovia Little Symphony in Winston-Salem, North Carolina. The orchestra, formed in 1978, was composed of retired symphony musicians, with an average age of sixty-three. The founder and conductor, a former music supervisor, brought together more than thirty players for each concert, from a pool of about ninety. The advantages seem obvious: intergenerational learning; performers eager to volunteer; great music brought into the schools; musicians available during the school day; and numerous opportunities for cultural connection and collaboration. Several funding groups supported the orchestra, and students, musicians, teachers, and administrators alike seemed happy with the program. I have often wondered why public education does not lean more heavily on its most experienced teachers once they retire. You would think they have so much to offer, yet non-musical and non-pedagogical concerns of schools boards and administrations seem to get in the way. At any rate, the good example here is certainly worth repeating, and perhaps a reader of this article will be inspired to do so.

—CR

* * *

THE SCHOOL SYSTEM in Winston-Salem, North Carolina has a new community music resource, a senior citizens' orchestra. Formed in August 1978, the Wachovia Little Symphony (Wachovia is the old Moravian name for what is now Winston-Salem) is comprised of a pool of ninety present and former symphony musicians with an average age of sixty-three. A rotating group of about thirty of the members perform two concerts a month for school children and for senior citizens.

Conductor-founder Robert A. Mayer, a retired coordinator of music for the Winston-Salem/Forsyth County Schools and a highly regarded musician in the community, has rallied most of the area's largely retired professional musicians and put them back to work. Concertmaster Earl Wolslagel, who served in that capacity with the North Carolina Symphony, brings fifty years of experience with some thirty orchestras to his position. Dr. Leonard Nanzetta, oboist, is a former member of the National Symphony. Trombonist Austin Burke is a former member of Ringling Brothers Circus Band. The piano soloist is Hans Heidemann, a former member of the First Piano Quartet. So it goes. Most of the members are either former or present members of the Winston-Salem, Greensboro, Charlotte, or North Carolina symphonies.

These peppy and talented oldsters maintain three basic repertoires, one for kindergarten through sixth grade, one for junior and senior high schools, and one for senior citizens' concerts. The 1978-79 season consisted of twenty-two concerts in the elementary schools, five in secondary schools, two concerts to raise money for the Winston-Salem Arts Council, six for senior citizens, and a benefit for the Winston-Salem Symphony that raised $26,000. There are no cobwebs on these instruments.

Dr. Mayer says that "The orchestra does not rehearse per se, due to the high caliber and experience of our musicians. Instead, we meet fifteen or twenty minutes before most concerts to read through any new numbers to be added that day. Since our mission is to stimulate and entertain our young and old clientele, our music is for enjoyment and is 'light' in nature. But it is artistically played."

A typical children's concert opens with the Stars and Stripes Forever, and includes a novelty such as the Sandpaper Ballet featuring sand-paper blocks, a piano and vocal soloist, and several movements from the Nutcracker Suite. The orchestra often performs pops concerts for its audiences of senior citizens.

The endeavor has the complete support of Dr. James A. Adams, Superintendent of Schools, who remarks, "The symphony offers our students the benefit of seeing the senior citizen in a role other than that of the stereotyped elderly person who is often misunderstood by youth." It has the equally wholehearted backing of C. Douglas Carter, Special Assistant for Instruction ("Our students have been fortunate to have these fine artists within the school environment"), and Dorothy Graham, Director of Urban Arts ("This is another way of giving quality art to school children and to senior citizens").

Three different funding groups have joined to assure appropriate financial support for the orchestra. Musicians are paid for each concert, and out-of-town players receive travel compensation. The group is on a thirty-six-week schedule. Fortunately, retired musicians are available during the daytime, when school concerts must be scheduled.

The symphony is good for its musicians and good for its audiences. With rehearsals scheduled just ahead of performances, the orchestra doesn't demand too much time, yet allows older musicians to sharpen their skills. One member of the orchestra with a wry sense of humor claims the symphony performs a public service for the musicians and the community. "It keeps the elderly off the streets," he says, "and cuts geriatric delinquency by half."

First cellist Amy Nanzetta finds playing in the symphony rewarding. "The informal, relaxed format of our programs encourages the children to respond and to participate. Their reactions are spontaneous and enthusiastic." For Dorothy Cooper, the white-haired grandmother who is soprano soloist, participating in the school concerts "has been the most rewarding experience I've ever had." Hans Heidemann, the piano solo-ist, says, "It gives me great pleasure and satisfaction to introduce good music to the next generation. They have little chance to hear live performances." Concertmaster Earl Wolslagel believes that "This type of opportunity should be made available in many communities throughout the country."

Principals and teachers who have attended performances are enthusiastic and sup-portive. Walter C. Joyce, Principal of Oak Summit Elementary School, says that the or-chestra "really made a hit" with his students. A teacher in this school, Mary Ferguson, points out how children benefit from such cultural experiences. "One of the greatest problems that we face in working with these particular children," she says, "is their lack of exposure to the many, many experiences needed to build concepts." As far as the schools are concerned, the orchestra has already established itself as a valuable community resource.

Children react to the experience by writing letters to Mr. Mayer and members of the symphony. "I wish they would come back," one declared, "so I could figure out how the instruments know when to come in." Some, like Beverly Galyean, an elementary student in Old Town School, are even inspired: "I liked the *Sandpaper Ballet* best of all. I also liked the march at the end of the program. I am going to play the drums next year in fifth grade." The idea of a senior citizens' orchestra is unique and the Wachovia Little Symphony may be one of a kind. But the endeavor is worthy of imitation.

28

PUBLIC UNIVERSITIES—THE NEW CULTURAL CENTERS

MUSICAL AMERICA 30 (July 1980)

A report was released in 1978 that outlined the state of the arts at public and land-grant universities. Supported by statistics and lists of numbers, the purpose was to outline what was happening at institutions of higher education relative to the arts. It turns out that universities have long been cultural centers, and this remains the case for many schools today. A current reader will find interesting the description of these institutions, how they were formed, costs for students at the time, how universities served as patrons of the arts, and the new and innovative programs available. Fowler, as always, raised some interesting questions to challenge why more was not being done to promote music and arts education in American society. Some of these relate to issues faced by artist-faculty; lack of student internships in the arts; the approach of courses in arts administration; lack of preparation for careers in television and theater; lack of research in performing and visual art; and the problem of reaching both non-arts majors on campus, and those in the rural United States. Overall, this is an interesting snapshot of music and the arts at the university level to compare with the situation today.

—CR

* * *

WE FINALLY have some statistics about arts programs in higher education. The Fine Arts Commission of the National Association of State Universities and Land-Grant Colleges conducted a survey of member institutions in the fine and applied arts in May 1978, and the data has just been released in a handsome, seventy-page document titled *The State of the Arts at State Universities & Land-Grant Colleges.*

As the publication explains, this survey documents the fact that state and land-grant universities offer broad access to quality arts programs at a very reasonable cost to the students. In 1978–79, the median charge to state residents for undergraduate tuition and fees at these public institutions was only $724. If it is true that the survey "shows that the state of the arts at member campuses reflects the state of the arts in our country as a whole," then the arts are, indeed, proliferating and flourishing.

In case you wonder, as I did, what a land-grant college is, the publication explains that under the provisions of the Morrill Act of 1862, Congress made land grants to the states of 30,000 acres for each member of Congress. On this basis, upwards of 11.4 million acres of land were given by the federal government to the states with the idea that income from sale of the land would endow and thus establish land-grant colleges and universities in each of the states.

Today, 3.2 million students attend these institutions out of a total U.S. higher education enrollment of 11.3 million. Land-grant colleges and universities include such formidable institutions as Cornell University, Purdue, the University of Illinois, Texas A & M University, Ohio State, Massachusetts Institute of Technology, and the University of Wisconsin, Madison. The survey was based upon responses from 106 of these campuses or almost fifty percent of the four-year colleges and universities that are members of this association.

EFFECTIVE ART PATRONS

The main impression conveyed by the data is that these institutions are eager and effective patrons of the arts. Collectively, they represent a national network of regional cultural centers that are accessible to all Americans, regardless of where they live. The document tells us that "Survey respondents reported totals of 4,036 exhibitions of art or craft works and 10,731 performances of musical recitals and concerts, theatre, opera, musical theatre, and dance productions presented on campus during one calendar year." That is a considerable amount of activity.

These institutions offer performance and exhibition opportunities on and off campus to students and faculty. The permanent collections and traveling exhibits of their art museums and galleries reach a wide general public. Of the almost four hundred college and university museums in the United States, one-fourth are on the campuses of state universities and land-grant colleges. Many of these, like Indiana University's Art Museum at Bloomington, designed by I.M. Pei, combine outstanding facilities with quality collections and expert staffs.

NEW PROGRAMS

The survey revealed four new programs of study at these institutions: arts therapy, arts administration, museology, and historic preservation. A total of 1,080 students were enrolled in these programs in the fall of 1977. Most of these students—sixty-five percent—were registered in some form of arts therapy, either in music, dance, art, or drama—all growing fields. Museology is the name given to programs in museum sciences, a recent offering dating from the mid-1970s.

Another section of the report deals with research. Among other items, the survey highlights some of the research collections entrusted to these institutions. Southern Illinois University at Edwardsville, for example, houses 150,000 pieces of sheet music, piano rolls, and old records in its Ragtime and Jazz Archive.

Another part of the survey investigated cultural extension, the public service component of these colleges and universities. The survey found, for example, that seventy-five respondents "reported a total of 1,620 continuing education courses in more than twenty-three arts disciplines in the fall of 1977." We learn that "Under state law, the University of Kansas must allow people over sixty-five years old to audit courses free," and that "The Pennsylvania State University offers workshops in improvisational acting to senior citizens."

Many of these institutions regularly bring the arts to elementary and high school students by means of touring companies and ensembles, and they offer these students opportunities for performance and exhibition at festivals, competitions, and other programs. The arts are also delivered to the public through campus radio and television stations.

Student enrollments in the arts are not only holding their own, but have been increasing over the past several years. In 1979-80, they are up 3.6 percent. "The number of students enrolled in dance classes at the University of Iowa, for example, has increased from 824 in 1975 to 1,500 in 1979."

QUESTIONS RAISED

These are just a few highlights of the survey report, which contains a number of tables and innumerable examples of the kinds of arts activities that are on-going at state and land-grant colleges and universities around the country. The report does provoke numbers of questions:

1. Do such institutions shelter their artist-faculty from the shocks of serving a real public, thus buffering them from the public tests that help artists to stretch their possibilities?
2. Why aren't there more student intern programs that place students in professional arts enterprises to gain real-life career experience for college or university credit?

3. Do courses in arts administration, which appear to be springing up everywhere, teach students to counter the prevalent and ingrained notion perpetuated by artists and arts institutions that the arts are by nature insolvent and require a handout for survival?

4. Why within the major curricula of these institutions is there little or no accommodation to preparation for careers in the entertainment field— recording, television, and the live stage?

5. Why isn't there more research in the visual and performing arts on these campuses?

6. Why aren't these arts programs reaching a higher percentage of the non-arts majors on their campuses?

7. Why isn't more effort being made by these institutions to bring the arts to rural America?

The report provokes these kinds of questions because it reveals the enormous potential of these institutions to enrich the artistic life on their campuses, in their communities, and across the country. As the report tells us, "Their achievements in the arts have made and will continue to make essential contributions to the quality of American life." One can only hope that, in spite of all they are doing, they strive to do much more.

29

REACHING KIDS, PART I: HOW SYMPHONIES DO IT

MUSICAL AMERICA 35 (February 1985)

Professional orchestras often do more than merely present subscription concerts to their patrons. Many times they play a significant role in community music and arts efforts, and education outreach is one important part of this puzzle. Most orchestras these days (as was increasingly the case in the mid-1980s) have developed savvy education programs to offer cultural enrichment to local school-children (it was likely not lost on symphony administrations that development of future audience members could be another valuable outcome of such out-reach programs). From 1983 to 1984, the American Symphony Orchestra League (ASOL) compiled information about education programs at numerous US orchestras nationally. The findings, titled *Orchestra Education Programs: A Handbook and Directory of Education and Outreach Programs,* was published as a book by ASOL in 1984. A fascinating summary and review of the book is put forward, full of relevant facts, compelling data, goals and objectives, and outreach materials. In all, the report provides a strong case for the value of the programs presented by American orchestras. The reader will likely find that the progressive nature of these efforts served as a template for many of the educational practices in place at many US orchestras around the country today.

—CR

* * *

AMERICAN symphony orchestras and opera companies are growing increasingly so-phisticated in their educational endeavors. These artistic enterprises are devoting more of their energies and resources to their educational programs, many of which are highly developed and effective. As such, they complement and supplement in-school music education programs by enriching and broadening the curriculum and by provid-ing students with a "real" and totally professional musical experience, something the schools would be hard pressed to offer on their own.

Symphony orchestras and opera companies are but two of the community arts orga-nizations that are providing educational opportunities in the arts. Dance and theater companies, museums, community schools of the arts, independent dance schools, and community bands and orchestras constitute an out-of-school educational infrastruc-ture in the arts that is unique among all the subject matters of education.

YEARS OF EFFORT

It has taken many years for the arts to develop such elaborate and astute community-based educational programs and establish the connections so that the in- and out-of-school programs function cooperatively. Significantly, there are no other subject matters in education that have achieved the comprehensive composite of community/school programs we find almost universally in the arts. Dr. John Goodlad, dean of the Graduate School of Education at the University of California, Los Angeles, credits the arts with providing "a glimmer of the potential" of what education might be if bridges were built between the schools and the community.

In the area of school/community cooperative educational programs, the arts are ahead of the rest of the subjects in the curriculum of American schools. Part I of this article surveys the educational programs and the network created by American sym-phony orchestras. Part II, next month, will look at what American opera companies are doing in education and how their work meshes with the schools. These programs are models for the way all educational programs should be conducted. As Goodlad says, "To continue with the myth that schools alone can provide the education we need is to assure their continued insularity and probably their ultimate irrelevance." The arts dispel that myth.

ORCHESTRA PROGRAMS

Last year, the American Symphony Orchestra League published *Orchestra Education Programs: A Hand-book and Directory of Education and Out-reach Programs*, a com-pendium of information and materials compiled from surveys it conducted in 1983 and 1984.

These surveys reveal the astonishing array of educational programs that symphony orchestras provide, from tiny tots concerts (for 1 to 4-year-olds); junior and senior high school, and family concerts; and preconcert lectures for adults; to open rehearsals, master classes, and young artist competitions. More than 250 education directors and education committee chairmen representing orchestras throughout the country submitted the information. Of the 576 orchestras sent the survey in 1983, forty-three percent responded. That shows considerable interest.

In 1983, these data reveal, sixteen percent of the major orchestras reported decreases in the size of their audiences. In 1984, that figure increased to twenty-five percent. This publication warns that symphony orchestras "have a monumental task in front of them. They have a community largely unaware of their product and unconcerned about their existence. If there is to be continued improvement in the current state of affairs, the symphony orchestra governing board . . . must become more involved in an orchestra's educational efforts."

Perhaps the most revealing questions asked were those concerned with the orchestra's basic commitment to education. Well over fifty percent of regional and metropolitan orchestras have a mission statement on education in the orchestra by-laws, have an education committee, and a specific line item for education in the orchestra budget. Oddly enough, less than fifty percent of major orchestras have a mission statement that supports education. This is explained by the fact that "The by-laws of many major orchestras were written long ago and may not reflect the orchestra's present commitment and sense of direction." This is evidently the case, because seventy-four percent of the major orchestras—more than any other category—have a specific line item for education in their budget, even though only fifty percent of these orchestras have an education committee within their board.

GOALS

Apparently, the purpose of an education program varies with the size of the orchestra. For example, major orchestras most frequently cited "achieving greater appreciation of symphonic music" as their primary purpose, while community orchestras cited "developing future audiences" as their major goal. In comparison, metropolitan and urban orchestras put "enhance the quality of life in the community" first. "Promoting the orchestra to all community members" was also ranked high as a goal by most of the orchestras.

Fifty percent of the budgets of these education programs go to youth concerts, fifteen percent to in-school ensembles, and thirteen percent to family concerts. Much smaller amounts go to support competitions, tiny tots concerts, youth orchestras, and other activities. And how many students do these orchestras reach? The National Symphony performed for 41,000 students during the 1983–84 school year, and one can venture to estimate that combined figures for all symphony orchestras would reach into the millions.

But this publication is far more than a compilation of statistical data. It is also a practical guide to organizing and carrying out orchestra education activities. For example,

Chapter 3, "Education Program Production," presents a good bit of the wisdom of these education directors in explaining exactly how to go about devising concert programs and administrating an educational program. Such concerts, they maintain, should achieve "a good balance between visual and musical elements" and keep the orchestra the "main attraction."

"BE FLEXIBLE . . ."

There is some astute advice here that sounds as if it may have been learned the hard way: "Be flexible about cutting pieces and excerpting single movements or sections. By doing so you may create a music lover and the composer will forgive you." And about the narration: "Don't bluff the kids. Children can spot a phony before the first cliché hits the floor." Orchestra personnel are advised to work closely with members of the educational community "to achieve common goals."

These education directors are quite blunt about programming popular music such as Top 40 hits and orchestral arrangements of Broadway show tunes: "There is a continuing controversy about whether or not to play this type of music in children's concerts. It is argued that children will like it, and therefore it will make friends for the orchestra." But they go on to say that there is "a superb body of time-tested music that is the mainstay of the orchestral repertoire. Playing this music is simply what orchestras do. Giving children orchestral arrangements of Top 40 hits, therefore, is cheating them and ultimately doing a disservice to orchestras."

It probably comes as no surprise that, in the major orchestras, only Zubin Mehta, music director of the New York Philharmonic and Charles Dutoit, music director of the Orchestre Symphonique de Montréal, regularly conduct education concerts. "Ninety-one percent of the major orchestras use associate conductors. In regional orchestras, thirty-six percent of the music directors conduct education concerts, while in metropolitan, urban, and community orchestras, the music director is the prominent figure."

HOW TO . . .

Included here are sample orchestra cue sheets, typical information sheets for the ushers, letters to the teachers that include the rules of concert etiquette, and an entire youth concert script produced by the Boston Symphony Orchestra. Scripts, by the way, are widely used at student concerts. Preparing them is something that the education director must learn.

Many orchestras (seventy-six percent of the majors) use teacher manuals or packets to prepare students and suggest follow-up activities. The Chicago Symphony Orchestra, for example, distributes teacher packets that include program notes for all three concerts (including information on all the pieces to be performed, short biographies of the composers, and a glossary of musical terms), guidelines for adult leaders and chaperones, reference materials such as a biography of the conductor and an explanation of the instrumental families in the orchestra, and forms for ordering prerecorded cassettes, docent (volunteer) visits, and multiple copies of the reference materials. The cassettes contain musical examples and conversation about the pieces as well as interviews with the young soloists who appear on each program. Recordings of some of the musical selections on each program are also available on tape at a nominal fee.

Chapter 4 is a detailed listing of the complete educational activities of more than 200 symphony orchestras in the United States and Canada, and Chapter 5 indexes the orchestras by the types of programs they offer.

The final chapter is devoted to young artist competitions. We learn here that "In 1984 symphony orchestras gave away more than $150,000 in cash prizes and scholarships and encouraged hundreds of people to learn their instruments well enough to make a solo appearance with the orchestra."

Obviously, this is a useful handbook for anyone who works with the education program of a symphony orchestra. It is also a useful tool for music education majors who aspire to becoming education directors of these programs, a position both exciting and challenging. As this guide states, to teach children that "there are nine entrances of the fugue subject in Bach's G minor Fugue is one thing, but to involve the children in the experience so that, at the ninth entrance, the hair rises on the backs of their necks is another." That's getting right to the heart of it.

30

REACHING KIDS, PART II: HOW OPERA COMPANIES DO IT

MUSICAL AMERICA 35 (March 1985)

Just as symphony orchestras were engaged in school-community partnerships, opera companies were strongly involved with such outreach programs, as well. Major arts organizations were dealing with declines in subscriptions, audiences, and supporters, and worked diligently to address these alarming developments. This, in conjunction with an interest in providing education and enrichment experiences for children, created a powerful opportunity to reach out in new ways and bring opera outside of the concert hall. Like the American Symphony Orchestra League (ASOL), Opera America (OA) produced a study that looked at current impacts of the genre, audience trends, public interest, educational efforts, and the like. The report was titled *Working Ideas: A Resource Guide for Developing Successful Opera Educational Programs,* and looked at various ways to engage communities and citizens, and thus encourage better appreciation for opera and its repertoire. Education was a central component of the report, and many models were highlighted in the publication. These include those by opera companies in Houston, New Orleans, San Francisco, New York, Miami, and elsewhere. As in many efforts in the arts and music education fields, collaboration is a principal key to success, and the work of ASOL and OA are two fine examples of how this can be achieved. Those reviewing the professional education programs in place today can look to these earlier models as incubators of our current practice. Perhaps these earlier iterations even offer ideas that are presently being overlooked (and at even lower cost).

—CR

* * *

LAST MONTH in Part 1 of this two-part look at school/community partnerships, this column focused on the educational activities and programs of American symphony orchestras. These orchestras are giving higher priority to their educational endeavors as an investment in their future. In 1984, one out of every four major orchestras reported a decline in their audiences. Survival means developing a greater appreciation of symphonic music among the public. Orchestras seem more eager than ever to interest young people in the powerfully expressive vehicle of the symphony orchestra and its rich and incredibly varied literature. Increasingly, they view themselves as cultural resources working hand-in-hand with schools to enhance the arts education opportunities provided to students.

Symphony orchestras are but one part of a vast network of cultural institutions, organizations, and community enterprises that assist schools in the process of educating students in the arts. The modes of delivering arts learning experiences to young people are proliferating. Not too many years ago, that delivery system in music consisted almost entirely of in-school music specialists and out-of-school private music teachers. Now there are chapters of YoungAudiences, Inc. in numerous cities that bring performers into the schools. The Artists in Education Program of the National Endowment for the Arts supports artist residencies in the schools in every state. Organizations such as the Junior League and Performing Tree, Inc. (in California) bring community arts resources and the schools into educational partnership. Today, the schools are seldom the only vehicle bringing the arts to children.

OPERA EDUCATION PROGRAMS

Like their symphony orchestra counterparts, opera companies are becoming increasingly active in educational programming. Last year, OPERA America, the service organization representing professional opera companies in North, Central, and South America, together with Learning About Learning Educational Foundation, published *Working Ideas: A Resource Guide for Developing Successful Opera Educational Programs*. This looseleaf compendium of proven ideas and educational processes is a first-rate educational tool that encourages and enables schools and opera companies to strike up mutually beneficial alliances.

The variety of educational programs described in *Working Ideas* and the astuteness with which they are carried out reveal a strong commitment on the part of these opera companies to educate young people. OPERA America was begun in 1970 by seventeen charter opera companies that just fourteen years later number ninety. Of these, eighty-four companies—or ninety-three percent—have active education programs. In

1980, sixty-one of the then seventy-six companies—or eighty percent—had programs. That percentage seems to keep increasing, no doubt because of OPERA America's own very active education efforts. These efforts began in 1977 largely through the commitment and leadership of Henry Holt, then principal conductor and education director of the Seattle Opera.

Today, OPERA America has its own education director, Marthalie Furber. At the inception of this program in 1980, the companies were surveyed about their education programs. At that time, the sixty-three companies that responded to the survey spent over $3 million, or approximately nine percent of their companies' budgets, on education.

Furber says that "At least forty companies have at least one designated staff person to oversee and implement their company's education program." Most, she says, are not called education directors because they usually have at least one other major responsibility. "Touring," Furber says, "is the most common shared responsibility, but marketing, public relations, and production managers/coordinators are also common overlaps." And she goes on to explain that "In some cases the education program is shared among various departments. In others, especially in smaller companies, the general director oversees the education program."

The important thing, she says, is that "the companies are committed to education, and they are becoming more sophisticated in their thinking about it."

A VARIETY OF APPROACHES

As proof of that sophistication, Furber says that in-school performances are now described in terms of the type: scenes, selected arias, informal discussions, or full productions. There is an increase in post-performance discussions with students. Pre-performance "Introductions" have increased by twenty percent. Outreach programs, too, are described as in the parks, brownbag lunches, street opera, senior citizen groups, or shopping center programs. There is more conscious age grouping, with programs designed particularly for those groups.

Working Ideas devotes more than a hundred pages to all the various types of opera education programs and how to develop and manage them. Many of these programs would have to be called exemplary. For example, the outreach program of the Houston Grand Opera, called the Texas Opera Theater (TOT), has toured 170 cities in thirty-six states. TOT is self-contained, traveling in a portable bus and truck that allows it to bring both full-length operas and one-acts (generally performed in English), lecture/demonstrations, and master classes to young people over a wide area. Before its arrival, TOT provides teacher workbooks about each opera.

New Orleans Opera Association uses life-size puppets, called "Oppets" to introduce pre-school children to opera. TOT, too, uses puppets. It performs "The Best Little Puppet Show in Texas" to introduce opera to elementary school children.

The Metropolitan Opera's In-School Program (complete with teacher training) involves students in creating and producing an original opera, from writing, composing, designing, and casting to staging, costuming, publicizing, and performing. Minnesota Opera's composer-in-residence program, Tucson's school project, and Michigan Opera Theatre's education program provide other models for student creation and production. Furber says that there are other such efforts outside opera companies—so many, in fact, that "We are starting a newsletter, *Kids Create and Participate* to communicate among these groups."

The STARS program is a summer artistic development program in which Willie Waters, artistic director for the Greater Miami Opera, works with talented high school students to refine performance skills in musical theater.

Boston Public Schools has a program in ten schools that involves students in a participatory program in which students perform works by well-known composers that were written for young people to perform.

The range and variety of educational activities within the various companies is remarkable. Since 1980, the number of member companies that offer in-house, mainstage performances for students has grown from twelve percent to twenty-one percent. While seventeen percent of companies in 1980 opened dress rehearsals to students, thirty-five percent of the companies in 1984 did. The increase in in-school performances by these companies is even more dramatic: twenty-two percent of the companies in 1980 to fifty percent of them in 1984.

Increasing numbers of companies are conducting teacher workshops. Houston Grand Opera, for example, has been extremely active in the establishment of the new Houston Institute, recognizing that teacher training is absolutely vital to the future of the art form.

TEACHING MATERIALS

In addition to all this effort, most companies now produce pre-performance materials that teachers can use to prepare students for the experience. These materials take on many forms. Mobile Opera, Inc. produces sophisticated teacher's manuals on each opera that students attend. San Francisco Opera provides a study guide for teachers with background information on opera, history, and production, and suggests units of study for the students. Sacramento Opera Association provides a kit for three-week periods. A demonstration workshop for school districts precedes distribution of the kits. Each canvas bag contains a complete recording of the opera, a film-strip, a teacher's guide describing the use of the kit, props and costumes for the students to use, bulletin board pictures, puzzles, and a copy of the book, *In Defense of Opera*.

Perhaps the most professional of all the materials are the Metropolitan Opera Boxes, a series of teaching materials made available to all schools by the Metropolitan Opera Guild. Each box focuses on one opera and includes background on the opera and the composer, a series of lessons, a handout for students that suggests various activities such as designing the sets or acting a particular scene, a recording of excerpts, a film-strip that might tell the story of the opera through photographs of a Met production, and a poster for the bulletin board. Nine operas are now available, including *Carmen, La Bohème, The Magic Flute,* and *Porgy and Bess.*

Much of the in-school work by opera companies, like that of the symphony orchestras, is carried out by volunteers and classroom teachers. Furber says that "At the time of our survey, almost fifty percent of the respondents indicated that volunteers implemented programs. A few were run completely by volunteers. Most were a cooperative effort between staff and volunteers." At least seventy-four percent of these volunteers in 1980 were opera guild members. The guilds also serve as a major source of funding for these programs.

OPERA America is continuing to encourage these educational initiatives. Three education task forces are now at work on educational materials development, pre-college artistic development, and appropriate repertoire to be performed for young people. The materials development task force has already launched the first phase of developing a generic opera education curriculum for students in grades K through 12 which will be site-tested and subsequently published.

COLLABORATION

Together, American opera companies and symphony orchestras are mounting a significant educational effort. Their work represents an acknowledgement, as John Good-lad reminds us, that "There is not one agency, but an ecology of institutions educating— school, home, places of worship, television, press, museums, libraries, businesses, factories, and more."[1]

In the arts, unlike other subject matters, we are learning to accrue maximum educational benefit from such school/community collaborations. This is a livelier, more vibrant way to educate—and to learn. The schools alone cannot provide these kinds of musical experiences. In this sense, then, the arts are out in front educationally. We are incorporating ever-broadening means to deliver the arts to young people.

Goodlad points out that "Networks in the arts all across this country educate in their own right as well as help the schools to educate in and through the arts." He sees the arts as a model for the kind of collaborations that ought to take place in all subjects. To establish "educative communities" and the "educative society," Goodlad says, we must "go beyond the schools." Toward these ends, our orchestras and opera companies are showing us the way.

---

[1] John I. Goodlad, *A Place Called School: Prospects for the Future* (New York: Harper & Row, 1983), p. 350.

31

WHOSE CULTURE SHOULD WE TEACH?

MUSICAL AMERICA 108 (July 1988)

The question of culture in American education and in music classrooms is certainly not a light one. Who should be represented when we teach music or discuss diversity in schools? Fowler tackled this critical issue in a book titled *Can We Rescue the Arts for America's Children?* (1988). This book was a response to a report he had written ten years earlier titled *Coming to Our Senses: The Significance of the Arts for America's Children* (1978), about the work of the Americans for the Arts Panel. In those publications and in this article, he examines the role of culture in education, and addresses the question of whose culture should be taught to children. Should we teach from a perspective of pluralism, emphasizing diverse cultures? Should the emphasis be more on single cultures: European, African, Hispanic, Asian, American? How should we present multiple cultures, and how do we present them in the best, most appropriate way when we do? These and other questions are discussed, and no doubt remain at the fore of current conversations about repertoire, pedagogy, and curriculum in the music education field.

—CR

* * *

This article is excerpted from a new book by Charles B. Fowler entitled Can We Rescue the Arts for America's Children? *published by the American Council for the Arts, 1285 Avenue of the Americas, New York (NY) 10019. The book provides an overview of the state of arts education today in light of the landmark report,* Coming to Our Senses: The Significance of the Arts for American Education, *published a decade ago. This update will be of special interest to readers who are concerned about the future of American music, particularly those who have followed Dr. Fowler's incisive reporting "On Education." (Musical America Editor)*

AMERICA'S culture is a vast and complex mosaic of arts of multiethnic and multinational origins. There are the arts of America's minority populations, and there are the arts of the majority, the latter representing the Western European tradition. The tension between those forces presents the public schools with a number of difficult choices. Which arts—whose culture—should be taught?

Ten years ago, the Rockefeller panel report, *Coming to Our Senses: The Significance of the Arts for American Education,* defined American culture as "a quilted fabric with numerous national minorities interspersed." The panel viewed the artistic creations of our ethnic peoples as "the most visible expressions of this variegated culture," and they saw these creations as "an invaluable resource for arts education."[1] The ethnic arts movement, they said, is "a central force in American culture," and they urged the schools to "take advantage of such programs to improve their own arts education efforts."

The explosion of arts in the inner cities since the mid-1960s tells us that Afro-Americans and Hispanic-Americans have their own characteristic cultural heritages. The panel expressed reservations, however, about the possible limitations of arts programs designed for those who share the same social or economic conditions. The danger, they said, is that "such programs can become isolated and segregated from the rest of the society, thus running the risk of stagnating without the interchange of ideas." Then, too, they felt that "programs directed at particular ethnic or racial groups may only temporarily satisfy the need to strengthen a sense of self or to articulate fully the messages and forms which derive from social and historical heritage."[2]

What was not said, and needs to be said, is that arts programs that tend to isolate people from the totality of American culture not only repudiate that culture but also, by the sin of omission, perpetuate continuing cultural deprivation. This is true whether the narrow vision of the world emanates from the minority sectors of the society or from the white, Anglo-Saxon majority. Such programs put blinders on children and teach them to see only their own footsteps.

We must be careful not to move toward cultural separatism, particularly in our cities. Here, where many children attend schools that do not provide adequate arts instruction and where they are not introduced systematically to prevailing traditions

---

[1] The Arts, Education and Americans Panel, *Coming to Our Senses: The Significance of the Arts for American Education* (New York: McGraw-Hill, 1977), p. 255.

[2] *Ibid.*, p. 189.

and practices of artistic culture, they are apt instead to be engulfed in the particular culture afforded by their community. For many children, this is the culture of the ghetto, often rich in its individual way, but certainly not representative of the larger society outside. Those who teach the arts have an obligation to assure that the many ethnic elements of our culture do not separate us, at the same time that they assure students access to the universal elements of culture that bind us as a civilization.

What we do not want in the United States is a dissolution of our many ethnic cultures or a fusion of them into one indistinguishable mass. The diverse riches of mind, spirit, and imagination make a dynamic whole, *but only if there is a shared culture at the base.* If we are not to be a country of many separate peoples, we must establish commonalities of culture as well as some understanding across our many distinguishable artistic legacies.

Shall we uphold a school district's right to teach mainly black arts, or Hispanic arts, or Asian arts, or European arts because of the particular ethnic demographics of the local population? E.D. Hirsch, Jr., author of *Cultural Literacy: What Every American Needs to Know,* says, "Our diversity has been represented by the motto on all our coins—E PLURIBUS UNUM, 'out of many, one.' Our debate has been over whether to stress the *many* or the *one."* And he further amplifies the argument for a balanced view of American culture:

> If we *had* to make a choice between the *one* and the *many,* most Americans would choose the principle of unity, since we cannot function as a nation without it. Indeed, we have already fought a civil war over that question. Few of us accept the extreme and impractical idea that our unity can be a purely legal umbrella, which formally contains but does not integrate our diversity. On the other side, the specific content of our larger national culture is not and must not be detailed, unchanging, or coercive, because that would impinge on our equally fundamental principles of diversity, localism, and toleration. A balanced, moderate position is the only workable American position, and it is bound to be the one that will prevail.[3]

We must know ourselves as both the many *and* the one. (Sometimes, we humans have to be reminded that we are far more alike than we are different, and it is the alike qualities that are so often overlooked.)

Hirsch, a professor of English at the University of Virginia, goes on to say that, above all, schools should teach the commonalities of mainstream culture, but he says:

> To acknowledge the importance of minority and local cultures of all sorts, to insist on their protection and nurture, to give them demonstrations of respect

---

[3] E.D. Hirsch, Jr., *Cultural Literacy: What Every American Needs To Know* (Boston: Houghton Mifflin, 1987), p. 96.

in the public sphere are traditional aims that should be stressed even when one is concerned, as I am, with national culture and literacy. . . . It is for the Amish to decide what Amish traditions are, but it is for all of us to decide collectively what our American traditions are, to decide what "American" means on the other side of the hyphen in Italo-American or Asian-American. What national values and traditions really belong to national cultural literacy?[4]

No doubt Hirsch would agree that the inculcation of national cultural literacy should take precedence over any ethnic considerations, but not that these subcultures should be homogenized or obliterated. On the contrary, people need to wed their personal cultural identity to a strong sense of national cultural identity. They must come to view their own uniqueness as an important slice of the whole to see themselves in the context of the larger world.

But defining that larger world poses difficulties. What exactly constitutes mainstream American culture? Hirsch offers a 54-page list of "What Literate Americans Know." An analysis of the terms on his list reveals about 154 words related to music, 53 to art, 37 to theater, 10 to dance, and more than 300 terms from literature or areas related to the arts. That is a total of about 555 terms representing the arts out of some 4,650 entries, or about 12 percent. But why Brahms and not Bernstein and Copland? Why Caruso and not *Carmen*? Why Gilbert and Sullivan and not Rogers and Hammerstein? Why Prokofiev and not Rachmaninoff, Verdi and not Wagner? Such questions, obviously, could go on endlessly with little prospect for agreement. Literacy would be better defined in terms of the broad traditions of culture—musical works, say, of many periods and styles, master composers through the ages, and familiarity with the traditions of music-making.

What Hirsch does not acknowledge in his book is that children should be introduced to the *uncommonalities* of artistic culture—humankind's extraordinary achievements in architecture, ballet, chamber music, drama, jazz, modern dance, opera, painting, poetry, prose, sculpture, symphonic literature, and so forth. But we must not make the mistake of believing, as does Allan Bloom, author of *The Closing of the American Mind*, that the distinguished elements of American culture derive entirely from the traditions of Greece and Western Europe. Eurocentrism is as unsuitable a view of American culture as the relativistic pandering to everything and anything. Nor is our culture tied primarily to literature and philosophy—that is, words—as both Hirsch and Bloom would evidently have us believe. All of the arts, including literature, are at the core.

By their nature, the arts in their totality give significant representation to a culture. They exude civilization. From this point of view, it may be more important for a largely Hispanic community to stress other aesthetic manifestations of cultural diversity than just the Hispanic element. The black person who knows only Afro-American music and the white person who knows only European painting and architecture are

---

[4] Ibid., p. 98.

equally deprived. Yet it must be acknowledged that this country has its roots deep in the Western traditions that emanated from Greece, Rome, and Europe. Every citizen of this nation has a right and an obligation to that heritage, just as we all have a right and an obligation to jazz, ragtime, and gospel. In this regard, our artistic eclecticism is an American fact of life, and the cross-fertilization between types and styles of art is the basis of much of our creative vitality. What helps to bind us as a nation and as a people are the universal elements of our pluralistic artistic heritage.

What, then, do the schools do? Should they pass on all the existing manifestations of art as though all are of equal value? To the extent that all these artistic expressions are part of our heritage, yes, they have a viable claim to a share of arts education. Indeed, the main function of arts education is to transmit to new generations the breadth and richness of American culture. But constraints of time and resources force arts educators to make certain choices. What, then, do we pass on, and what do we pass over?

Children vary widely in what arts they have been exposed to and what they have come to understand. From this standpoint, communities and schools will differ in what they need to stress. People should understand their own ethnic culture as well as the cultural traditions of the nation. But arts curricula do not need to stress what students already know and like. Young people do not need the schools to introduce them to popular culture. They quite often *do* need the schools to give them an opportunity to understand their own ethnic artistic heritage and to introduce them to the artistic heritage of other cultures, including the European traditions that are the basis for so much of our artistic expression. To these ends, arts education is the irreplaceable conduit for conveying the artistic heritage of Afro-, Asian-, European-, Hispanic-, and Native Americans to citizens of the next generation. For if these arts are not a part of arts education in the schools, many American children will not have access to them at all.

A second criterion of delimitation and choice involves the degree of abstractness or difficulty of the artistic "language." If a particular example of an art form is simple to perform (or readily understood), students may not benefit from studying it. Some popular folk art is immediately decipherable. These artistic codes are deliberately in the public vernacular. In comparison, understanding African sculpture, Asian dance, Greek theater, Hispanic literature, or European artistic traditions poses challenges comparable to learning a foreign language. These codes tend to be more complex, more highly structured and developed, or sometimes more subtle, profound, or sublime in content. From this standpoint, they demand more *attending to* in education. We have to know *more* to get the message, like the extra trouble it takes to understand Shakespeare or Spenser or Milton. ·

The fact of our pluralistic artistic culture, then, does not translate into equal claims on the educational curriculum. Every citizen should have the means to understand the greatest artistic traditions of America, those that represent the ultimate human achievements. Students should be given all the pieces of the cultural puzzle, not just those they easily relate to, are already familiar with, or are already interested in. Some of those pieces are especially representative of the range, character, and concentration of American arts; some are difficult to understand. The curriculum must be adjusted accordingly. As citizens, we are all heirs to both the majority and minority cultures of the nation. That is a uniqueness of American citizenship that cannot be taken lightly in today's schools.

Music Education and Professional Reform

32

THE MUSIC EDUCATORS NATIONAL CONFERENCE (MENC): DAVID FACES NEW GOLIATHS

MUSICAL AMERICA 26 (April 1976)

The music education profession has long faced challenges of many sorts. MENC, as the professional body representing music teachers in the United States, played a uniquely important role in addressing the issues. Fowler had an intimate connection with MENC (now NAfME), having served for six years, from 1965 to 1971, as editor of its flagship publication, *Music Educators Journal.* Here he offers a brief history of the organization, highlights its specific role in the oversight of music teaching and learning compared with professional organizations, and mentions some of the good work they have done over the years. An important focus of the article, however, was to bring to light some of the significant challenges MENC faced in the mid-1970s, and to recommend solutions to address them. Among the difficulties were issues relating to finances, reform, diversity, elitism, administration, and policy. As for recommendations, he suggested that music education have a more open and accepting view, bring more children to music education, think more creatively, incorporate more diversity and pluralistic viewpoints, and act more boldly on its own policy proclamations and ideas. This piece is worth a read on many levels, but perhaps it is most valuable as an opportunity to hear the voice of an experienced insider who knew and cared about music education as much as anyone.

—CR

* * *

THE UNITED STATES was not only the first nation to require free public education for all its citizens to assure the development of an informed and therefore responsible public, but also the first nation to perpetuate a democratic view of the arts as being good for all citizens and therefore a part of basic or general education. Initially the introduction of drawing or "picture-making" in American schools during the Colonial period was done for the purpose of preparing people for industrial employment. What music there was in Colonial schools was taught in order to train people for singing in church. Music received its first formal acceptance as a part of the public school curriculum in 1838 in Boston. As the post-Civil War industrialization made leisure time available to the middle class, the fine arts, taught for cultural enrichment rather than for some more practical purpose, won general approval. Neither the acceptance of music as part of public education nor of the arts as part of general education for all students has come easily.

Innovations of this magnitude require the force and persuasion of advocacy groups working diligently for the cause. One such group that has worked sixty-nine years for the advancement of music education in the United States is the Music Educators National Conference.

Organized in Keokuk, Iowa in 1907 as the Music Supervisors National Conference, MENC (the name was changed in 1934) has grown from sixty-nine members to more than sixty-three thousand at present. As a national, nonprofit organization whose membership consists of music educators and administrators on all levels from pre-school through college and university, the organization has assumed a unifying voice for music education in the United States during the better part of the twentieth century. In contrast to "professional" organizations such as the American Medical Association and the American Bar Association, the MENC has fulfilled this role primarily by functioning as a collector and distributor of information, rather than operating as a policy-proclaiming, project-oriented, or action-taking body.

The earliest form of information sharing began with the first conference in 1907 and developed into the proliferation of meetings and conferences that now take place on the local, state, regional, and national levels. Beginning in 1910, published accounts of these meetings were made available, but by 1914 the 350 members received, free of charge, copies of the *Music Supervisors Bulletin* (now the *Music Educators Journal*) which remains the bulwark of the Conference's information distribution system.

OUTWARD TURNING

If the Conference concentrated its focus largely upon its own membership, encouraging the development of a missionary spirit of advocacy on the part of individual music teachers in their own communities, it also struck up profitable liaisons with other organizations in education in order to seek and win over the support of the power structure in education. The affiliation with the National Education Association, which is at present all but severed, began in 1908 and grew to the point that MENC became a department of the NEA in 1938 and moved from Chicago to Washington, D.C. to be housed in the

NEA building itself in 1956. Down through the years, sporadic collaborations with the American Association of School Administrators, the American Federation of Musicians, the National Association of Secondary School Principals, the National Association of Schools of Music, the American Association of Colleges for Teachers Education, and other associations have helped to promote the cause of music education in the schools.

Beginning in 1910 with the report of the Committee on Formulation of a Music Course for High School, committees, councils, and commissions of music teachers within the MENC, working on a voluntary basis, have studied particular problems, proposed possible solutions and, through the Conference's publications program, made the results available to the field at large. A public relations program, established in 1966, has also given substance and range to the advocacy and information functions, reaching out to the public to ask them to "support music in your schools."

MENC TODAY

Where is the organization today? Vast changes appear to be called for in the last quarter of the century. In 1975 MENC moved into its own new building in the Center for Educational Associations at Reston, Virginia. But the strain on financial resources caused by the building project, coupled with general inflationary pressures, has resulted in curtailment of some activities and programs at a time when music education faces increasingly severe problems. With current declining enrollments in the public schools, cuts in public budgets for education, and public demands to go "back to basics," music teachers are finding that, even after all their work during the past three-quarters of a century, music is among the lowest subjects on the educational totem pole, being easily cut or even totally dispensed with in too many school systems across the country. While older music teachers are attempting to hold on to their jobs through seniority, new teachers are finding few opportunities for employment.

The Conference's own Tanglewood Symposium in 1967, which examined "The Roles and Functions of Music in a Democratic Society," declared that music be placed in the core of the curriculum. It also recognized the need to broaden the base of music taught in the schools to include jazz, pop, rock, electronic, and virtually all forms of music. Official advocacy in favor of the democratic right of citizens to evolve their own musical tastes rather than mimic the preferred "classical" tastes of the old-style music teacher has been slow to win favor and done much to fan the flames of the zealous missionary-elitists who still proclaim the primacy of the European-based musical art.

THE OTHER EIGHTY PERCENT

Music programs, particularly at the high school level, have been geared largely to the talented, with the emphasis on participation in band, chorus, and orchestra. While much verbiage is given to "concern for the other eighty percent," few programs have moved to accommodate the vast majority of students, and little action has been taken by the national organization to lead the profession toward serving a larger constituency. High schools, it seems, are particularly difficult to change.

Meanwhile, the other arts are on the move proclaiming, rightfully, that *all* students deserve opportunities to develop their emotive and aesthetic selves; that, indeed, all students should have access to some art form that they can handle successfully. Where music teachers have often found themselves fighting with art teachers for the last few crumbs of the school budget, they are now faced with the challenge of working cooperatively with the other arts in evolving aesthetic education programs that reach the entire student body. For music teachers, who have become accustomed to their art form dominating the public school arts scene, slicing the dwindling financial pie in more (and smaller) pieces may not be viewed as progress. Although cooperative solidification of the arts could win music a status and priority in education equivalent to, say, the social sciences, music teachers are not apt to take kindly to this invasion of their limited but comfortably insular domaine. Neither elitism nor isolationism dies easily, even when faced with the probability that no single art will make it to the core of the curriculum alone.

In no small sense the problem that the Conference faces as it approaches the last quarter of the century is to give direction to a field that is burdened by its reverence for tradition. No other art form is so passionately past-oriented. While theater students do not neglect Shakespeare; nor art students, Rembrandt; nor architectural students, classical forms; these arts basically are focused on the present and the future. Technique is learned primarily through involvement with contemporary idioms. Unless music education accommodates itself more to the present, it cannot assure the viability and evolution of the art form. Creativity must be given a status equal to performance.

It seems apparent that the Conference's greatest achievements in the past ten years have been connected with major policy pronouncements, such as those that emanated from Tanglewood. These have been rare but welcome occurrences, for all too often in mediating between opposing factions, consensus-taking has sought middle ground that would not offend—or help—either group. But coloring policy beige may not satisfy the exigencies of the present situation. Diversity of opinion is characteristic of America's cultural pluralism, and strong but opposing views must be given voice. Minority professionals in music, for example, may well find their own solutions in the inner city that may or may not apply in suburban or rural situations. But they need a voice in and the support of the national organization that gives identity and thrust to their profession.

The stakes are high. America seems to be teetering on the brink of either cultural atrophy or renaissance. Intensification of MENC's advocacy role, particularly with the public and the educational power structure, coupled with active programs and projects designed to directly assist the field, could bring important national dividends. The Conference, as one of the largest arts organizations in the world, could be a telling factor in determining whether famine or feast will characterize the cultural future. A commitment to the latter—and soon—would be a momentous gift for all Americans.

33

THE TANGLEWOOD SYMPOSIUM REVISITED

MUSICAL AMERICA 28 (July 1978)

In 1967, a symposium was held to debate the most critical issues facing music education in a century. This meeting, known as the Tanglewood Symposium, was arguably the most important gathering of the music education profession in the twentieth century. The Tanglewood Declaration, which laid out the agreed-upon philosophical goals and tasks to move the field forward, has been a Declaration of Independence of sorts for music education. At the time Fowler wrote this article ten years later, several of those in attendance believed that the objectives of the original meeting needed to be revisited. This second meeting, held in 1978 at the University of Wisconsin–Milwaukee, brought together major figures to raise these noble issues, and to help determine a modified path forward, given the changing landscape of the 1970s. Fowler, who was in attendance and participated at both meetings, ably writes a review of the events, provides background and analysis, and even reprints the original Tanglewood Declaration to offer the reader a broader understanding of the symposia. Many notable figures spoke at the second meeting, including Will Schmid, Gerald McKenna, David Searles, David McAllester, George Duerksen, Donald Shetler, Mary Hoffman, James Standifer, and Charles Hoffer, among others. The winds of reform were certainly blowing during the 1970s, and keeping the flame of Tanglewood alive was an important goal of the music education profession. There have been similar meetings since, yet it is unclear if most music teachers (or the profession) have taken notice.

—CR

* * *

TEN YEARS AGO the Music Educators National Conference held a symposium at Tanglewood that analyzed the role of music in American society in light of the turmoil of the 1960s. That meeting did much to alter the focus of music in American education during the next decade. It set forth a rationale intended to make music more relevant to the needs of students. It asked that a larger variety of musics be taught and that more of the students be reached. It suggested that teacher education programs be broadened and that music join the mainstream of education.

The issues raised by the symposium and the pronouncements that came from it have been guideposts for music educators ever since. But the times have changed. Two enterprising professors at the University of Wisconsin in Milwaukee, Will Schmid and Gerald McKenna, felt that the moment had come for a reassessment. They organized "The Tanglewood Symposium Revisited," held March 10–12, to reexamine the state of music education today.

THE VALUE OF INTROSPECTION

As a participant in both the original symposium and this revisit, I was struck again by the value of such introspective exercises. Too seldom do the formats of meetings and conferences of music teachers provide opportunities for discussions that delve into the depths of the major problems and possibilities that face the field. One outcome of this meeting is the recommendation that the National Executive Board of the Music Educators National Conference take action to update the original Tanglewood Declaration.

The state of the arts in society today is considerably different from that of ten years ago. David Searles, deputy chairman for Policy and Planning of the National Endowment for the Arts, identified four trends: a much greater willingness to support the arts in all segments of society; the attempt to assure quality at the same time that the base for the arts is extending outward in all communities; recognition in the non-arts world that the arts are a powerful tool to accomplish their non-arts objectives; and the increasing visibility of the arts in all segments of society. He expressed the fear that with all the sound and fury, "there is the possibility that art itself will become obscured," and he recommended that greater consideration be given to the artist and to creativity.

A PRODUCTIVE CROSS-FERTILIZATION

David McAllester, professor of anthropology and music at Wesleyan University and a participant in the original symposium, presented a view of culture as "the contagious commodity." Increased contact between cultures has created a cross-fertilization of traditions, a mingling which hopefully retains the best of all worlds. He encouraged further broadening of the music taught, because it is an effective bridge between peoples. "Surely at no time in history," he said, "has cultural understanding been more necessary than in these perilous times."

In response to McAllester's presentation, Ben Johnston, a composer and theorist from the University of Illinois, raised the fundamental question, "Why should every child have music?" He answered by saying that music is a remarkable way of making your own culture understandable to yourself and others. However, he pointed out that contemporary music has become artificial. It's too obviously invented. The mingling of cultural approaches, he suggested, provides a way through. "As educators," he said, "we should help people realize all these possibilities."

George Duerksen, chairman of the department of music education and therapy at the University of Kansas, pointed out that music is used for a wide variety of purposes and that the old idea of the conservatories—that music can't survive if we don't conserve it—is no longer credible. Arts education, he stated, should help people learn how to use the arts in a variety of ways to change their environment.

"But is there a danger that we have substituted gamelon bums for Beethoven buffs?" asked Jerry Olsen from the University of Wisconsin in Madison. "The more bums, the better," McAllester replied. "We've taken music out of the elitist camp. It is not a matter of substituting one kind for another." McAllester, Johnston, and Duerksen all felt that high schools, like colleges, can offer all kinds of musical experiences. In the same way that physical education is offering lifetime sports, there can be lifetime music.

A TANGLEWOOD UPDATE

Donald Shetler, head of music education at the Eastman School of Music and also a participant at the first symposium, came down hard on the need to update the findings at Tanglewood. He chided the field for its failure to communicate the objectives of aesthetic education to the public. Basic education, he reminded the audience, is in worse shape than the arts and music educators are not responsible for teaching the basics. He noted the rarity of music teachers who share contemporary music and ethnic musics with their students or who understand the relation of music to other arts and to the community. The reform of institutions of higher education, the improvement of teacher education, and the need for basic research were seen as major issues.

In response to Shetler's talk, Mary Hoffman, president-elect of MENC, made a plea for programs that stretch from cradle to grave. She agreed that music educators need to get out into the community. If schools do not want the responsibility for providing music education, "maybe the town has to afford us." We have a tendency, she felt, to save the programs even when they are second rate. There must be an attempt to broaden programs, and she suggested getting people to help in areas where the music teacher's own background is insufficient.

The final major speaker, James Standifer of the University of Michigan, pointed out that music education is in serious trouble in the cities in spite of all the symposiums, conferences, and pronouncements. "We are in worse shape now than ever before," he said. Standifer looks to computerized instruction as one possible means of absorbing the mechanistic parts of teaching, thereby freeing the teacher for the human relationships that are now being neglected, particularly in the cities.

In response to Standifer, Eunice Boardman, professor of music education at the University of Wisconsin at Madison, noted that whereas once society threw the problem of the arts to the schools, "now they may be deciding to take it back." Music educators, she said, should decide what society is not providing in the way of arts experiences and offer those in schools. She made a strong case for treating the arts as process rather than products. Handing students musical products rather than involving them in creative and re-creative experiences has caused sterility.

Charles Hoffer, president of the North Central Division of MENC and professor at Indiana University, opened his remarks with a question: Why have performing groups in high schools become so prevalent? Is it that the students like them? The teachers? The parents? We don't know enough, he said, about nurturing creativity in the arts. Little consensus exists about the value of music in education. Hoffer spoke in favor of more emphasis on art music which, he feels, has generally not been taught well: "Utilitarian music is going to take care of itself; the art music needs help."

In the discussions that followed, the music teachers in attendance attempted to regain a sense of their own functionality and the usefulness of music education in the schools. They tried to get at the heart of what music education is all about and determine what would be a convincing case to bring to the public. Out of the anguish of such a search comes insight. Michael George, supervisor of music in the Wisconsin Department of Public Instruction, took exception to the first major point of the Tanglewood Declaration: "Music serves best when its integrity as an art is maintained." He asked, "What does that mean to the music educator who is trying to decide whether or not to provide experiences to meet the special needs of the handicapped?"

While it was not the intention of this revisit to duplicate the scope of the first symposium, it seems clear from the many questions that were raised and the depth of thought generated that the time has come for MENC to mount a vast reassessment in the near future. Like the Tanglewood meeting, it could provide a focus and set directions that will determine the effectiveness of music education in the decade ahead.

Does it need updating?

THE TANGLEWOOD DECLARATION

The intensive evaluation of the role of music in American society and education provided by the Tanglewood Symposium of philosophers, educators, scientists, labor leaders, philanthropists, social scientists, theologians, industrialists, representatives of government and foundations, music educators and other musicians led to this declaration:

We believe that education must have as major goals the art of living, the building of personal identity, and nurturing creativity. Since the study of music can contribute much to these ends, *we now call for music to be placed in the core of the school curriculum.*

The arts afford a continuity with the aesthetic tradition in man's history. Music and other fine arts, largely nonverbal in nature, reach close to the social, psychological, and physiological roots of man in his search for identity and self-realization.

Educators must accept the responsibility for developing opportunities which meet man's individual needs and the needs of a society plagued by the consequences of changing values, alienation, hostility between generations, racial and international tensions, and the challenges of a new leisure.

Music educators at Tanglewood agreed that:

(1) Music serves best when its integrity as an art is maintained.

(2) Music of all periods, styles, forms, and cultures belongs in the curriculum. The music repertory should be expanded to involve music of our time in its rich variety, including currently popular teenage music and avant-garde music, American folk music, and the music of other cultures.

(3) Schools and colleges should provide adequate time for music in programs ranging from preschool through adult or continuing education.

(4) Instruction in the arts should be a general and important part of education in the senior high school.

(5) Developments in educational technology, educational television, programmed instruction, and computer-assisted instruction should be applied to music study and research.

(6) Greater emphasis should be placed on helping the individual student to fulfill his needs, goals, and potentials.

(7) The music education profession must contribute its skills, Proficiencies, and insights toward assisting in the solution of urgent social problems as in the "inner city" or other areas with culturally deprived individuals.

(8) Programs of teacher education must be expanded and improved to provide music teachers who are specially equipped to teach high school courses in the history and literature of music, courses in the humanities and related arts, as well as teachers equipped to work with the very young, with adults, with the disadvantaged, and with the emotionally disturbed.

34

MUSIC IN OUR SCHOOLS: AN AGENDA FOR THE FUTURE

MUSICAL AMERICA 31 (March 1981)

A few years prior to writing this article, in 1978, Fowler presented an agenda for music education at the Tanglewood Symposium Revisited (an important reform conference modeled on the original Tanglewood meeting in 1967). He brought years of experience and innovative ideas to his talk, and here offered his major themes to move the profession forward. Three principle themes were highlighted: democracy, creativity, and purpose. The larger concepts were: (1) *Music education should be democratized;* (2) *Creativity in music should be given as much emphasis as performance;* and (3) *Music education must serve the purposes of American education and the needs of American society.* These were bold suggestions, to be sure, but also sorely needed when talking about music teaching. They had also been on the mind of MENC and others, but with how much impact? While the influence on the profession cannot be quantified, it is clear that these topics are right at the forefront of music-education reform in the early twenty-first century. Should we be pleased to learn that these compelling ideas are not new, or disappointed that we are still fighting for them?

—CR

* * *

MARCH 9–15 has been designated by the Music Educators National Conference as Music in Our Schools Week, a national celebration of the import and impact of music in American education. The occasion affords an opportunity to take stock and to look ahead.

Music was the first art form to be incorporated into the public school curriculum, well over a hundred years ago. If its beginnings in the Boston schools were somewhat tenuous and limited to singing, it soon spread to other school systems and enlarged its framework to include instrumental music study as well. The growth during all these decades has been nothing short of remarkable. There is no question that today, music education is available in some form in every school system in the country. The quality of America's school bands, choruses, and orchestras surpasses by far those of most other countries in the world.

With that said, I would like to propose an agenda for music education in the final two decades of this century. I first proposed this agenda at a symposium at the University of Wisconsin, Milwaukee, in March of 1978.

Music education should be democratized. It may seem like a truism to say that the study of music should be made inviting and accessible to every student at every educational level, yet it is a goal that has alluded [*sic*] us. While few music educators would disagree with the motto, "Music for every child, every child for music," many have steadfastly focused the music programs—particularly those at the secondary level—upon selective and restrictive performing groups and on teaching the talented.

It must be acknowledged that, in music, many students are eliminated early from the main events. The determined search for talent, though it may start within the general music study provided for every student in the elementary school, soon zeros in to concentrate on performance specialism by the secondary level. It's practically unheard of to offer beginning lessons on an instrument at that level, let alone to offer courses in music that meet *the interest* of all students. Music on the secondary level, for the most part, is a team sport reserved for the few who have already demonstrated that they know how to carry the ball.

Providing a broader curriculum that would open music study to all students would require that music teachers make their peace with the quality versus quantity dichotomy. Would proliferation of arts study move the arts toward mediocrity? I see the development of greater numbers of interested musical amateurs—and here I refer to listeners and song writers as well as performers—as a way to keep music in general alive and vibrant. When he was Chancellor of the State University of New York, Samuel Gould said, "I do not subscribe to the theory that a democratic nation, concerned for all its citizens, cannot work in the interests of excellence."

First and foremost, then, I believe that the agenda for music education must embrace a democratic philosophy and open the art of music to every student. That some students have music and others do not is blatant discrimination that should be eliminated in public education.

Creativity in music should be given as much emphasis as performance. The greatest failure of American music education is that music, by and large has not been taught as a personally expressive medium. Unlike the other arts, musical expression is generally restricted to re-interpretation. By limiting musical expression to the re-creative, music becomes a secondhand art.

Performance and interpretation, of course, can be somewhat creative. I say "somewhat" because there are strict limits upon just how much interpretation is permitted. Transgressions of "taste," as we call these interpretive borders, are quickly admonished. Consequently, the range of self-expression in music is apt to be considerably narrower than that permitted, say, an actor who is interpreting a role on the stage. In music we are stifled by tradition to the point of near suffocation. One manifestation is that we have become print-bound. Most musicians tend to be slaves to the printed page. In high school and college programs that have finally added jazz after all the years of resistance, what is the approach? The students are taught to read the charts. Yet this music originated as a primarily aural and improvisory art—a true medium of self-expression. Indeed, music itself must have originated in this manner.

To achieve a creative orientation, I propose that improvisation be given major emphasis to the point where it becomes a deliberate and important part of what every student learns in the music classroom. As one of the gates through which students gain access to music as a self-expressive art, improvisation is central to what music education is all about.

In my way of thinking, we should be giving students the opportunity to play with sound in the same way they play with paint. In this way, students are not the mere recipients of a rigid and finished musical commentary on the world as it was; they are participants in evolving a musical expression of their world as they feel it and envision it. And this applies as much to college and university curricula as to the public schools. I, for one, cannot comprehend how degrees can be given in music without requiring even one course in composition.

Music education must serve the purposes of American education and the needs of American society. Music should enter the bloodstream of the school and the community. Part of the reason music exists on the periphery is that music educators are content with compartmentalized isolation and insulation. Too many music teachers champion their own purposes and allow their courses to stand outside the primary goals of education and the interests of the American people.

I believe that achieving the first two goals set forth above—to reach every student and to bring more of a creative emphasis to music teaching—will help this cause. But they will not suffice. There is an old saying that the last thing a sea fish discovers is salt water. Music education's salt water is education and the community.

For this reason, I believe that music educators should take the lead in establishing the arts in the context of all kinds of new educational and social *transactions*—between the arts between arts specialists and classroom teachers, between the arts and other subjects, and between the school and the community. That is a new kind of dynamism.

Students need options, not only in the study of music, but also in studying all the arts. I see music educators taking the lead in establishing comprehensive arts programs in all schools. Theirs was the first art in the schools and is the most organized. They have the established base to promote the arts as a curriculum area comparable to the sciences. Every child growing up in the United States has the right to understand the kind of perceptions about the world that the arts afford. By broadening the focus to promote aesthetic as well as musical sensitivity and understanding, the case for music itself would be strengthened.

By adopting these three basic modes of operation—commitment to democratization, to giving creativity as much emphasis as performance, and to placing music in the service of education and society—I believe music education will begin to reach the people and the power structure and establish a broader public constituency So, as we acknowledge the achievements of music education during the week of March 9, let us also celebrate the possibilities for the future.

35

CHANGING SCHOOLS THROUGH THE ARTS

MUSICAL AMERICA 32 (April 1982)

The JDR (John David Rockefeller) 3rd Fund was an important supporter of music and arts education in the 1970s. The Fund's work included proposing and authoring legislation; preparing detailed reports; testifying before Congress; recommending curricular changes; advocating for arts education; and lobbying politicians, government and cultural institutions, and members of the business community. In 1982, one of the Fund's former associates authored a book that offered clear insights into utilizing arts education to improve schools. The book, titled *Changing Schools Through the Arts: The Power of An Idea*, was written by Jane Remer and published by McGraw-Hill. The author writes in plain terms about the value of arts and music study, and provides suggestions for how schools might better incorporate instruction in music and the other arts. She also highlights various benefits of artistic study, including improved student attitudes, better attendance, higher motivation for learning, more community support, and stronger morale. A number of useful suggestions are offered; current schools and music teachers could use ideas in this book as a model to advocate for their own reforms in contemporary context.

—CR

* * *

Changing Schools Through the Arts: The Power of an Idea is a relatively short book (165 pages) that tells in plain and unencumbered language how the arts can be—and have been—used as agents for making schools better places in which to learn.

That the arts can make schools more effective is, for many parents and educators, a rather startling idea. Since the quality of education is their perennial concern, this book should make for interesting—and instructive—reading for both groups. The narrative documents how the idea was born, how it first came into practice in thirty-two schools in New York City, and how it subsequently spread to schools in Hartford, Little Rock, Minneapolis, Seattle, Winston-Salem, and elsewhere.

The concept of school development through the arts is viewed here from the perspective of planning and establishing a comprehensive Arts in General Education (AGE) program. This approach, which strives to bring all the arts to all the children by infusing them into the daily teaching and learning process, brings about both school reorganization and revitalization.

Unlike the usual school art and music program, this approach encompasses dance, theater, creative writing, even architecture, and involves the entire school—all the students, teachers, administrators, and parents. The influx of all the arts into all that goes on in the school transforms the institution and the educational process itself. How and why it happens are what this book is about.

IMPROVED ATTITUDES

The author, Jane Remer, formerly associate director of the now defunct Arts in Education Program of the John D. Rockefeller 3rd Fund that supported the development and testing of this hypothesis, claims that these programs improve attitudes toward school, attendance, morale, motivating for learning, and support and involvement of the community. Remer tells us that such programs encourage the development of new instructional approaches and materials in all areas of the curriculum, the arts included, and they use the talents of school personnel and the resources of the community more effectively.

Those are awesome claims, derived, the author says, from experience with these programs and observation of them. Although Remer admits that what is needed is "a comprehensive research and evaluation effort to illuminate, reinforce, or temper our experiential confidence," she is cautious about making assertions as to how the approach affects learning in the "basics":

> This list [of claims] deliberately omits the claim that basic achievement skills rise solely because of the presence of the arts, or that standardized test scores and minimum competency ratings improve because of an AGE program. Variables influencing these assessments have yet to be isolated, let alone controlled. It stands to reason, however, that if a school becomes a better workplace and the people in it are proud and comfortable, productivity and general learning should improve.

Remer's experience with these programs verifies that learning in the basics "tends to be strengthened."

That's what I like about this book. The reader is given a very personal and candid account, one gleaned from seven years of close involvement with both the development and dissemination of the idea. Remer obviously knows what she is talking about, and is not afraid of letting us in on all the problems involved.

She says, for example, that it "took a lot of talking to convince people that we did not have a pre-packaged program designed to improve basic skills whose results would be measured in easily quantifiable and impressive numbers."

Remer also admits that "AGE does take money." She says, "AGE may or may not look like a Santa Claus project at the outset, but the programs *have* attracted federal, state and private resources and it would be naive and misleading to leave the impression that participants commit to it solely for intrinsic rewards."

In the course of the book, we are taken on a tour of an AGE Demonstration School—P.S. 152 in Brooklyn—where we observe its effects on the school environment and the teaching and learning process and where we meet some of the teachers and begin to see how crucial the role of the principal is in the execution of this plan.

FACING THE OPPOSITION

As with any new idea, there are skeptics and detractors, and Remer faces them head on. She says that a number of her friends in the arts world "wince every time I refer to the arts as tools, catalysts, agents, or instruments for school change." These people believe that "if the arts are used for other purposes, especially social ends, they will be bastardized and distorted beyond recognition." They also don't want to admit that the arts are within everyone's reach. The notion that *all* the arts are or should be the province of *all* the children "is a populist but still not very popular idea."

The book makes clear the important role that artists and arts specialists must assume in initiating and sustaining an AGE program, in spite of the fact that much of the process of incorporating the arts into teaching and learning must, of necessity, rely upon the daily work and commitment of the classroom teacher. Remer says, "Unless teachers are comfortable with the arts, given time to discover artists, and other 'how-to-do-it' consultants, AGE will not materialize."

Still, there are arts specialists around the country who remain skeptical about the effects of AGE programs on the already existing art and music programs. Remer admits that, "Unfortunately, all too often, AGE programs *have* served to fill a vacuum *after* the specialists were let go *en masse.*" But she goes on to say that "Where AGE programs have survived ... the result is that more specialists are hired and more arts courses are offered."

LEAGUE OF CITIES

This volume provides an historical record of the national network known as the League of Cities for the Arts in Education, a group of urban centers that entered into partnership with the JDR 3rd Fund to learn together how to adapt this idea to their differing needs and circumstances. As such, it can serve other school systems as a how-to manual for establishing an AGE program.

I would guess that parents and educators who venture to read this lively and enthusiastic account will, no doubt, be tempted to want to see for themselves what positive effects the arts might have upon the development and improvement of their own schools.

36

THE LACK OF PROFESSIONALISM IN HIGHER EDUCATION

MUSICAL AMERICA 32 (June 1982)

Fowler did not shrink from dealing with controversial, serious issues of the day. The role of musicians, performers, teachers, professors, and composers is the topic here. Defining these roles, especially in the context of higher education, was a bit of a challenge, and one that surely ruffled feathers. The main subject is based on another *Musical America* article from the previous year, in which the American Society of University Composers (ASUC) conference is reviewed. Issues raised in this piece focus on the nature of teaching versus performing (or creating), whether university professors can claim to be artists as well as teachers, and the effects of this self-definition (as artist or teacher) on curriculum, and the wider implications for students. A central issue is whether a professor is a teacher, a creator, or a performer, and the fact that the environment inside higher education is not closely connected with the professional world outside it. In short, do faculty really provide the education that music students need to be successful in a real-world context, and do they have the necessary background to teach it? Another important question is the role of creativity in music teaching and learning: is the profession truly taking note of it? An interesting topic, to be sure, and for those in higher education, likely still at the forefront today, over thirty years later.

—CR

* * *

THE ARTICLE by James Chute on the national conference of the American Society of University Composers (MA, August 1981) and the public debate it sparked between Richard Brooks, chairman of the executive committee of ASUC and Clifford Taylor of Temple University (MA, February and March 1982, Letters) have brought to the surface issues that have important implications for education. While I did not attend the conference, I would like to enter these critical discussions with the following observations from an educational perspective.

The cause and effect relationship between university subsidized composers and their sometime failure to communicate with the public is not the dilemma of composers alone, but is a situation infecting the arts in general in higher education. Professors who claim to be sculptors or painters on the basis of mounting a show of their works every other year for their students and colleagues also fail to reach—or interest—a real public audience in any significant number.

A DEEPER PROBLEM

The problem here is deeper than the mere fact of communication or the lack of it. It resides in the raw-boned way these people view their professionalism. Most define themselves first and foremost as "artists." Ask them what they do for a living and they will say, "I am a pianist," not that "I teach piano."

Taylor points out this subterfuge and the problems it incurs when he says: "Since we are supported socially and economically as teachers and not as composers these days, at least in most cases, we mix our roles in our own minds. We do not live by our composing, but by our teaching, so we can afford to avoid that unpleasant matter of public acceptance of and payment for our efforts. Unfortunately, should this be our attitude, we influence most prospective composers when they are students. We encourage them to also avoid the commercial necessities of a composer who might not also be a teacher, on salary."

Such teachers perpetrate a false view of the realities and exigencies of the profession they claim to represent. As a result, students are deluded about what it takes to, say, be an actor, a scenic designer, a playwright, a dancer, a concert pianist, or a composer.

Unwittingly, attitudes are conveyed and ingrained that often thwart a student from attaining true professional status. For example: the idea of commerce in the arts—of producing or designing to sell to a broad audience—is generally disparaged. Students learn: art that sells is not as good as art that doesn't sell or art that appeals to only a highly select audience. (Teachers justify the fact that their own art doesn't sell.)

One might well ask how professors of piano can teach a student to be a concert pianist when they themselves have never had the experience—understanding the necessity for and role of the agent, concert management, the trials of touring, etc. The actor who, on campus, is given two or more months to learn a role is hard pressed to enter television where roles must be mastered in a week. This situation is the precise reason why some artists institutions—the Rhode Island School of Design is a good example—require their architectural instructors to earn half their livelihood as practicing architects. The same is true of some—not enough—schools of music, the California Institute of the Arts, for example.

UNREALISTIC CURRICULUM

Unrealistic attitudes toward commerce in the arts manifest themselves in the arts curriculum itself. In most colleges and universities we see an almost total lack of attention given to courses that would permit students the option to learn how to become arrangers or performers of popular music, writers of teleplays actors on television, or Broadway dancers—in spite of the opportunities for employment in these a reas. If the idea of communication itself is suspect, the thought of communicating with a broad public in an outright "popular" way is abhorrent. The ivory tower gets in the way of any need for accommodation.

The fact remains that the art of music—and all the arts, for that mater—is one of communication. Earning a living through performance of through composing necessitates the mastery of communicating with a public. Professionalism in this regard involves—as it does in every profession—earning a dollar by serving somebody else's interest. The problem with many of the so-called composers on campus—those whom I would call the "unprofessionals"—is that they are subsidized to dabble without any regard or necessity for communicating with anybody, one reason we hear so much vapid music from this source.

My observations tell me that too many college and university arts faculty profess to a professionalism to which they cannot and should not lay claim. Such "artists" do a great disservice to their students.

Webster's defines "profession" as "a vocation or occupation requiring advanced education and training, and involving intellectual skills, as medicine, law, theology, engineering, teaching, etc." A "professional" is one "engaged in a specified occupation for pay or as a means of livelihood (a *professional* writer)" and "a person who engages in some art, sport, etc. for money, especially for his livelihood, rather than as a hobby."

Clearly, a professor's profession is teaching. The fact that a teacher may act, direct, design, sculpt, paint, choreograph, conduct, compose, sing, or play does not a profession make. By all means, teachers should do what they teach; that makes them better at their profession—teaching.

EGOS

The difficulty with this notion, of course, is that it apparently bruises egos. There are, after all, some artist-faculty who earn part of their living practicing their art. And if you think about it, they are aptly named—"artist-faculty" or "composer-teacher."

Actually, a person's true profession is usually defined accurately for the Internal Revenue Service on one's income tax form.

Now all this may sound quite perfunctory except for the fact that the deceptive way people define themselves has its direct and deleterious effect on the student. I would suggest that "prestigism,"* laying claim to being a professional that one is not, is a deceit tantamount to plagiarism. They both make false assertions, the first about what one is, the second about what one has done.

Perhaps we should pause for a moment and consider which is the best model for the student—the inspired teacher who has chosen that profession, the struggling artist who is still striving to enter the profession, or the established professional artist? It seems to me that the answer might not be any one, but all, provided that the model is based on honesty. Integrity, after all, is a fundamental underpinning for communication through the arts. Higher education would benefit enormously from having more faculty who are frankly committed to teaching as a profession.

WHAT'S IN A NAME . . .

I was interested in the fact that one of the ASUC conference's most heated issues was whether to take "university" out of the organization's name. The issue went undecided and probably for good reason. An American Society of Composers would—if the name were strictly interpreted—eliminate most of the ninety percent of the current membership who are affiliated with universities. At least the term "university composer" conveys the idea of a combination of roles.

My contention here is that many of these people who label themselves as "composers" are not composers at all. In some cases, they are people *trying* to be composers—just as a composer of songs working as a waiter is an *aspiring* songwriter. The problem is labeling oneself by intention rather than by fact. I would suggest that "university composer" is one more example of a coupling of terms that connotes a counterfeit world, in a league with "military intelligence" and "marital bliss." Perhaps a more accurate name would be the American Society of Teachers of Composition.

Brooks make the point that the ASUC should not become involved in matters of taste or esthetic content lest the organization become dictatorial in the manner of the U.S.S.R.'s Composers Union. Well, I see no reason why such an organization cannot discuss any issue of concern to its members' welfare—problems of ethics and communication included. Obviously, the members are already doing so, if this conference report is any indication. For the sake of more effective education and concern for the future of American music, I would hope that this organization would get to the bottom of such matters.

---

* The term is coined to evoke the original French and Latin derivation of "prestige," meaning illusion or deception.

As part of the conference, Pauline Oliveros made a number of recommendations for consideration by the ASUC, among them two that have direct bearing upon educatio She suggested that the organization "identify and analyze the qualities and processes of the so-called master teacher," certainly a worthy endeavor. And she recommended that the ASUC "establish contact with the National Music Teachers Association [*sic*] for the purpose of encouraging children to compose."

About the latter, I would suggest that a strong case could and should be made for turning music education around so that as much emphasis is given to creativity as to performance. Music, unlike dance, painting, sculpture, even theater, is now largely taught as a re-creative art. Both the Music Teachers National Association and the Music Educators National Conference should be prompted to move music education into a more creative mode with, perhaps, improvisation rather than composition at the core. If music could be approached from the start as a personal means of expres-sion rather than a second-hand art, perhaps the ASUC would not be faced with its present dilemmas.

37

THE LACK OF PROFESSIONALISM IN HIGHER

EDUCATION—CONTINUED

MUSICAL AMERICA 32 (September 1982)

An original article was produced on this topic in June 1982 and apparently raised the ire of many who read it. It seems there are university composers and others in higher education who disagreed with the definitions of professionalism outlined in the first article. Many of those opinions were written as letters to the journal, and others directly to the author and editor. One of the major points raised focused on the need to combine liberal-arts training with vocational preparation for a life in music and the arts. It would be difficult to argue against strong career preparation, and incorporating the real world as much as possible. Also up for debate is the question of audience: just who are composers writing their music to enlighten (or, who should they be writing for)? This is also the case in music education when we train students to understand their classrooms better in order to teach better. Overall, the argument may be boiled down to whether those who consider themselves artists first, are really teachers (professors) first, and would rather not be labeled that way. Is being an educator not a noble enough profession? Perhaps, too, the question centers on who gets to decide one's professional identity—maybe this is even the larger conundrum?

—CR

* * *

THE AMPLE and candid exchange of views stimulated by my column on "The Lack of Professionalism in Higher Education" in the June issue is highly gratifying. While there is honest disagreement, I find the opinions expressed to be of substance—in spite of some misinterpretations of my remarks—and offer the following response to several of the more controversial issues that have been raised.

HAVENS OF ACADEMIA

I have no quarrel with composers like Jacob Druckman, Vincent Persichetti, and Gunther Schuller who have established reputations in the musical world outside the universities. They are professionals—and artists—in the best sense of those terms. My thesis was not directed at them, although I believe they have a stake in these discussions.

There is the problem of "artists in colleges and universities who gain their promotions largely by doing their art within the confines of their own institutions. These faculty tend to create havens of academic arts, and they then perpetuate them, while ignoring the practical realities of the outside world. I believe that the arts schools must not become stands unto themselves, training people for more of the same. And I maintain that it is reasonable—on the basis of concern for our musical future—to criticize both the schools and the composers for furthering this situation.

As I indicated in the original article, the problem is far larger than composers alone. A recent evaluation of theater management programs in higher education, for example, found that "many of the respondents [managers in the field] felt that the faculties of the degree programs do not have enough professional contact or credentials to prepare and acquaint the students with the real world." The vocational thrust is clearly evident, as is the need for practical application to supplement theory. In this regard, an internship was viewed as "a vital link between educational training and professional application."

While it is not exactly equatable to the composers' situation, this study of arts management programs does point up the tendency of colleges and universities to ignore the marketplace, the world outside, call it what you will. In my mind, there is no question about the dual importance of a liberal arts education that will allow students to adapt to change and live a better life, combined simultaneously with professional specialization that will provide students with skills needed for the world of work.

As a freelance writer, I have enormous built-in empathy for the plight of today's artists, but the need to make a living that has brought countless artists to the soothing arms of higher education has taken its toll. Apparently, for some, the comfort afforded by security and a steady paycheck, coupled with the demands of teaching, have sapped the creative energy and diverted the talent.

But, by and large, the composer on campus is America's composer for today and tomorrow. For that reason, composers must begin to see what influence higher education is having upon them. (Someone once said that the last thing a sea fish discovers is salt water.) The corruption is contentment, approbation, and finally self-aggrandizement. I'm suggesting that the vision of our artists who are caught up in education must reach out beyond the universities.

Beethoven was a part of his world, totally involved in it, certainly politically. True, his music expresses his personal vulnerability and indomitable will, but it also—in its vast emotional range and intensity—expresses a new sense of human power and enlightenment that characterized his time.

Perhaps an organization such as the American Society of University Composers should sponsor a project similar to the Music Educators National Conference/Ford Foundation Contemporary Music Project which placed composers in community settings where they composed for community musical groups. Universities, colleges, and conservatories with majors in music composition could sponsor their own internship programs on the community level or connected with specific performing groups. (Music schools already have a model for internships in their student-teaching programs.) In his letter, Thomas Jordan testifies to the value of his experience as an Artist-in-Schools composer. The point is that music has to get to people.

WHICH AUDIENCE?

In my thinking, audience communication is at the heart of our current contemporary musical dilemma. When we ask why our concert audiences tend not to be receptive to much that is new in contemporary music, we must consider at least the possibility that some of the problem may lie with the music itself. Composers must address this question, rather than laying all the blame elsewhere. Such an exercise in introspection could prove highly worthwhile.

My own thoughts about musical communication run like this: The composer has every right to communicate with any audience (however large or small) that he chooses, or even no audience at all. But if he chooses the latter course and is satisfied to create his art totally for himself—vis-à-vis Milton Babbitt: "There is no reason in the world for one to write for others" (MA, June 1982, p. 18)—then I say, when he descends the tower stairs, he shouldn't complain about the lack of public interest, the dearth of performances of new music, and the indifference of performing groups and conductors.

Why should the musical world attempt to realize communicative or expressive meaning that was never intended in the first place? How can such a composer rightfully expect a public to support his private world?

Conversely, I believe we need more composers who write for a public—even the established musical public—in the larger society beyond the university. At the same time, I completely understand the resistance of artists to the term "entertainment," a word that, from their viewpoint, has too many popular connotations. But in the larger sense, all musical performance is a form of entertainment, whatever the public. I doubt that, even as a non-profit enterprise, Composers Recordings, Inc. would still be in existence today if people did not find enjoyment in its product.

The problem of contemporary composers communicating with an audience is acknowledged by composers themselves. John Duffy, president and director of Meet the Composer, an organization that is working to make contemporary music more accessible to a wider range of audiences, says that this organization "was founded to reclaim composers as active members of society and shapers of our musical culture." A recent article states that Meet the Composer "has contributed a great deal to the reexamination and reassessment of the role of the composer in our society—not only how we perceive the composer, but also how he regards himself and his work—by bringing audiences and composers (and their music) together."

What is wrong with the notion of arts, artists, and composers serving communities? Serving audiences? If we are going to bring a new dynamism to musical art, we need to establish a whole new spirit of *transaction* between music and society, something that all the inbreeding and cloistering in higher education doesn't seem to allow.

COMPOSERS WHO AREN'T

My biggest quarrel is with those who, in the role of professor, masquerade as composers or artists. In effect, their claim to title maligns the true professional, swelling the ranks and usurping their hard-won prestige. It is simply that many people compose who are not composers, sculpt who are not sculptors, paint who are not painters. I have little patience with dabblers who cloak their identities with undeserved nomenclature.

What are the criteria for labeling oneself a "composer" or "artist"? That question needs to be addressed by the arts community, if only to tighten the reins and bring clear-cut definition back to these terms. I don't pretend to have all the answers, but my contention is—and perhaps I could have stated it more clearly—that the universities are sheltering many so-called "artists" who do not have credence as such. They aren't really all that serious about their art. They aren't true practitioners. They lack integrity about who they think they are. I simply object to their legerdemain.

ARTISTS WHO ARE

Obviously, the trials of great aritists who strived on in spite of their financial plight and failure to make a living at their art, does not negate them as artists. Their struggle provides us with a strong clue to the true meaning and definition of terms. Perhaps it is the quality of their dedication and commitment that dignifies them as true aritists. Perhaps it is their self-motivation and integrity, their innate need and determination to say something and be heard. There are no token recitals, art shows, and performances here, no necessity for the motivating carrot of publish or perish. When you think about it, every piece of music written says what music is, what it can express, and why it deserves to be valued. The responsibility of the composer is awesome. It's not easy to be an artist; it's not a title that one easily appropriates.

25

EDUCATORS WITHOUT APOLOGY

Some arts faculty are ashamed of being educators; if they weren't they would use their teaching title proudly, as their credential. Unfortunately for their students—and for themselves—they view the profession of teaching on a lower echelon of respect. Their pretense as artists is the last vestige of their own failed and frustrated aspiration.

Yet teaching is an honorable and necessary profession that deserves their respect and devotion. If these "artists" on campus treated teaching as an art, whole new cadres of master teachers might develop in our arts departments across the country. But, first, these artists and composers must see themselves and accept themselves for who they really are—teachers. I think they would be better teachers and their students would be better students, if they admitted it.

38

MUSIC EDUCATORS MEET—BUT DO THEY MISS THE POINT?

MUSICAL AMERICA 34 (September 1984)

Reading this review of the MENC 1984 National Conference, one could easily be reading one of a similar meeting in the early twenty-first century. Primary purposes of these events include bringing music teachers together, presenting sessions on topics related to music teaching and learning, hearing performances of fine young musicians, debating the principal topics of the day related to music education, and helping to move the profession forward by re-energizing music teachers in the field. It seems that while all of this was technically covered in the printed program, the conference itself mostly fell short of the goal. A number of constructive criticisms and recommendations are offered, which touch on session presentations, guest speakers, primary and secondary topics, attendees and their interests, and looking at the relevant macro and micro issues. While the overall sentiment of the article is seemingly negative, it is intended only to help the profession and solve some of its most pressing problems. While MENC was not happy about the evaluation, whether or not they took it to heart is unclear. Music educators are teachers, after all, and one of our primary tasks is to help students become better through compassionate, critical assessment. Are we not able to take a dose of our own medicine?

—CR

* * *

I HADN'T ATTENDED a national meeting of the Music Educators National Conference (MENC) for ten years—since the one in Anaheim in March 1974 (see MA, July 1974). Perhaps that is why the changes I saw and felt at this year's conference in Chicago (March 21–24) were so startling—both reassuring and disturbing at the same time. Much has taken place in that decade that has altered the impact of music as an educational force and as a profession.

A convention of this size is staggering to take in, let alone report. With nearly two hundred workshop sessions and ninety performing groups, there is no way that one individual can see it all. So, I don't pretend that this is a summary. Call it some personal impressions—observations made, one hopes, with objectivity—and, based on these, a few suggestions.

LORIN HOLLANDER

There are always high points at an MENC conference, and this one certainly provided some. Pianist Lorin Hollander, for example, gave an inspired address at the opening general session. Although I've heard him speak on the same subject at least three times before, his thoughts remain provocative. Hollander views music from the perspective of the awesome problems of the world—the threat of nuclear annihilation, over-population, starvation, pollution. "If these problems are going to be solved," he reasons, "they will be solved the way problems have always been solved—by creative people. He maintains that the root of our educational crisis today is that "We are not nurturing creativity."

There is considerable and persuasive scientific substantiation, Hollander says, to show that music is a profoundly human force, that it is a universal phenomenon as human as breathing. But, he says, "Music is not being seen as the basic it is." People question the value of music education at the same time that Hollander believes "Music teachers are in an ideal position to nurture creativity in children."

What Hollander doesn't explain is why people don't make the connection between music education and creativity. They don't make the connection because the rhetoric about nurturing creativity through music study is far ahead of the reality. In truth, the public has not experienced any significant creative thrust in their own music study or in the music education provided to their children. They don't see the connection because, quite simply, it generally doesn't exist. I wish Hollander had made this point and challenged the music teachers to realize the creative potential of their subject. Still, his was a fine and worthwhile presentation.

EXTENDING OUR SYMBOLS

Another high point, for me, was the good sense and humanitarian message delivered by Ernest Boyer, former U.S. Commissioner of Education and now president of the Carnegie Foundation for the Advancement of Teaching. Introduced as "the most powerful voice in American education," Boyer spoke about the educational report of the Carnegie Foundation (See MA, March 1984), reiterating its thesis that "We communicate not just with words but in nonverbal ways as well." Like Hollander, he shared with the audience the inner core of his own moral code: "I genuinely believe God planted within us the capacity to extend our symbols of communication to match the feelings and ideas in our heads and hearts." Boyer defines language broadly to encompass literacy in all our symbol systems, including the arts.

At the height of his address, Boyer made the following statement to resounding applause: "A civilization is defined by the measure of the symbol systems that it holds and cherishes and protects. And anyone who suggests that art is a frill and that it can be denied is, in my judgment, dismantling the civilization." He also made the point that, "Excellence is for all our children, not the elite few." Perhaps there was a slight nudge in that line, I'm not sure. I wanted him to go on and focus the issue. I wanted to hear him say, "Music is for all the students, not just the talented. Now get to it." Music teachers need to be challenged on this issue as well.

GENERAL MUSIC TEACHERS

On this point, there is a renewed commitment on the part of general music teachers—those who do attempt to reach all the students—to assert themselves and their philosophy within the profession. These teachers have formed a new Society for General Music within the superstructure of MENC that was highly evident at this conference. This group has all the zeal and enthusiasm of converts. Its quarterly publication, *Soundings,* is full of stimulating ideas and thought-provoking methodologies. And the Society presented sixteen sessions at this conference on such topics as "Eliciting Creative Responses in Children," "Jazz Improvisation," "Creating Opera," Music Textbooks," "Orff-Schul-werk," and "The Computer as a Tool."

Now I'm certain that all the efforts of this Society are extremely worthwhile, but I'm left with a nagging question. In light of MENC's already fractured constituency—there are eight associated organizations and some twenty-five major committees—I cannot help but ponder the merits of yet another enclave, off doing their own thing. Isn't general music—that is, the reaching of all students through the music program—the business of *every* music educator?

Be that as it may, the general music teachers, it must be acknowledged, have an enthusiasm and excitement and dedication that one can literally feel. It's like electricity in the air, a quality I found noticeably lacking in most of the rest of this conference. From that standpoint alone, this Society has something valuable to share with the entire profession.

COMPUTERS & CONCERTS

Computers and computer technology were pervasive at this meeting. Music teachers appeared hungry for knowledge about how these miracles-of-technology could be used to assist the learning process. They crowded into sessions demonstrating these new instruments and their programs, and they eagerly experimented with the many new electronic machines on display in the music industry exhibits and elsewhere. These teachers were embracing something new, and that was reassuring. Exhilarating.

And I was again, as I always am at these conferences, stunned by the unexpectedly beautiful musical performances that emanate from unexpected places. A few examples: the Concert Choir of the University of North Dakota; the Houston High School of Performing and Visual Arts Symphony; the Rocky Mountain (High School) Singers from Fort Collins, Colorado; the Hardaway High School Symphonic Band from Columbus, Georgia; the Husky. Singers (they weren't) of Northwest Junior High in Atlas, Oklahoma; and the Southern Methodist University Symphony Orchestra from Dallas—a stunning orchestra. And who could ever forget the Singing Seniors from New Kensington, Pennsylvania? Their average age is 77, but their vocal solos and dance steps are as sprightly as a teenager's.

"One thing that amazes me," a former MENC president told me, "is that these performing groups can still afford to come, and from such distances." Yes, I agree, but it is even more amazing to me in light of the poor audiences that attended many of these performances. Some of these groups came hundreds of miles at enormous expense and hours of effort only to find themselves performing for a handful of people. One little girl brought it all home to me. I was congratulating her after a fine performance by her high school band when, all of a sudden, she broke into tears. "Why didn't they come to hear us?" she sniffled. "Don't they know how hard we worked to be here?"

Well, of course, this situation is easily remedied by setting aside specific times for performance when nothing else is scheduled. If performance is worth having, then it's worth attending.

I had another bad moment at one of the concerts. It was during the performance of Donald Erb's *Music for a Festive Occasion* by the Southern Methodist University Symphony Orchestra. Four students—I'm not certain whether they were high school or college—sitting with what appeared to be their music teacher, laughed and derided the music all the way through the performance to the evident approval of the teacher. They were probably at the conference to perform themselves, yet here was a gross lack of decorum and respect and an obvious total ignorance of any contemporary music. It made me wonder what these students are learning.

MISGIVINGS

There were, for me, two other more disconcerting observations about this conference. The first struck me in the lobby one day as I was walking through the throngs of music educators to another session. The music education profession is getting older. In contrast to a decade ago, there is a noticeable lack of young teaching professionals. And with the loss of those young teachers has gone a tangible bit of the profession's zealous spirit. There are also a good deal fewer people in attendance. Whereas the Anaheim conference drew upwards of 8,000 teachers, Chicago commanded about half that number.

I know that many explanations can be given for this slump in attendance—curtailments of music programs that have reduced the number of music teachers and openings for new music teachers, and budgetary constraints affecting many school systems and institutions of higher education that have restricted the number of teachers who can travel to such meetings.

Still, I got the impression from talking with many of the teachers who attended that there is another explanation, and this is my other reservation about this conference. Quite simply, the content of most of the conference does not meet the real needs of the profession. To be sure, there were sessions on sundry subjects that focused on all levels of education, instrumental and vocal. But I didn't find a great deal of enthusiasm or eager participation at many of these sessions.

SQUANDERED ENERGIES?

It seems to this observer that the energies of the profession are being squandered and dissipated by numbers of narrow specialisms that shouldn't isolate, but do. And many of these specialisms are no longer new and fresh enough to command the same interest or generate the same excitement they once did. The conference reinforces these specialisms rather than discourages them. Perhaps that is deliberate, but the result is a fractured profession, one that lacks cohesiveness, vision, and an invigorating spirit.

It is interesting to note how all these various sessions come about in the first place. They are planned by some twenty-five committees comprised of various interest groups in the field—people representing such areas as audiovisual resources, buildings and equipment, gifted and talented, instrumental instruction, the handicapped, keyboard instruction, teacher education, and the like.

But what these committees plan are sessions devoted to their own specialty. Perhaps this is commendable, but what I find missing here is a higher order of concern. There is little evidence that these committees went back to the fundamental questions: What are the major problems facing music education today that must be addressed by the profession? And, recalling Hollander and Boyer: How can the creative potential of music be realized? What can be done to assure that music reaches all the students at all levels? But there are other questions as well: What kinds of curricular changes are needed in order for music education programs to serve all students? And, in response to the recent flood of education studies, what kinds of rationales substantiating the need for and value of music in the schools will be most effective in sustaining and improving programs, K-12? What groups can help us muster the necessary support and how do we organize these efforts? How can instruction in music be improved?

NARROW FOCUS

Instead of these generic concerns undergirding the organization of the conference and forming its substance, the committees tend, because of their narrow focus, to have a parochial influence. Sessions, rather than addressing the major issues facing the profession at large, address improvisation, technology in guitar design, how best to help the horn section in the school band, the training and development of electronic musicians, melodic perception, and the like.

To be sure, there were excellent sessions on government relations, teacher education, and excellence in education that were more generic. But these were probably not perceived as such because the printed conference program does not distinguish between macro and micro issues. All the sessions appear to be of equal importance. And that is simply not the case.

I'd like to see an [sic] MENC conference organized around these larger themes so that the highly specialized sessions are viewed in the broader context. Keyboard instruction would then be seen as part of the major concern for improving instruction. Sessions on government relations and excellence in education would be viewed as related responses to the challenges of the recent education studies and the curricular changes being proposed and implemented in the states.

After all, these national meetings are billed as "inservice" conferences, the idea being that you attend a conference to learn and that teachers can even earn college credit through participation in such a meeting. Well, I'd like to see a real working conference that concentrates the energies of those in attendance on solving the enormous and difficult problems that plague the profession. This is what many other fields do, and I think music teachers would respond positively to such an approach.

BELOW THE SURFACE

We learned at the Eastman conference (See MA, January 1984) that the music education profession is seething beneath the surface. Music teachers are concerned—deeply troubled—by the cutbacks and curtailments of the past decade and the possible threats they face from the conflicting recommendations of recent educational reports, at least in the area of the arts. They need to have the opportunity to work out their frustrations and get on top of their problems. I believe they are eager to work and will welcome the challenge.

But basing a conference on the larger issues will have another advantage. By emphasizing tracks of general interest and concern that avoid the enclaves and specialisms and cut across all the strata of music education, MENC would be taking a deliberate and positive step to reunite the profession as one force. In working together to solve mutual problems, the conference, instead of reinforcing fractionalization, would encourage the development of unity and cohesiveness—the common cause approach advocated by Charles Leonhard. The profession can only profit by relying upon its collective wisdom.

Now I would hope that the conference organizers do not take offense at my observations and suggestions but accept or reject them in the spirit they are engendered. I do firmly believe that MENC can function as an enormous power for improvement in the entire field of arts education. I just want to see this organization and this profession excel.

39

ARE TEACHERS OF THE ARTS GOOD ENOUGH?

MUSICAL AMERICA 35 (October 1985)

Few would argue against the importance of teacher preparation to the field of music education. This does, of course, apply to all arts disciplines, and a symposium held in May 1985 was focused on addressing this very issue. The meeting, Teachers in the Arts: A National Symposium, was sponsored by Louisiana State University. A main focus was on the current state of music and arts teacher preparation, current challenges and opportunities, and suggestions for how to improve training and development. Several notable speakers offered their thoughts, including G. Leland Burningham (Utah Superintendent of Public Instruction), Kathryn Martin (Dean of the School of Fine Arts at University of Montana), Lin Wright (Chair of Theatre Arts at Arizona State University), Gerrard Knieter (Dean of Fine Arts at University of Akron), and Harlan Hoffa (Associate Dean of the College of the Arts and Architecture at Pennsylvania State University), among others. While a number of critical assessments were levied, the major goal was to help improve the mechanisms and protocols of teacher training at the time. I can tell you from experience that this conversation clearly continues today, and that reforms of music teacher training are numerous and beneficial. While there is still work to be done, for once, the profession heeded the call, as evidenced in the early twenty-first century.

—CR

* * *

THE EDUCATIONAL reform movement of the 1980s is reevaluating every rock in the foundation of American schooling. That complex process has not—cannot—overlook the arts. To make certain that their voices are heard and that their own field is scrutinized and reconstituted judiciously, arts educators are entering the process with determined forthrightness. Such was the underlying tenor of the national symposium, Teachers in the Arts, held at Louisiana State University in Baton Rouge in May.

The arts education theorists and practitioners who presented papers at this meeting recognize a simple truth: educational reform is directly related to and dependent upon changes in teacher education. Excellence, the call-word of the reform movement, cannot be achieved without concomitant quality of teaching. That equation is the crucial mortar that binds arts education programs to the schools. Unlike most other subject areas, the arts depend upon their own projected vitality and worth to justify and maintain their existence.

WHY REFORM?

To put it bluntly, arts education programs just aren't good enough. That was the message of G. Leland Burningham, superintendent of public instruction in the state of Utah, and it may account for why the arts have not atttained the status of an educational basic or realized their educational potential. Burningham points out two major problems. First, he says, few students "gain a broad, in-depth view of the arts." And second, even if they are exposed to a broad array of the arts, "the content of some arts courses, or courses with components in the arts, is questionable." Burningham elaborates:

> The visual arts, particularly at the elementary level, are too often a series of gimmicky projects that have no sequence and no valid reason for their inclusion. The cognitive aspects of the visual arts are essentially ignored and in many cases instruction is purposely withheld for fear of destroying the child's natural creativity.... Music programs are better, but elementary teachers, who are not prepared to teach the basics of music education, simply have their students "sing along" with records and tapes. Even students who have sung in elementary school choruses and played various Orff or percussion instruments sometimes cannot read music and do not recognize the names of great composers or their works. Dance, if taught at all, is part of the physical education program, and drama, for the most part, receives token time in the language arts program, largely removed from the development of critical thinking skills.

Furthermore, Burningham backs up his evaluation by citing the results of the National Assessment of Educational Progress in art and music. These assessments of student achievement and attitudes toward the arts, administered to 9-, 13-, and 17-year-olds, show that "most students did not know how to perceive or respond to the arts in anything but a superficial manner."

If arts programs sometimes slight their subject matter, they also suffer from problems inflicted by society. The conditions of teaching are changing. One in five children in America lives below the poverty level, and the same number now lives in a home with no father. Many 'latchkey' children go home from schools to parentless homes. Five times as many children are born out of wedlock today as in 1970. These problem children simply do not learn as easily or as well. They are more difficult to reach. Arts teachers, like their counterparts in other subjects, now face such problem children as a matter of routine.

Then, too, ethnic and racial minorities in the United States are increasing rapidly. By 1990, minorities will constitute more than thirty percent of the total U.S. school-age population. In Texas, 46 percent of the students are now minority; in New York, 32 percent.[2] Teaching these children successfully often requires special know-how, different methodologies, and new materials.

WHAT TEACHERS SHOULD KNOW

There are certain common skills, knowledges, and understandings that all arts specialists should possess. Kathryn Martin, dean of the School of Fine Arts at the University of Montana, identifies four areas in which there should be basic knowledge: 1) aesthetics of the discipline; 2) studio art (or music, or drama, or dance performance); 3) the history of the art form; and 4) criticism. In addition, she says, the arts specialist should possess "some knowledge of the arts disciplines outside the discipline of the major."

There is a need to develop thoughtfully sequenced curricula in each art form. Without this, arts teachers are at a distinct disadvantage. One of the symposium's responders, Lin M. Wright, chairperson of the Theatre Arts Department of Arizona State University in Tempe, points out that no sequenced curricula now exist in either dance or theater. Such curricula are necessary for effective, in-depth programs in the arts.

Brent Wilson, professor of arts at Pennsylvania State University, says that schooling exists "primarily to assist students in gaining a sufficient degree of mastery of the various symbol systems to enable them both to study others' ideas about the world, and to build their own symbolic conceptual models of the world." And the arts, he says, "play a special and unique role in this symbolic worldmaking process."

He explains:

In the arts, it is possible to see mirrored ourselves; our vision of the beautiful, the good, the desirable; our aspirations and our challenges; the problems and dilemmas that we feel we must resolve.

To understand this "indispensable" capacity of the arts to construct the realities of our existence is endemic to teacher education. Arts teachers, Wilson maintains, should know (1) which works from the histories of the arts are the most important for students to study; (2) how to guide students through a knowledgeable study of these works, (3) how to guide students to make sensitive and insightful interpretations of the essential meanings of these works; and (4) how successfully to assist students to create or re-create their own artistic and aesthetic visions and versions of the world.

Gerrard L. Knieter, dean of fine arts at the University of Akron, also advocated greater knowledge of the discipline. "An arts teacher should be able to explain to others what particular facet of human experience is captured through that particular art," he says. Knieter believes that courses in the history and theory of the arts should deal with "why the art has a special impact on the individual." He, too, urges that students become familiar with the other arts, and he is critical of traditional instruction that is limited to Western civilization. History and theory classes, he says, should "cultivate broad knowledge and experience in non-Western traditions."

What should arts teachers know? Knieter says:

> They should know the content of their art in all styles, periods, and cultures, and they should have a working knowledge of the other arts. Arts educators should be knowledgeable about education and psychology so that they can share the common bond that exists among all who teach. They should be especially gifted as teachers so that they can model the best image for students to emulate. Such teachers should share the common wisdom of those who are liberally educated so that they can appreciate the significant contributions that others have made in the social sciences and humanities.

How can all this information be crammed into a four-year college curriculum? Neither Martin nor Knieter believes that it can be. It sometimes takes a lifetime to create a great teacher. However, additional time could be made in the teacher-education program, Martin says, by "restructuring existing courses and dropping those professional education courses which are simply not as important as the increased work in the arts."

TEACHING EXPERTISE

Education courses were hard hit at this conference. Stanley Madeja, dean of the College of Visual and Performing Arts at Northern Illinois University, calls departments of education "self-serving." He says, "Requirements of education departments may reach forty hours and have no relation to what students must know and do." He believes that prospective arts teachers should "concentrate on the discipline itself and pick up pedagogy later."

Knieter echoes these thoughts: "Those who teach primarily in the public schools find little or no value in the education courses they have taken." Martin agrees:

> Frankly, the arts methods classes as they are primarily taught within many pre-service programs are a waste of time, particularly when the emphasis is on the cutting out of turkeys, Christmas trees, etc., rather than the development of studio skills and the exploration of the concepts of perceiving, exploring, and creating.

Knieter, too, distinguishes between mere activities and the development of aesthetic sensitivity which he sees as the central purpose of education in the arts. What this distinction insures against, he says, particularly at the elementary level, "is the mistaken notion that the manipulation of a medium, or what are often called 'activities,' can be viewed as authenttic encounters with the arts."

In his summation of the symposium, Harlan Hoffa, associate dean of the College of Arts and Architecture at Pennsylvania State University, noted that one of the common themes "was an insistence that teaching students to paint pretty pictures or sing pretty songs was no longer enough—if it ever was." According to Hoffa, the symposium educators said

> ... that the history of the arts—and especially the development of refined critical skills—had to be emphasized if the arts were to take their rightful place among "the basics," and they insisted that a more systematic and orderly approach to arts curriculum planning had to be undertaken. And ... they seemed to agree that teachers of the arts have suffered the results of their inability to communicate clearly, convincingly, and effectively with almost anyone except their peers and colleagues—with other teachers, with parents, with those who govern and control education, and sometimes, it seems, with students themselves. In effect, they were making a concerted case for something that looked and sounded very much like "discipline-based" arts education. "Discipline-based" arts education does, in fact, seem to be the rallying cry of the 1980s ...

Indeed, Marilynn Price of the Getty Center for Education in the Arts, gave an entire presentation at this symposium on discipline-based arts education. The problem here is the possible misapplication of this very useful view of visual arts education to the field of music. The problems in the visual arts are quite different from the problems in music—just about the opposite, in fact. While visual arts programs often stress creativity to the neglect of history, theory, technique, and criticism, music programs often stress the latter and neglect creativity. In the matter of teacher education, we must not make the mistake of making hasty applications across fields.

The actual process of teacher training, Martin says, "must begin with an exploration of the learning process." There is a craft to teaching and learning. In Martin's words:

> Learning ... is primarily the ability to discover, to experience, to analyze, and to synthesize. Thus a critical responsibility of the teachers, the educators, is to assist in the development of the environment which makes possible facilitating the processes that lead to discovery, experiencing, analyzing, and synthesizing.

She believes that more effective ways of teaching pedagogy must be discovered and that some of this could be taught by example, instead of through the usual education courses. To these ends, some teacher-education programs are now requiring a year of apprenticeship as a condition for certification.

CLASSROOM TEACHERS

The role of classroom teachers in teaching the arts poses a dilemma for arts educators. The greater the emphasis given to substance, the less likely it is that classroom teachers can successfully teach the arts curriculum. They simply do not have the background. The lack of the arts in the preparation of classroom teachers is historic practice bordering on custom. This prevailing deficiency was precisely why arts specialists were called for in the first place. The argument to maintain arts specialists in the elementary schools has credence so long as elementary teachers are unprepared to teach the arts. That's the irony. If arts specialists fight for a better arts education for the classroom teacher and achieve it, they do themselves out of their jobs.

Still, the prevailing situation does not preclude the greater involvement of classroom teachers in arts education. When they are provided with some background and assistance, classroom teachers can become expert at integrating the arts into their regular subject-matter teaching.

One of the responders at this symposium, Carol Koukendahl, assistant superintendent for curriculum in the Houston Independent School District, believes that "The arts support academic learning and cognitive growth by developing the ability to use symbols, to make meaning, to handle intricate processes, to stick with tasks, to perceive." Young people, she says, "will develop none of these abilities unless they are taught."

Arts specialists, Martin says, "should be prepared to assist the classroom teacher in the pedagogical use of the arts." She says this is not to suggest that the arts should serve solely in a support position within the curriculum. But, she asks, if the arts provide the best pedagogical support for some aspects of early learning, "Why should not the arts be used in that capacity?" She also questions why the arts are not integrated into history and literature, since they reflect social and political history. Another of the responders, Al Hurwitz, director of teacher training at the Maryland Institute– College of Art in Baltimore, asked, incredulously, "Can you imagine being a social studies teacher without ever having the arts?" Again, this longstanding lack of the arts in many people's education is a large part of the problem. Martin says, "The arts must be considered basic because they are substantive areas of knowledge as well as creative pursuits."

Martin believes that classroom teachers should be provided with a far more thorough background in the arts:

> The pre-service training of the elementary classroom teacher includes little or no background in the historical and critical domains of the arts, and marginal amounts of work in the areas of aesthetics and studio art of creative expression regardless of discipline! For classroom teachers and art specialists to be successful, this simply must be adjusted.

But, on this issue, Knieter expresses another view. "The haunting questions for colleges and universities," he says, "is whether or not courses in the arts should be given for these teachers":

> Many adults will not draw, sing, or act today because of their experience in elementary schools. Yet, there are some classroom teachers who are quite capable of doing excellent work on a limited basis. It is educationally folly to force a teacher to teach any of the arts with which they feel uncomfortable, for what they will teach is their lack of enthusiasm for the art in question, in addition to quite a bit of misinformation.

In such cases, Knieter maintains, no instruction at all "is not necessarily a bad option." Knieter believes that "The most sensible approach is to have professionally certified arts teachers in all of the schools do the teaching."

One of the crucial issues, brought up by Madeja, is how to get the arts into the elementary curriculum. In many schools, language arts alone constitute sixty percent of the school day. There are incredible demands being placed upon elementary teachers that cannot help but affect their relation to the arts. Madeja calls upon state education departments and institutions of higher education to become involved in solving this problem.

Implementation of the plethora of ideas presented at this symposium implies, as Hoffia noted, that educators must "revamp much more than the teacher-education programs themselves. Nothing less than a wholesale reconstruction of the entire arts education system would be required." That appears to be the only way that the arts can become a solid rock in the foundation of American schooling. This symposium was directed by David W. Baker, professor of art at LSU, and managed very capably by a number of his graduate students.

40

EDUCATIONAL REFORM: FERMENT IN THE ARTS

MUSICAL AMERICA 36 (April 1986)

In 1985, the National Endowment for the Arts, along with the Rockefeller Foundation and the US Department of Education, funded a large-scale analysis of arts education in US schools. The report, titled *Arts, Education and the States: A Survey of State Education Policies,* was comprehensive in nature, and included data from all fifty states and almost every US territory. Topics addressed were general education goals, curriculum, testing, textbooks, graduation requirements, funding, and current trends, among others. A number of important points stand out: curriculum guidelines were available in forty-three states; forty-two states mandated music and arts education; twenty states had graduation requirements in the arts; many states had clear teacher certification requirements; and most states required that the arts be listed as basic elements in the larger curriculum. The final report included a number of suggested recommendations to outline an agenda for the states moving forward. This type of clear thinking with specific guidelines would be most welcome in a contemporary context. The primary question, however, would anyone listen?

—CR

* * *

A RECENT survey of state education policies conducted by the Council of Chief State School officers—those who head the nation's state education departments—reveals that the education reform movement is causing enormous ferment in the arts, much of it positive. William F. Pierce, executive director of the Council, states at the outset:

> We think this document makes the case that whatever your personal objective for American education may be, the arts make a significant and important contribution, and that the states play an essential role in ensuring that the contribution of the arts to the total system is made available to all of the children and youth of our nation.

Each of the fifty states and all but three territories completed the questionnaire for this study—an extraordinary ninety-five percent response. This means that we now have a fairly exact accounting of what states are doing—and not doing—in all the areas affecting the arts: general education goals, curriculum, testing, textbooks, graduation requirements, state funding provisions, and the influence of current educational trends. Overall, the developments are favorable to the arts, but there are some trouble spots to be sure.

Only thirteen state boards of education specify the arts within their formal statements of educational goals. But the good news is that almost all the states are currently revising policies in ways that should positively affect arts education. They are contemplating changes or new initiatives in such areas as graduation requirements, teacher training and certification, curriculum and course offerings, and funding. About the latter: one-third of the state agencies indicated that they increased general funding for arts education, one-third decreased funding, and another third made no change. This is about as good an indicator as we have for measuring the overall status of the arts in education throughout the United States.

Curriculum guidelines for arts instruction are distributed by forty-three states. In response to current trends, the most recent guides are competency- and discipline-based. Typically, they define specific skills and competencies to be acquired by students in a particular subject at a particular level. They allow the local school districts to determine how such skills and competencies will be taught. As expected, a majority of the states (36) publish guidelines for visual arts and music. But more than twenty states have developed guidelines for theater,[1] dance, and creative writing.

Forty-two states mandate instruction in the arts in elementary or secondary schools, but the requirements are limited in most states to visual arts and music. Twelve states require that dance and/or theater be offered at the secondary level.

Twenty states now have graduation requirements in the arts, and all but two of these states have adopted the requirements within the past five years. Unfortunately,

---

[1] This report uses the term "drama" rather than "theater," the latter being the generic nomenclature I prefer and have substituted throughout. I take my cue from the American Theatre Association which uses the term "drama" to signify the written art, "theatre" to refer to the art form itself. Thus schools have a curriculum in theater that may include a course that explores the dramas of Shakespeare.

ten of these states offer students alternative options in vocational education or a foreign language that fulfill the same requirement. This means that at present there are just ten states that require every high school student to complete some study of the arts for graduation.

This report admits that these requirements have, on occasion, worked against the arts: "Local districts have not generally adjusted schedules to accommodate additional electives, which sometimes prohibit interested students from enrolling in arts courses." What has happened in states like Florida is that requirements in other subjects such as English, social studies, mathematics, science, and foreign language have so filled the students' schedules that there is no longer any time left for electing courses in the arts. Then, too, forty percent of the states reported that the emphasis being given to vocational education is "harming the efforts of those seeking adequate arts offerings." The effect on the arts of growth in course-offerings was viewed as negative by thirty-eight percent of the states, positive by forty-two percent, and neutral by twenty percent.

States such as New York have found a possible solution to a crowded curriculum that tends to elbow out the arts. They have increased the number of periods in the school day so that even though students have more required courses they still have time to take electives. But, then again, some states noted that when students are given broad choices and the fine arts is only one option, they often avoid an area in which they have had little course work since the elementary school. This observation points to the need to establish the arts as part of the core of learning for all children at all levels—one of the recommendations made in this report.

Goals and requirements are but two of the factors affecting the quality of arts programs. Standards for the education of teachers is another. Forty-two states maintain standards for the certification of K through 12 teachers in two or more of the arts, generally visual arts and music. Where the arts are in trouble is in establishing certification for arts specialists in theater, dance, and creative writing. Only twelve states and Puerto Rico certify teachers in theater for the elementary school, and less than half the states (23) certify teachers in theater for high school. Only nine states certify teachers in dance for elementary, thirteen for secondary. Creative writing teachers are certified in only three states for elementary, in five states for secondary schools. This is a baseline problem: without certified specialists in these art forms, they are inevitably either poorly taught or neglected altogether.

The problems of certification in the arts are insidious, and this report only begins to hint at them. Only twenty-six states require specific hours or units in the arts for regular elementary classroom certification, even though many school districts in these states give some responsibility for teaching the arts to these teachers. The report does admit that "Although states may grant certification, they are not always able to discern whether certified art teachers or regular classroom teachers are providing arts instruction." The report states that most states do not know who is teaching arts courses "because of their lack of access to data at the local level." In this matter the report is too lenient. If states are interested in maintaining standards of instruction, and certification is one way to do it, then such standards should be enforced. The report does recommend that states should ensure quality instruction by arts teachers who have been "certified in their subject area, or classroom teachers qualified to teach the arts," but this strikes me as not nearly strong enough.

Only ten states employ standardized testing to assess achievement in the arts on a statewide basis. But this is a marked increase, and other states indicate that they are actively pursuing the development of such assessment programs. The report states that this shows "a definite trend toward standardized testing in the arts." Such tests are generally limited to art and music and administered at the traditional testing levels for academic subjects, usually grades 4, 8, and 11.

This report does more than just hint that such testing may be necessary to establish the arts on a par with other subjects. Noting the increased emphasis on standardized testing in general, fifty-five percent of the responding states voiced concern about the negative effects of such testing on the arts. The report states that "As this testing [in basic subjects] has come to be tied more securely to the identification and testing of discrete skills mastered at particular grade levels and through individual courses, the knowledge and accomplishments of an arts education have been slighted." Along these same lines, the most negative trend for arts education, as cited by sixty-seven percent of the respondents, was the "back to basics" movement.

What is most important about this report is the commitment the chief state school officers make to the arts. They emphasize that new policies at the state level "should define the arts as basic to the K-12 curriculum." And they recommended a commitment at both the state and local levels "to fund and otherwise enable schools to provide qualified instructors to teach the arts (in all subject areas), to offer sufficient numbers of courses to reach all students, and to ensure that the arts are included as a part of solid academic preparaton for a well-rounded, precollegiate education."

The report concludes with ten recommendations that were developed by the project's advisory committee in response to survey results and to discussions with chief state school officers during a national meeting on the arts in Boston in May 1985. In effect, these recommendations outline an agenda for these state agencies to establish the arts as an essential component of the education of all children at all levels, to develop and implement a sequential, K-12, competency-based arts curriculum for all arts subject areas, to establish graduation requirements, to infuse the arts into other academic subject areas, to provide adequate time, space, and materials for arts instruction, and to incorporate the arts into state assessments.

Maryland state superintendent of schools David W. Hornbeck, who served as chairman of the arts advisory committee for this study, states in the preface: "The arts are central to the school's role to educate.... [They] can provide us and the students in our charge with special insight and sensitivity about the planet on which we live and its people. We need to get on with the task of seizing the 'arts opportunity' on behalf of our students." This report was funded by the National Endowment for the Arts, the Rockefeller Foundation, and the U.S. Department of Education.

41

TEACHER OVERHAUL: CAN WE DO IT?

MUSICAL AMERICA 107 (July 1987)

Pre-service teacher preparation is likely one of the most important tasks of the music education profession. Without good and qualified music teachers, students will not learn and programs will not flourish. It seems safe to say that public school music education in the United States essentially began with the idea of teaching. Had Lowell Mason not offered a free teaching and learning model to Boston, we might not be where we are today. The way we train teachers, of course, is bound to be cause for debate, controversial by nature, and complex to solve. In the late 1980s, the move for reform of music teacher preparation was at a fever pitch. Standards were changing nationally, individual states mandated differing requirements, licensing varied from state to state, college curricula were myriad, and decisions about the most important aspects in a degree program were under serious scrutiny. Not surprisingly, MENC, along with a number of other institutions, was in the middle of these debates. This is a lengthy, detailed, and structured article that outlines the many issues and aspects of how music teachers are trained in the United States. For the casual reader, seeing the entire arc will be fascinating. For the trained music educator, this is a must-read that will reignite your thinking about the critical task of how we prepare pre-service teachers for a career in music education.

—CR

* * *

QUALITY TEACHING is prerequisite to quality education. That truism is as inescapable for the arts as for any other subject. Increasingly, those who are determined to improve education are looking at how to improve the preparation of teachers. The two go hand-in-hand.

Like every other subject in the public school curriculum today, music teaching and learning are under close scrutiny. But why should the preparation of music teachers be altered? In what ways should it be changed?

Teaching today, by all accounts, is getting more, not less, demanding, largely because the conditions of teaching are changing. One in five children in this nation now lives below the poverty level, and the same number live in homes with no father. Increasing numbers of "latchkey" children go home from school to houses without parents. Five times as many children are born out of wedlock today as in 1970. Children from such problem situations consistently fail to achieve in school at the level of children from non-problem situations. Yet all teachers, including those who teach the arts, face children from problem situations as a matter of routine.

By 1990, more than 30 percent of the total school-age population in the United States will be minorities. That no longer means blacks. In the schools in Arlington County, Virginia, for example, there are 200 more Hispanic students than blacks (2,317) and almost as many Asian students as blacks (2,020). In nearby Fairfax County schools, Asian students now outnumber blacks. And in the District of Columbia public schools, there are now more Hispanics than whites. I was in an elementary school in New York City recently in which more than 50 languages are spoken. Communication alone requires extraordinary efforts. Teaching these students music—or any subject, for that matter—presents new challenges to any teacher.

As if the changing population of students doesn't present enough new challenges, teachers of every kind are being asked to demand more of their students and to motivate and maintain higher standards of achievement. In various forms and in varying degrees, curricular reform is being introduced in states and school districts throughout the country. As demands for excellence in student achievement reach fever pitch, pressures for better teaching and better-prepared teachers increase accordingly. Like other teachers, music teachers are, clearly, going to have to be better at what they do, and they are going to have to be accountable for what their students do and do not learn.

The nationwide movement to create a curriculum of more substance and rigor is also having an effect upon the arts. Many people believe that by giving the arts broader and more demanding content, the arts will attain greater credibility in the curriculum. As the reasoning goes, by making the arts more academic, we win the status accorded other academic disciplines. Are the arts undervalued in American education because they aren't as academic as other subjects? Perhaps, in part, they are. But this question at present is irrelevant. Arts education is on the move and is being nudged ahead by the current trends.

Given the penchant for making all subjects more cerebral, there is pressure to alter the arts curriculum accordingly. In visual arts, the Getty Center for Education in the

Arts is promulgating a broadened "discipline-based" curriculum to include art history, art criticism, and aesthetics, along with art production. Similarly, music programs in many states are being urged to broaden performance curricula to include aspects of style, history, theory, criticism, and culture.

Particularly in states that now require some credit in the arts for high school graduation, there is a growing sense that music courses must be provided for all students. The profession seems to be acknowledging the fact that all those bands and choruses in America's public schools have not produced a great public for music. They are beginning, in earnest, to address not just the select 30 percent, but all 100 percent of the students at the high school level. This not a simple about-face. It is a major change in philosophy that will require substantial changes in music teacher education.

The commitment to performance in music is deeply ingrained. Teaching appreciation is far more difficult. Yet, with all the difficulties it poses, there is a surge of new interest in the general music curriculum. As national chairperson of the Society for Music Teacher Education and a member of MENC's Task Force on Music Teacher Education, Irma H. Collins, professor of music at Murray (Kentucky) State University, has stated, "At present, general music appears to serve the performing groups; that is, it is thought of as a means to an end." Taking that reasoning one step further, Harry Broudy, professor emeritus of education philosophy at the University of Illinois, states that the major issue in the music curriculum today is "whether performance is an end in itself or whether it is ancillary to something else." There seems to be a growing commitment to teaching music so that it has a lasting effect on the whole of later life.

In discussing the trend toward being more academic, Thomas Regelski, professor of music education at Fredonia (New York) State College, says, "It could mean that the band, chorus, or orchestra become a class in general music through the medium of performance. They would assume a general music class approach and not simply be a model for the transfer of musicianship and musicality through eight years of conquering a given repertoire. Students would emerge from the program at least minimally prepared to be intelligent audience members, which is not necessarily the consequence of being in the ensembles as they are now conducted."

This transition will not be easy. Collins notes that "Students do not choose music for its academic emphasis." She says, "When asked, the students will tell you that they select band or choir for enjoyment. They don't think of either of these as being academic." Such student expectations will have to be altered if music courses are to be counted as credit toward graduation. And music educators will have to adjust their ego rewards as directors so that they can obtain as much satisfaction as teachers.

The implications for preparing music teachers are enormous. Reaching all the students will require new modes of education at the college level that stretch well beyond performance. Winning the back rows of students to music will require the acquisition of enormous musical in-sight, teaching expertise, and pure chutzpah.

It is not uncommon today for music teachers to be asked to supervise music programs taught by classroom teachers, to plan and teach music to those teachers through in-service education programs, to serve as cultural coordinators within the school district, to organize comprehensive arts education programs, to develop more academically oriented curricula to meet new graduation requirements, to work in magnet-school settings, and to direct advocacy efforts to win broader support for music and arts education. Obviously, if music educators are going to function more broadly, they should be more broadly educated.

One of the possible stumbling blocks to changing music teacher preparation is state certification. States differ in their standards for the certification of teachers to teach music, and these standards are not easily changed. In numbers of states, certification to teach music is granted automatically upon completion of the bachelor's degree, but states differ widely in their regulations for distribution of semester credits among courses in music, education, general education, and practice teaching. Some states first offer provisional certification with permanent certification being granted after the teacher attains the equivalent of a master's degree and a required number of years of teaching experience. Obviously, such state certification standards as now applied can affect the adequacy of academic preparation. Enforcing those standards through testing the prospective teacher is becoming increasingly common. Some 29 states now require a test for initial certification, and nine additional states will require testing by 1988.

There are other difficulties with certification when one surveys the entire arts field. While state certification in art (visual arts) and music is well established, certification in dance and in theater generally falls under the headings, respectively, of physical education and English. Only 13 states certify professional specialists in dance, and only 11 states certify professional specialists in theater. Such certification practices tend to thwart the teaching of these art forms, put up barriers to the arts curriculum being viewed in its broad outlines, and blur the relationship between those disciplines and teaching.

Another possible obstacle to changing teacher education programs in music is the departmental battles on campus. The funding of departments based on the numbers of students enrolled in a department's courses tends to reduce curricular discussions to economic issues. Change does not come easily between departments vying for the credits that will sustain them. These vested interests do not operate on the basis of what courses make good sense for the prospective teacher. They operate protectively and politically to preserve the department.

Considering the changing conditions of teaching, the need for curricular reform in music, and the changing function of music teachers, what solutions are being recommended? First, there are numbers of general recommendations coming from organizations such as the National Education Association and the Carnegie Foundation that may have some affect upon music teacher preparation. Then, too, there are specific recommendations from organizations in the arts. If this conglomeration of interests sounds confusing, that is an accurate assessment. Not all these parties agree. But some trends in thinking are emerging.

General Recommendations. The National Education Association recommends four practical steps to encourage outstanding teaching. The NEA belives that prospective teachers should first complete a basic liberal arts curriculum and maintain at least a 2.5 grade-point average before being admitted to a teacher education program. Once accepted into such a program, teacher candidates would master the professional knowledge of teacher education and apply this "in progressively more demanding student teaching experiences." They would then complete a teaching internship with experienced teachers. After this, as a professional teacher, they would be evaluated annually and provided with in-service educational opportunities.

This proposal is less radical than many. The Carnegie Foundation has proposed the standardization of certification requirements throughout the country. They propose a national test to assess teaching over a period of time, including provisions to correct inadequacies. The Foundation recommends that the undergraduate program concentrate on general and specific subject matter. This, in turn, would be followed by a master's degree program in professional education and an internship teaching program guided by a master teacher.

Reaction to teacher tests has been mixed. Generally, teachers do not believe that such tests can measure the ability to teach. But Kathryn Martin, dean of fine arts at Wayne State University, points out that "Degrees are not the indication that people know how to perform or to teach." Perhaps some form of group observation and evaluation of teaching practice, as instituted in Georgia and Florida, can provide a basis for certification.

Generally, reformers call for more emphasis on subject matter and less on methodology. Some call for learning teaching skills and knowledge after acquiring a liberal arts degree. Many suggest a period of internship working with a master teacher. Most make some provision for continued study, recognizing that everything cannot be accomplished in a four- or five-year program.

Specific Recommendations. What is the music education field itself saying about its own teacher education programs? A statement by the Working Group on the Arts in Higher Education maintains that "The focus on subject matter in teacher education is a tenet strongly held by arts faculties and administrators in American higher education. Statements by national organizations representing these groups (the Music Educators National Conference, for one) recommend that at least 50 percent of the teacher preparation curriculum for arts specialists [should] involve studies in the art form." In addition, this Working Group informs us that:

> Specialist arts teachers must understand the pedagogy of their discipline and the educational context in which their discipline and its pedagogy will be housed. . . .
> Teacher preparation curricula for arts specialists should also develop a sense of understanding about intellectual life as a whole and the role of art within it. Skill in the use of language, in-depth understanding of psychology, and familiarity with the historical roots of American civilization are essential for specialist arts teachers.

This is a tall order, but one that can be substantiated.

The Working Group goes on to make more controversial statements. For example: that "Specialist art teachers must have the basic skills of a professional artist" (p. 9); that "Keeping art at the center [of teacher education programs] may become increasingly difficult" in light of demographic shifts that "can result in programmatic goals for arts education that see cultural orientation rather than art itself as the central focus of the curriculum" (pp. 24 and 25); and that "Education is not needed to support the existence of mass culture" (p. 26). This last statement expresses the fear that teaching music as a discipline and as a high art will disintegrate if tainted by popular connections with leisure and entertainment. It is as though the Sondheims and Lionel Richies of the world don't need any education in music.

All these statements tend to point the field toward developing classically oriented musicians who teach—a goal not far removed from where many teacher education programs in music are today. But I question whether music teachers in the public schools need the same basic skills as professional artists. I'm reminded of a conversation I had with a fiddler who plays during the dinner hour in a local Italian restaurant. I asked him how many requests he gets to play *Ziegeunerweisen*. He laughed. "Many," he said, "and if I could play that, I woudn't be playing here." It isn't a matter of "Those who can, do; those who can't, teach." Teachers have a great deal else to learn besides musical technique. And one of those areas is the relationship of music to the various cultures from which it arises. One simply cannot teach well in today's classrooms without that knowledge.

I sense a rigidity in the statements of this Working Group. No wonder people such as Kathryn Martin point out the "need to get away from the restrictions of accreditation agencies." This would permit institutions to get out from under fixed models, invent more ingenious solutions, and serve local needs.

The recommendations of the Task Force on Music Teacher Education for the Nineties, of the Music Educators National Conference, are somewhat more progressive. This report, backed by 18 months of deliberations, recognizes the urgent need for change in the preparation of music teachers and states that "The time to act . . . is now."

The report offers guidelines to identify prospective music educators, proposes a curricular program for teacher certification in music, provides a cooperative plan for professional teacher development, and suggests options for the improvement of college teaching. But, in the main, the uniqueness of this report is in its call for the partnership of college and public school music teachers in the process of teacher education. This "new sense of community" acknowledges that the responsibilities for music teacher preparation must be shared among music education professors, cooperating elementary/secondary school music educators, and all college music teaching faculties. The mechanism for this process is a Professional Development Plan which amounts to a life-long career guide to professional growth. This approach promises to have the right mix of the ideal and the real, the theoretical knowledge and the practical experience that are necessary for one to become a good teacher.

It is important to realize that MENC has no power to implement these ideas and suggestions. Jeffrey S. Kimpton, director of music education in the Wichita public schools and a member of the Task Force, believes that the partnership process may run into some snags. He says, "Some, I think, fear that interrelating musical disciplines and utilizing ad hoc faculty who are experts in the field will jeopardize collegiate curricular autonomy and tenured positions." That never was the purpose, he says, and suggests that the idea "needs far greater clarification in terms of how it would be implemented in courses and departmental relationships." He believes, in hindsight, that the report "skirted the issue of really underscoring the need for competent preparation in teaching *general* music, a critical problem today."

Perhaps this oversight, which is very serious in terms of present trends, would have been avoided if the MENC Task Force had given more emphasis to the changing conditions of teaching, the ramifications of the educational reform movement, and the deficiencies in theory and practice within current programs. But the report, if not the whole answer, begins seriously to address some of the major problem areas of teacher education.

In weighing the current recommendations, Robert L. Erbes, chairperson of music education at Michigan State University, believes that the most valuable are "the calls for more careful selection of students, a more thorough and intensive period of training, continuing education based on meaningful professional training rather than more earned credits, and improved salary and working conditions." Out of the current ferment, he believes that we are likely to see more rigorous training, better assessment instruments and techniques, some form of career ladder for the advancement of teachers in all states, and more consistency in state standards for certification.

Out of the push and pull between the competing interests and viewpoints of the field will come some movement and change. Kimpton points out that Jerry Olson, chair of the MENC Task Force, "did a masterful job of balancing the sensitivities of the various constituencies of music teacher education." But the tone of this report is so positive as to invite inaction. If the need for change is as great as I belive it is, compromise will not suffice to satisfy that need. Bold and imaginative new initiatives are called for. Courage and experimentation will go further than caution and excuses. Will leadership rise to answer the call?

Diversity and Pluralism in Arts Education

V

Diversity and Pluralism in Arts Education

42

POVERTY: AN INGRAINED IDEA

MUSICAL AMERICA 26 (June 1976)

The concept of poverty takes many forms. Sometimes it may be financial, sometimes philosophical, and at other times, ethical or practical. Connecting poverty to the arts and music education is unfortunately not a difficult stretch. However, even though arts institutions and school districts may struggle to support their programs, the problem may be just as much ideological as financial. It is true that many artistic and educational endeavors could use more funding, but perhaps a rethinking of how to approach the business aspects of making music and teaching could help to solve many of the problems. Questions that are asked here include: What is wrong with making money in the arts? Are we not providing a service for our compensation? Shouldn't music education be supported, given the value it provides to students and society? Why are we avoiding the practical aspects of our profession? Why should success not be rewarded? While the idea of career-oriented thinking and business-minded operation is more common today, much more could be impressed upon those studying music, those in public and private institutions, and students training toward a career in music education.

—CR

* * *

THE ARTS in education are poverty stricken. That is the dire message from most administrators and teachers of the arts in every state, whether they are part of private or public institutions. Lack of funds is a problem that seriously hampers existing programs, forcing cutbacks at a time when people, especially the young, are showing more interest in the arts than ever before.

The arts do not command much status when budgets are adequate, let alone when they get tight. They are apparently easy and vulnerable victims of declining local tax revenues and inflation, too often being cast aside because of pressures to draw in the belt. Large cities seem the most affected. Los Angeles, Seattle, and New York, for example, have all made substantial cutbacks in music staff, but many smaller districts have also suffered losses.

Nor does there seem to be any place to turn for assistance. The arts educator who goes to the National Endowment for the Arts for financial help is redirected to the Office of Education. Yet there are scant funds at the Office of Education that can support the arts in education either. The Humanities Endowment also offers little hope of assistance in this area. Arts education has no home among the government agencies. What funds are available go largely to support artists who are already established, not to those people who are still trying to find their artistic legs in the educational process.

A CASE OF MALNUTRITION

Why are the arts, more than other subjects, affected by financial malnutrition? There are many reasons, but perhaps the most fundamental is that the American people tend to be functionally oriented. They view education in the same practical terms that they view the world. Unfortunately, people do not realize the economic and environmental contributions of the arts. They fail to understand what artists do. The fact that many people make a living at the arts and that design is a consideration in the manufacture and marketing of most products sold, does not occur to the majority of people, certainly to many of those who make the decisions about how public funds will be spent.

Administrators, members of boards of education, and parents who still think of the arts as frills do so because the arts have, in many cases, been taught as frills. Seldom do artists or arts educators stress the practical, materialistic, and functional aspects of the arts. The thousands of people who are making a substantial and satisfying living at some facet of the popular music industry—composing, arranging, performing, recording, managing, promoting, sound engineering, publishing, instrument manufacturing, retail sales, etc.—are rarely given any consideration or visibility in music education curricula or even in vocational education programs.

Arts educators have concentrated on teaching the nonfunctional aspects of their subject. They have deliberately stressed the esoteric and aesthetic aspects instead of the purposeful or useful. This is one reason the arts have not been held to be very important in education or valued in the scheme of American life.

Artists do not differ from others in making a living: they sell a service to the public. Dr. Paul Salmon, executive director of the American Association of School Administrators, says, "If the American people could see the arts as a good possibility for employment, then they would favor them in the curriculum. It is unfortunate that the picture of the starving artist is what the people see." Of course there are starving artists, but there are also many who are making a good living. Indeed, musical performers are among the top-salaried people in the United States. Yet it seems that visual vestiges of the bohemian struggling for acceptance is what hovers in the public mind as the image of the artist and the whole field of the arts.

THE STIGMA OF SUCCESS

"Commercialism" is the name applied to anything in the arts that pays for itself. If a performer has a best-selling album, he or she is relegated to the "commercial" realm. The term is often transformed into a barb hurled by the less successful (often elitist-oriented) artist at those musical performers who have attracted a larger public following.

So ingrained is the idea of poverty in the arts world that it has become fashionable to expect artists and arts organizations to operate in the red. At a meeting of administrators of community schools of the arts, for example, the reports of financing went something like this: "I had a $25,000 deficit this year; I must be doing something right." (Laughter.) Next report: "I had a $50,000 deficit this year; I must be doing something even more right." (Laughter.) Next report: "I had a $100,000 deficit; I must be a genius." (More laughter.) Next report: "I hesitate to say this but my school not only broke even, we made money. What am I doing that isn't right?" It is an old syndrome: if the artistic enterprise is in the black, there must be something wrong; if art sells, the standard must somehow be at fault.

THE PUBLIC NEEDS TO KNOW

The truth of the matter is that artists and their counterparts, arts educators, feel uncomfortable about money. "Art organizations must learn to function as businesses," says Gerry J. Martin, national executive director of Young Audiences, Inc. "Many administrators do not know where to go for funding, nor how to deal with funding agencies. Some have a lack of simple logic and common sense, while others feel that they are owed support."

Arts educators need to become better and more convincing salesmen. They need to build a constituency among the public in solid support of the arts in education. Out of this will come new support at the state and federal levels. The public needs to know how critical the situation has become. The problem is bigger, and the responsibility broader, than the arts community alone. Does the public really want the bland and ugly environments that would necessarily ensue if the world were devoid of the arts? How much is the quality of life affected by the artful, and what is that worth?

A reordering of priorities seems to be called for, as Alvin C. Eurich informs us in *Reforming American Education* (New York: Harper & Row, 1969, page 122): "We cannot tolerate another generation that knows so much about preserving and destroying life, but so little about enhancing it. We cannot permit our children to come into their maturity as masters of the atom and of the gene, but ignorant and barbarous about the ways of the human mind and heart."

But perhaps the poet Vachel Lindsay said it best:

> Let not young souls be smothered out before
> They do quaint deeds and fully flaunt their pride.
> It is the world's one crime its babes grow dull,
> Its poor are ox-like, limp and leaden-eyed.
>
> Not that they starve, but starve so dreamlessly,
> Not that they sow, but that they seldom reap,
> Not that they serve, but have no gods to serve,
> Not that they die but that they die like sheep.

The arts could do much to alter that picture, but only if they are given the priority and the support that could bring them into the mainstream of education.

43

SEX BIAS IN THE MUSIC ROOM

MUSICAL AMERICA 26 (December 1976)

The problem of sex bias (*gender bias* or *gender discrimination* in current language) is a serious issue that deserves attention. However, in order to truly provide equal treatment and address transgressions, those in leadership roles must be educated enough to create reasonable solutions. Here is a case of good intentions gone awry. In the mid-1970s, the US Department of Health, Education, and Welfare (HEW) was working diligently to uphold requirements of Title IX, an educational amendment from 1972 designed to protect people (primarily women) from discrimination in schools and other institutions receiving federal funding. In many cases there was a clear need, and Title IX provided valuable support to women pursuing their education and related activities. There were oversights, however, as in this case of a boy's choir in Connecticut which was under pressure because girls were not allowed to sing in the group. The ensemble or its teachers were not discriminating, but it was misinterpreted in this circumstance. There were sound historical and musical reasons for the male-only membership: the choir was specifically started to help boys become more interested in singing, so as to eventually create larger, mixed-gender choruses. Nevertheless, HEW still felt obliged to intervene. The story is compelling, and can lead to larger discussions of gender bias or related issues in other musical classrooms and ensembles. The problem does exist, it just did not in this case.

—CR

* * *

MOTHER-DAUGHTER father-son banquets aren't the only things that officials at the U.S. Health, Education and Welfare Department have to complain about these days. An all-boy choir in Wethersfield, Connecticut has been declared in violation of HEW's rules on school sex discrimination.

The most recent dispute involves an after-school choir of fifth and sixth grade boys which the department's stance for Civil Rights says should be disallowed unless it results from "requirements based on vocal range and quality." Under this ruling, single-sex choruses are only permitted if the other sex cannot fulfill the range and quality requirements. Conceivably, if a girl can sing tenor or bass (and some do), she must be permitted to join the male chorus. In like manner, if a boy can sing soprano or alto (and some do), he must be allowed to join the women's chorus. What those traditional musical groups will be called in the future remains to be seen. Non-compliance with this regulation could lead to the withholding of federal school funds.

In the case at hand these young boys' voices haven't changed yet. They sing in the same high range as the girls, so that by the law as interpreted by HEW officials there is no reason to bar girls from the group. According to Wetherfield school officials, however, vocal range and quality were not the reasons for justifying the all-boy choir. Vaughan Howland, the school system's director of elementary and secondary education, said the choir was begun in order to get boys interested in singing and in joining the mixed choirs which are now predominately female. Ironically, their intention was to get a better sex mix in those choruses, which is precisely the intent of Title IX of the sex bias law. Boys at this age tend not to want to be part of a girls' singing group.

OVERZEALOUS BUREAUCRATS

The school system wrote to Rep. William R. Cotter (D.—Conn.) and to their two state senators asking about the legality of the boy choir, because they didn't want to be in a position of noncompliance. Cotter said the case "may illustrate what happens when well-meaning but overzealous bureaucrats get hold of a good law and make it absurd." It also illustrates what a vice-like hold the federal dollar has over local school systems. Cotter has now brought the caseto the attention of HEW Secretary David Mathews and the Office or Civil Rights director, Martin Gerry, and urged them to include the issue in a review ordered by President Ford after the recent father-son, mother-daughter controversy in Scottsdale, Arizona.

A number of school districts have been told by HEW officials that their boys' choruses illegally exclude girls from participating solely on the basis of sex. The application of this law to athletics is just as controversial. The President has declared that, if

HEW officials who review the Scottsdale case uphold the original interpretation, he will immediately seek an amendment to the law.

What is disturbing is that officials and legislators who make and enforce these narrow regulations do not possess the musical understanding that could enlighten them on the difference between a boy and girl soprano at this age. By tone quality alone—and in complete compliance with the law as stated—a boy choir would be justified, because boys at this age sing with a clear, bell-like sound. In contrast girls tend to sing with a breathy, more reedy sound. Range, too, is different. Young boys can easily be taught to sing up to high C. By contrast, few girls the same age find this natural. Witness the use of boys' choirs or choirs of men and boys in churches over the past several hundred years. The reasons for this choice and preference is the particular quality and range of sound that can be achieved by no other means. A boys' choir and girls' choir of the same age would have an entirely different sound. The sexes are vocally different.

VIVE LA DIFFÉRENCE

So the law as it reads is, in actuality, meaningless. In barring single-sex choruses unless they result from requirements based on vocal range and quality, the law fails to recognize the real differences in vocal range and quality that exist between the sexes. A girl singing tenor sounds entirely different from a boy. A boy singing alto sounds entirely different from a girl. Upon the basis of tone quality alone, this law, the way it reads, ought to permit single-sex choruses instead of disallowing them. One sex cannot fulfill the range and quality requirements of the other.

It is obvious that none of the officials at HEW have had enough musical education to avoid making such laws in the first place. The blatant ignorance displayed by this regulation demonstrates the need for more, not fewer, single-sex choruses, so that people learn to savor the significant and aesthetically satisfying differences between them. It is no folly that composers over the centuries have scored specifically for boys' choir, children's chorus (mixed), women's or men's choirs, or mixed chorus, depending upon the particular expressive dimension they sought. Sex bias had nothing to do with it.

Schools should also be permitted to explore all the possible expressive combinations at hand, instead of being limited by a law that is misdirected. Sex bias is a legitimate concern, but the focus of it is hardly the music classroom.

44

SPECIAL TREATMENT FOR THE GIFTED

MUSICAL AMERICA 27 (April 1977)

Students have multiple experiences and interests, and the better that instruction can be tailored to their unique needs, the more effective and meaningful the curriculum. While there is more attention paid to this today than in the past, there were notable programs attempting to reach every child several decades ago. The example here, the Riverside Center for the Arts, was a magnet school in Harrisburg, Pennsylvania. Started in 1971, the school provided opportunities in music and arts education for students in grades 7–12 (originally 5 and 6). Emphasis was placed on creative and imaginative thinking, academic and artistic ability, plurality of backgrounds and genders, student and family need (in some cases), and other factors. The mission, purpose, application process, general curricular goals, and related matters are outlined here. While the magnet school seems like nothing new today, at one time it was an innovative idea that supported bringing diverse students and abilities together for a common learning opportunity. It seems that music education has done this for quite some time, though most music educators do not wish to relegate music classes to central schools and elite programs. They should be happy to continue this trend, and open their doors to wider and broader opportunities.

—CR

* * *

SCHOOL SYSTEMS are learning how to develop diversified programs to meet the special interests and needs of their students. Some cities, like New Orleans, Philadelphia, and Houston, have developed "magnet" schools with curricula focused on the arts and programs specifically designed for students who show exceptional artistic ability. New York City's High School of the Performing Arts is a prominent example. These schools are open to all qualified city students.

There is evidence that this trend is spreading to smaller cities and school systems. In 1971 the Harrisburg School System in Pennsylvania set up the Riverside Center for the Arts, a public school for the arts that at first catered to talented students in grades five and six and is now concentrating on the seventh to twelfth grades.

ENCOURAGING ARTISTIC EXPERIENCE

With the help of federal funds the Riverside School provides an environment and staff that encourages exploratory and in-depth experiences in art, dance, drama, music, photography, and television.

The Harrisburg story grew out of the ferment that typifies many school systems today. In the midst of redeveloping the school district in 1971, the Riverside Elementary School was abandoned. It was situated away from the mainstream and, with its nine rooms, was considered too small. The building represented a resource that might be used in some new way. It was Benjamin F. Turner, now Superintendent of Schools and then Deputy Superintendent for Program Planning, who had the vision to establish an arts center for city students. The school board gave approval, and the plan was underway.

Harrisburg is an urban school district with students from many diverse cultural, racial, and economic backgrounds. The 26.6 percent of the school population that is white consists of students of German, English, Jewish, Italian, Greek, and Slavic extraction, while 69.4 percent of the population is black and 4 percent are non-English speaking. The arts center was developed to bring together these groups in a way that encourages understanding, appreciation, and celebration of their differences.

SPOTTING TALENT

Identifying the talented, particularly when students come from such diverse ethnic backgrounds and vastly different home environments, is not simple. In 1970 the U.S. Commissioner of Education, Sidney P. Marland, Jr., together with an advisory panel, defined gifted and talented children as "those identified by professionally qualified persons who by virtue of outstanding abilities are capable of high performance. These are children who require differentiated educational programs and/or services beyond those normally provided by the regular school program in order to realize their contribution to self and society."

At first students were identified through an application form which could be submitted by a teacher, principal, counselor, parent, friend, or by themselves. Later, after the Center had been operating, the staff devised a list of characteristics of successful participants which became the basis of a new form to be filled out at each student's school. Among the desired characteristics sought are these: imagination and a sense of humor, self-control, the ability to deal with abstract ideas and to formulate original and divergent ideas.

Teachers, guidance counselors, and principals rate students on a scale of one to five on each characteristic. A test for creativity is also administered to all applicants. Students who rate high are then interviewed and asked to participate in specialized activities in the various arts. A student's art products or performances, interest and motivation, awards, and indications of leadership ability are also taken into account. Final selection is made on the basis of all the identification methods with a policy of inclusion wherever there is doubt about a student.

These procedures are still being refined, particularly to assure the discovery of the creative student from minority or disadvantaged groups. For many of these students, opportunities to explore their talents must be made available through the school or they will not be made available at all.

TIES WITH THE COMMUNITY

While discovering students with potential in the arts is one of the primary aims of the program, there are other important objectives. The Center is determined to create an exciting program and environment conducive to exploration and learning through the arts. The faculty introduces students to the arts process in all its aspects and provides them with across-the-arts experiences. The Center has also developed ties with community arts organizations including the William Penn Memorial Museum and the Harrisburg Symphony Association.

Barbara McGeary, project director, says, "Our community has a rich offering of people and resources that can be used to help broaden student exposure to all the arts. Community artists act as supplemental teachers at the Arts Center. Community resources such as museums, galleries, theaters, playhouses, orchestras, and dance studios serve as out-of-school classrooms."

One evidence of this bond between talented young students and their community counterparts is the soap opera the students are developing for the local television station with the help of professionals from the community. Called "Fond Memories," the show is written, directed, acted, and filmed by the students.

A resident string quintet provides opportunities for students to work directly with professional musicians. The Center houses a piano laboratory and students have the use of a synthesizer for the creation of electronic music. Up to 150 students spend half of every day studying the arts at the Center. They take their other subjects elsewhere.

The Project is financed in part by local school funds, in part by funds from Title IV of the Elementary and Secondary Education Act. With the Center the Harrisburg School System has taken concrete action toward meeting the specialized needs of its students.

45

MORE ARTS FOR THE HANDICAPPED

MUSICAL AMERICA 27 (June 1977)

The goal of music and arts education for everyone really hits home in this piece about opportunities for special-needs students. The results of offering arts programs to students with special needs were remarkable and children were learning and growing in ways thought unimaginable in other areas. Some students spoke with greater clarity, others sang or played an instrument, still more learned better reading and writing skills, all in addition to the emotional and spiritual benefits. Several groups were contributing at the time, including the Very Special Arts Festival, Alliance for Arts Education, and National Committee of Arts for the Handicapped. Jean Kennedy Smith (sister of the late President Kennedy) was deeply involved, and a longtime champion of arts education for those with special needs. There is a particularly moving segment on the price for survival that instigates serious thought about the role and importance of arts and music for children dealing with mental disabilities. While this area of research and practice has grown significantly today, there are still large numbers of students who need more support for their participation in musical activities. The more we understand as a profession, the better student lives and experiences can be in the larger picture.

—CR

* * *

MARION, barely able to talk, sang the *Star Spangled Banner* like it had never been sung before.... One boy with cerebral palsy got so excited after a successful rendition, he flailed his arms and legs and almost fell out of his wheelchair.... It was hard to keep a dry eye when Allen, confined to a wheelchair, strummed the guitar with his toes while a teacher lying prone fingered the chords and sang *Feelings.* The culmination of the program was several beautiful songs, including *God Bless America,* sung by a boy on a four-wheeled cart. He had short arms, no legs, and a big heart."

Very Special Arts Fair

Those are excerpts from a report on the State of Washington's Very Special Arts Fair, one of the first of its kind, designed to demonstrate the impact of the arts in developing artistic responsiveness and increasing general learning achievement among handicapped students. Held in May of 1976, this fair is serving as a model for some twenty other states which will hold Very Special Arts Festivals during 1977.

The festivals are drawing the public's attention to an area of national neglect. When it comes to the arts, it has been estimated that only one million, or twelve percent, of all handicapped children out of approximately eight million enrolled in schools receive any instruction. Yet the arts are activities that could bring some measure of joy and a sense of achievement to persons who too often lead drab and desolate lives.

A recent study in Connecticut, under the banner of Project SEARCH, an acronym for Search for Exceptional Abilities Reachable Among Children with Handicaps, revealed through extensive and innovative testing that twelve percent of the handicapped children who were studied were gifted—*roughly three times as many as in the general school population,* according to the same, largely subjective norms. Alan J. White, director of the project, stated that "This group has exceptional potential for growth and training and creative activity in the arts." Unfortunately, such talents and capacities are often overlooked or ignored.

Jean Kennedy Smith, the late President's sister and a long-time champion of the cause of the mentally retarded and handicapped, recognizes the need for arts programs for these children: "More and more we are learning to understand that for every artist who has painted a picture, composed music, or written poetry, and for all the teachers who have educated students in the arts, and for all of us who have enjoyed the genius of artists, there have been others who have been excluded from even the chance to see the portrait, hear the song, or read the verse. They have been excluded because we have branded them 'Handicapped' or 'Retarded' and therefore have considered them 'Unappreciative.'

"Every child is a gift of God and every child of God has a potential for talent; a capacity for creativity; and a right to enjoy to the fullest the beauty and vitality of the arts. These talents can enrich us all."

A Nationwide Program

Fortunately there are a number of signs that point to improvement. In June 1974, the Joseph P. Kennedy, Jr. Foundation provided the funding for a National Conference on

Arts for the Mentally Retarded which drew national attention to the value of the arts in the education of these children. One outcome of the conference was the formation of the National Committee, Arts for the Handicapped, originally spearheaded by Mrs. Smith, which is now coordinating the development of a nationwide program of arts for all handicapped children. This year they have held three regional meetings in conjunction with the Alliance for Arts Education, one of their funding sources, to pursue their three major goals: to research and disseminate information about curriculum and instruction in the arts for the handicapped; to exemplify model arts programs that may be successfully used with the handicapped; and to increase the number of handicapped students served by arts programs by two hundred thousand per year for five years.

One of the strategies used to implement these goals is the concept of the Very Special Arts Festival, an activity in the arts comparable to the Special Olympics. These festivals illustrate through live demonstrations how music helps handicapped children to read and count, how video taping enables them to explore and document their world and sharpen their communication skills, how movement and dance increase their awareness of mind and physical movement, how making puppets leads to writing and acting original playlets, and how the visual arts and crafts awaken perception, increase physical control, and provide creative release.

Whereas in 1976 New York State sponsored three regional and one all-state festival with ten thousand handicapped students participating, this year there will be nine regional festivals and a two-day all-state. The State of Washington will hold eight regional fairs and one all-state this year. They are instituting teacher training programs to help teachers learn how to use the process of the arts to help these children learn. Through the arts some remarkable results have accrued: autistic children are learning to speak; those who couldn't move are learning to crawl; children with poor self-concepts are being given hope; students with learning difficulties are finding a way through. The reason that the arts work is that they provide a non-competitive challenge, yet are engaging and fun.

OUTSTANDING PROGRAM

In the past few years some outstanding programs have sprung up across the country. The Alan Short Center in Stockton, California, founded in 1975 and opened in April of 1976, uses the arts to teach socialization and pre-vocational skills to handicapped students eighteen and up. The center uses group art projects to help students come out of themselves and relate to each other. Photography helps them see what they otherwise might miss. Weaving teaches motor skills. Cooking, pottery, guitar playing, square dancing, singing, printmaking, creative drama, and interpretive dance are part of the curriculum.

In the fall of 1974, the Rockford, Illinois Park District commissioners were asked to consider a recommendation by Webbs Norman, park district director, that "the park district establish a year-round program for handicapped area youngsters." The result is

"Camp Sunshine," an arts program that accommodates upwards of sixty handicapped youngsters. Miriam Perrone, director of the program, acquired her creative approach to reaching these children through efforts to educate her own son, now eighteen, a victim of Down's syndrome, a severe form of retardation known then as Mongolism. The breakthrough with her son, who has an IQ of 49, came when she noticed that, in response to music, he moved, listened, and tried to make sounds. That was the beginning. Paul will graduate from high school this year with a diploma specifying that he meets basic standards in reading and writing, among other things. Mrs. Perrone's summer program is an outstanding example of what can be and is being accomplished for handicapped children through the creative use of theater, dance, and music.

THE PRICE FOR SURVIVAL

Mrs. Perrone is devoting part of her time to helping other arts teachers learn how to use the arts as a way to intensify the handicapped child's responsiveness to learning. At a Denver conference, sponsored by the National Committee, Mrs. Perrone spoke poignantly about the urgency of the work that must be done:

"Every human being pays a price for survival. That price has a wide range. Sometimes it is an advertising executive in an office dreaming about sailing a boat. Instead, he writes copy about it. Then there is the garment worker who spends forty years in the industry and has arthritis in both hands. That is a price for survival.

"The handicapped pay the highest price of all to survive, because they sacrifice their identity. At least other people find identity through the choices they make. The handicapped have no options; they are never allowed to make choices. They do not have that freedom or even the anxiety that goes along with it.

"The handicapped are dehumanized. They are called 'totally innocent,' 'God's little angels,' vegetables, and menaces. It seems to me that such attitudes have only changed an inch since my son was born.

"The arts are only one option we can offer these people, albeit an important one. If people will gain strength in their own identities—love themselves more—then they will not be threatened by the handicapped. Maybe if they can find their own security, they will be able to reach out and love a person who happens to have a handicap. It is everybody's responsibility to value other humans for what they are. If we build on those values, the handicapped will have the opportunities and freedom they so desperately need and deserve."

PUBLIC LAW 94-142

Besides the many outstanding programs being developed throughout the United States and the many competent and dedicated teachers, like Mrs. Perrone, who are at work, the cause of the handicapped has been further enhanced by the enactment of the Education for All Handicapped Children Act, Public Law 94–142 in November of 1975. The new bill calls for a massive expansion of grants to the states to a possible annual total of more than $3 billion by 1982. The magnitude of Congress's concern is clearly evident. An excerpt from the Senate report on the legislation makes a strong commitment to the arts:

"The use of the arts as a teaching tool for the handicapped has long been recognized as a viable, effective way not only of teaching special skills, but also of reaching youngsters who had otherwise been unteachable. The Committee envisions that programs under this bill could well include an arts component and, indeed, urges that local educational agencies include the arts in programs for the handicapped funded under this Act. Such a program could cover both appreciation of the arts by the handicapped youngsters, and the utilization of the arts as a teaching tool per se."

46

BLACK PARTICIPATION AT THE KENNEDY CENTER:

GOALS ARE SET FOR CULTURAL DIVERSITY

MUSICAL AMERICA 29 (August 1979)

Increasing awareness and understanding of diverse points of view among myriad constituencies is an important goal for a national performing arts center. By the late 1970s, the Kennedy Center still needed a gentle push and community support to move toward these goals. Roger Stevens (Chairman of the Center) established a commission and requested a report to study issues of African American participation and engagement. The report, titled *Cultural Diversity and Quality in the Performing Arts,* made eleven recommendations, along with twenty-four operational goals focused on issues of cultural diversity and related programming. More specifically, these suggestions supported better involvement of the black community in arts and music events presented at the Kennedy Center. Another outcome was the National Black Music Colloquium and Competition in 1979, with $10,000 total prize money. While issues of inclusion and understanding are critical to any organization, it seems the Kennedy Center stepped up to address the concern, and in collaboration with the very constituencies the initiatives were designed to support. Note that while some language here may appear a bit dated, the respect for multiple audiences, backgrounds, and viewpoints is ever clear in Fowler's writings. In fact, he had been raising issues of equality for many years as an author and editor. It is likely that similar ideas today could help bridge misunderstandings and bring more (and diverse) audiences to great performances of music, education, and related arts opportunities.

—CR

* * *

THE FIRST racial issue the John F. Kennedy Center faced came in the early planning stages. Where would the Center be placed, uptown where it would be accessible to the local Washington population or on the Potomac River where bridges provided easy access to the suburbs? The rationale for selecting the Potomac site was that this was to be a "national" center for the arts and that the overriding concern was not to serve just the Washington audience.

Located as it is, the Center is not easily accessible by means of public transportation, nor does Washington's new subway provide a convenient connection. It is not surprising, then, that the local, largely Black, population was not in evidence among audiences there. The Blacks did not feel part of this Palace on the Potomac, isolated between the Watergate complex and Memorial Bridge to the north and south, the river and a freeway to the west and east.

THE BLACK RESPONSE

Well, the national center idea has now come full circle. In taking notice of their own absence from events at the Center, the Blacks mounted a campaign to rectify the situation. In response, Roger Stevens, Chairman of the Center, appointed a "National Commission to Expand the Scope and Constituency of Black Participation at the JFK Center for the Performing Arts." After two years of work, the Commission's Report is now in.

Called *Cultural Diversity and Quality in the Performing Arts*, the report defines what it means to be a national arts center: "Cultural diversity . . . is a philosophy which recognizes that America is comprised not of one, but rather of a great many different cultural groups. This diversity rejects the melting pot ideology which holds that all Americans should strive to conform to a single mold of Americanism. Instead, it maintains, the beauty of America is in its diversity and, therefore, American peoples should be encouraged to maintain their distinct cultures. In this manner, all are free to be who they are and, as a result, all Americans may learn from and appreciate the broad range of cultures which together make America."

Lest this be interpreted as a lowering of standards, the Report warns that, "Quality in the performing arts . . . is superiority not only of style but also of the substance of art," and calls for the Center to combine "depth of quality with the freedom of cultural diversity."

By letter and phone and through hundreds of personal meetings the Commission, led by Archie L. Buffkins, surveyed a wide constituency of arts agencies, organizations, artists, and arts educators, as well as the public—both black and white. Based upon this survey, the Report and four separately bound appendices set forth the recommendations of the Commission, the actions they have initiated to implement those recommendations, and the projects they have begun. The Commission's Report should prove to be of value to other arts centers and its work should serve as a model for other arts commissions.

OPERATIONAL GOALS

The Commission's accomplishments are nothing short of extraordinary. The Report identifies twenty-four "Operational Goals" the Commission has set for itself, then specifies the actions taken to achieve those goals, as well as a perception of the impact those actions have had. For example: One of the Operational Goals is, "To improve the information delivery services of the Kennedy Center to the Black community." Among the actions the Commission has taken to bring this about: "A more extensive mailing list was developed for the Kennedy Center including Black newspapers, periodicals, radio stations, social clubs and professional societies." As a result, "More Blacks feel that the Black community is welcome at the Kennedy Center; The Black community is being better informed of Kennedy Center activities by the Black media; More Black social clubs and professional societies are aware of and will consider making use of Kennedy Center facilities for their functions."

Other actions included contact with many elements of the Black community to increase their involvement with the Center's programs. In this sense, the Commission serves as a national clearinghouse for disseminating information about the Center's activities.

The Report briefly describes more than a score of Kennedy Center and national projects sponsored by the Commission. These range from specific events such as concerts by violinist Sanford Allen, jazz musician Nathan Davis, and the Urban Philharmonic Orchestra to long-term demonstration projects conceived on a national scale. The latter include a Black Theater/Playwright project that has awarded major funding to six Black theater companies and playwrights to mount new productions and Black Music Colloquium and Competition (see end of article).

Model projects range in diversity from sponsorship of a radio series entitled "Soul of the Classics," devoted to the music of Black composers, to a visit by Black schoolchildren to a special preview of the Stuttgart Ballet's *The Sleeping Beauty*. They have given substantial emphasis to the encouragement and development of new talent and the production of new works, both through national projects and specific grants such as commissions for compositions by George Walker and Roque Cordero.

In order to further fulfill the overall purposes of the Commission, eleven major recommendations are directed to the Kennedy Center. They ask that the Center establish a permanent committee to monitor the development of ongoing Commission projects and to advise the board of trustees on matters relating to all aspects of the concept

of cultural diversity within the performing arts. They ask the Center to institutional-
ize selected projects initiated by the Commission, to continue allocations from the
Kennedy Center Corporate Fund to sponsor projects that will foster the concept of cultural diversity, to explore creation of an Office of Education and Community Affairs,
and to continue affirmative action practices now in operation at the Center.

1979 National Black Music Colloquium and Competition

The John F. Kennedy Center and its National Black Commission are sponsoring
the National Black Music Colloquium and Competition. This new music project
is designed to find talented young pianists and string players across the United
States and provide them with a unique opportunity to gain national recognition.
Prizes total $10,000 and regional auditions are scheduled for September in Atlanta,
Chicago, Houston, Los Angeles, New York, and St. Louis.

The project will culminate in January 1980 with master classes, the colloquium, and finals of the competition at the Kennedy Center. Two national
winners—a pianist and a string player—will receive $2,000 each and be fea-
tured in a joint concert at the Center's new Terrace Theatre. Regional winners
will receive $500 each.

To be eligible, artists must not have reached their 36th birthday by application
deadline date, August 1, 1979 and must be prepared to present a solo recital drawn
from standard repertory and music of Black composers.
Technical assistance and administration of the competition are being provided by
the National Music Council.

47

THE CHRISTMAS CAROL HASSLE

MUSICAL AMERICA 29 (September 1979)

The title of this article likely describes what many music teachers have faced when programming their concerts throughout the year. Many musical works throughout history have been based on sacred texts or religious purposes, which in a more modern context can provide learning opportunities through their performance. However, this may often seem at odds with the practices of public educational institutions, though it is usually about pedagogy rather than religion. An interesting case arose in 1978, when the American Civil Liberties Union (ACLU) pursued action against a South Dakota school district that was presenting traditional Christmas carols at some of its programs. The school district explained that the preparation and performance of this music was strictly educational, and that no pursuit of religion was intended or endorsed. The good news is that the courts agreed, though the ACLU considered an appeal. In the meantime, the United Presbyterian Church weighed in on the matter, stating that performing sacred texts and carols in schools was an affront to the meaning of the music and the religion behind them. It seems that music teachers cannot win sometimes. The more important issue for the reader, however, is that if one wanted a succinct and clear overview of this common scenario, the article here provides it. Whether in 1979 or current context, all the facts that matter are laid out clearly.

—CR

* * *

IN A SUIT by the American Civil Liberties Union to establish a permanent injunction prohibiting the singing of Christmas music in the Sioux Falls (South Dakota) School District, U.S. District Judge Andrew Bogue ruled that the policy and rules governing religion in the curriculum adopted by the Sioux Falls School Board do not violate the Establishment Clause of the First Amendment to the United States Constitution. The ACLU had tried to prevent twenty-nine carols it considers too religious from being sung in 1978 public school assemblies.

In his sixteen-page opinion, Judge Bogue provides, for the first time, a clear interpretation of the law as it applies to the use of religious music in public schools. The Establishment Clause of the First Amendment provides that "Congress shall make no law respecting an establishment of religion. . . ." Many of the multitude of cases that have interpreted this clause have involved the issue of the allowance of religious exercises or activities in public educational institutions.

Judge Bogue states: "From these cases, a three-part test has emerged which is to be used in evaluating cases arising under the Establishment Clause. The test was articulated by Chief Justice Burger . . . as follows: 'First the (activity) must have a secular legislative purpose; second, its principle or primary effect must be one that neither advances nor inhibits religion; finally, the (activity) must not foster an excessive government entanglement with religion.' In order for a challenged practice to pass constitutional muster, each part of the test must be met."

Because the Sioux Falls case posed in the judge's view "an extremely close question of law," his opinion provides a detailed interpretation that should be of value to all school systems and to music teachers in particular. In essence the ruling states that, if a school system's adopted rules and the programs and treatment of religious subjects that occur pursuant to those rules do not constitute inherently religious activities, then they are constitutional.

The ACLU had particularly objected to Rules 1, 3, and 4 of the School Board:

(1) *The several holidays throughout the year which have a religious and a secular basis may be observed in the public schools. . . .*

(3) *Music, art, literature and drama having religious themes or basis are permitted as part of the curriculum for school-sponsored activities and programs if presented in a prudent and objective manner and as a traditional part of the cultural and religious heritage of the particular holiday.*

(4) *The use of religious symbols such as a cross, monorah, crescent, Star of David, creche, symbols of Native American religions or other symbols that are a part of a religious holiday is permitted as a teaching aid or resource provided such symbols*

are displayed as an example of the cultural and religious heritage of the holiday and are temporary in nature. Among these holidays are included Christmas, Easter, Passover, Hanukah, St. Valentine's Day, St. Patrick's Day, Thanksgiving and Halloween.

The Supervisor of Music for the Sioux Falls School System testified that Christmas songs with religious content were taught and performed for purposes of providing students with a complete musical education. Witnesses further testified that the simple *studying* of Christmas songs with religious content in a classroom setting would not provide the student with a complete musical education because an integral part of studying music is *performing* it.

In regard to the school system's Rule No. 1, the judge stated: "The rule makes it abundantly clear that schools in the Sioux Falls School District may observe holidays which have *both* a religious and a secular significance. This rule appears to distinguish between holidays with a purely religious significance, such as Pentecost, Ash Wednesday and Good Friday, which may not be observed in the public schools, and those holidays such as Christmas and Easter, with both a religious and secular basis, which may be observed."

While the ACLU agreed that students may study various religions and holidays in the public schools, they argued that permitting schools to present Christmas assemblies which contain songs with religious content goes beyond the realm of study and involves the schools in the impermissible activity of promoting the Christian religion. Rule 3, they said, allows the schools to involve themselves in inherently religious activities.

The judge disagreed. "Rule 3 seeks to ensure that schools may present holiday assemblies which contain religious art, literature or music as long as such materials are presented in a prudent and objective manner. The rule recognizes that much of our artistic tradition has a religious origin. Religious texts are frequently used in Christmas music. Much of this art, while religious in origin, has acquired a significance which is no longer confined to the religious sphere of life. It has become integrated into our national culture and heritage. To allow students *only* to study and *not* to perform such works when they have developed an independent secular and artistic significance would give students a truncated view of our culture."

He then quoted Justice Jackson's concurring opinion in a 1948 in Illinois:

Music without sacred music, architecture minus the cathedral, or painting without the scriptural themes would be eccentric and incomplete, *even from a secular point of view.* . . . The fact is that, for good or for ill, nearly everything in our culture worth transmitting, everything which gives meaning to life, is saturated with religious influences, derived from paganism, Judaism, Christianity—both Catholic and Protestant—and other faiths accepted by a large part of the world's peoples. (Emphasis added)

In Judge Bogue's opinion, "To rule unconstitutional a policy which allows Christmas assemblies to contain material having religious significance if such material is presented in a prudent and objective manner would leave the schools in the position of only being permitted to present programs that are eccentric and incomplete."

He further states that "The purpose of the policy and rules is to expose and involve the student in the full spectrum of our Western musical tradition. Music is selected for its inherent musical value. Performance is an intrinsic part of a musical education."

According to his ruling, the Courts cannot evaluate the effect of school Christmas assemblies containing *some* religious material on each and every individual. "... This Court finds that the performance of Christmas music with religious content does not constitute a religious activity per se. "The effect of Rules 3 and 4 is not to promote religion.

"Furthermore, this Court cannot find that the school system provides any aid to religion or to any religious institution through its policy and rules. ... It is true that an individual's religious sensibilities might possibly be kindled by participating in a school Christmas assembly in which songs with religious texts are sung. It is also possible that religion might be equally 'promoted' when a Christmas song with a religious text is studied objectively in the classroom. The school cannot guarantee that exposure to various religions and religious ideas will not aid religion in some cases. Similarly, the school cannot guarantee that the type of exposure and participation allowed by Rules 3 and 4 will not benefit, in some fashion or other, any religious institution by the acquisition of a convert. The type of 'aid' which the policy and rules might afford is not the variety which a Court should or can attempt to control."

When asked about the Court's opinion, Deming Smith, attorney for the school district, said, "Naturally I feel overjoyed. The opinion is in favor of the constitutionality of the schools' policy and specifically of the use of Christmas carols in school programs." The ACLU is contemplating an appeal.

CAROL-SINGING IN SCHOOLS IS OPPOSED BY CHURCH

In a direct challenge to the ruling by U.S. District Court Judge Andrew Bogue described in the adjoining article, the United Presbyterian Church in Sioux Falls filed a brief in May opposing the singing of Christmas carols in public schools on grounds that such activity debases religion.

The church has joined with the American Civil Liberties Union, which led the unsuccessful fight against the carols earlier in the year. The ACLU maintains that students should not be subjected to religious influences as part of public schooling. Judge Bogue's ruling, which now stands, maintains that singing "Silent Night" in a school Christmas pageant does not violate the constitutional separation between church and state.

48

ARTS BY THE HANDICAPPED

MUSICAL AMERICA 29 (November 1979)

Addressing music and arts education for students with special needs is an important task. For far too long, those with handicaps (exceptionalities in contemporary language) were not given the attention or focus they deserve. Among the efforts to address this concern were those by the Kennedy Center and the National Committee of Arts for the Handicapped. While they worked in many areas to provide artistic, educational, and enrichment support, they also sponsored a Very Special Arts Festival in April 1979. Hosted by the Kennedy Center, some 750 youngsters took part in various activities that introduced them to and immersed them in musical and artistic experiences. A number of well-known artists joined to effort, including Jamie Wyeth, Andy Warhol, Domenico Mazzone, Linda Bove, and Jacques d'Amboise, among others. In addition to details about specific learning and performance activities, there is also further commentary about the value a festival like this holds for children. Indeed, the more we nurture those with special needs, the more we realize the change such nurturing and opportunity can bring to their lives. After all, is that not a major goal of music education in the first place?

—CR

* * *

WHAT IS A National Very Special Arts Festival? It's a celebration of the arts by handicapped youngsters. There are dance and dramatic presentations by the deaf; musical performances by the visually impaired; ceramic and sculpture displays by the mentally retarded; painting demonstrations by the orthopedically handicapped. (Some of these students paint with the brush in their mouth.) Children with oral communication problems and learning disabilities can be reached through the arts—through puppet shows that motivate them to talk and movement exercises (reaching to touch the clouds to understand the term "high") that open the doors to the mind.

The arts are a way through. They invite participation. They excite the imagination. They stimulate the physical self. They provoke happiness. They celebrate the human being. Consequently, they are proving to be a powerful tool in the education of handicapped children, a potent force for learning that has only recently been recognized.

In April, more than 750 handicapped youngsters from across the United States took part in a National Very Special Arts Festival at the Kennedy Center. The National Festival, hosted by the National Committee, Arts for the Handicapped (NCAH), served as the culmination of festival programs held in forty-seven states that involved more than 1.5 million handicapped children and youths.

At these festivals the children not only learn from each other, but they also participate in special arts workshops. Jamie Wyeth and Andy Warhol taught painting; Domenico Mazzone taught sculpture; Tammy Grimes sat on the floor and told stories; Linda Bove and Ed Waterstreet of the National Theatre of the Deaf and "Sesame Street" presented a drama workshop; Jacques d'Amboise showed how he has taught deaf children to dance.

CLEARING MISCONCEPTIONS

One of the purposes of these festivals is to clear away public stereotypical misconceptions about the handicapped. There are those who believe that the handicapped, by nature, lack ability and talent. Not so. The physically handicapped—no matter how severely afflicted—may be both bright and gifted. Some people believe that the handicapped generally have compensating talents, that the blind automatically hear better and therefore have a ready affinity for music. This is not necessarily the case. As Jacques d'Amboise said, "You must challenge the handicapped. That is the only way compensatory talents can emerge."

And the festivals accomplish one other important feat. They put the handicapped out in public where people can begin to relate to them and overcome whatever phobias they may harbor regarding them. It used to be that handicapped children were hidden away—"warehoused." There was a certain shame surrounding them. This is quickly dispensed by the festivals, where the activities invite camaraderie and where the inner warmth of these people—perhaps born of the burden of being different—engulfs us and reminds us that we are all of one human family—all handicapped to one degree or another.

The Special Festivals are organized by the NCAH, an educational affiliate of the JFK Center for the Performing Arts. Congress has authorized the U.S. Commissioner of Education under the Special Projects provision of the Elementary and Secondary Education Act to "carry out a program for the purpose of identifying, developing, and implementing model projects or programs in all the arts for handicapped persons" through arrangements with this organization. For this purpose, the Congress has appropriated $1 million, hardly enough funds to touch the thousands upon thousands of children who are, in one way or another, handicapped—estimated at ten percent of the population. Besides this contract arrangement for discretionary monies, the NCAH, founded four years ago and spearheaded by Mrs. Jean Kennedy Smith, receives additional project funds from the Bureau of Education for the Handicapped.

DEVELOPING A CURRICULUM

The Special Arts Festivals are only one part of the efforts of the NCAH. Wendy Perks, executive director of NCAH, says that "Currently we are completing a three-year research project to develop a curriculum for the handicapped that incorporates all the arts." Janie Goldberg, the present project coordinator, explains that the curriculum is designed to use the arts to teach basic skills. During the first year of the project, teachers in five elementary schools in the Clover Park School District of Tacoma, Washington, collected student data and assembled detailed lessons. The data suggest that the use of an arts-infused curriculum by handicapped children contributes to increased academic achievement.

The curriculum is now being field tested in thirteen sites. The Arts for Learning Guides that have been developed show the teacher how to infuse the arts into the established curriculum of handicapped children. Responses of teachers to the materials will be studied and the Guides revised accordingly. They will then be published and made available to teachers across the country. During the first six months of the new curriculum, students in the program produced significantly better achievement test scores than did the control group.

In addition to the Arts in Education Project described above, the NCAH has contracted two other projects. An Arts in Service Project is now in its third year. The project uses conferences and workshops to identify and develop leaders on the state level who can effect change in education for the handicapped. Another project, Arts for the Severely and Profoundly Handicapped, is in its first year. This project proposes that in three years it will develop a model arts program within three local education agencies which serve the severely and profoundly handicapped child.

A SENSE OF FREEDOM

Why all this activity? Can the arts really have a major effect on the handicapped? Perks answers: "The handicapped have been restricted. Many have led very isolated lives. The arts provide a sense of freedom where children can develop and express their imagination and thus bring creativity into their lives." Dr. Louise Appell, associate director of the NCAH, says, "The handicapped child needs to learn how to function better and how to enjoy living. The arts provide an exciting means to stimulate interest and activity and, at the same time, to teach such basics as motor control, perception, language development, and social skills."

Appell believes that the arts and the handicapped are natural partners. The National Very Special Arts Festival provides a means to demonstrate this dynamic relationship. A group of deaf Hawaiian adolescent boys and girls using sign language to "dance" the lyric of a song can illustrate for the public the marvel of talent, warmth, genuineness, courage, and sensitivity that emanate from these children, traits that make them honorable members of the human race.

49

OLDER AMERICANS—A NEW RESOURCE OF CREATIVE TALENT

MUSICAL AMERICA 30 (August 1980)

There are many groups outside of public school classrooms who have an interest in the arts and music education. While the profession is finally getting around to recognizing the value of all people who wish to participate in creative activity, we were generally less enlightened in our past practice. There certainly were exceptions, however, and we have some good examples in the report here. A number of experts working with older people—some in gerontology, some in theater and music, and others in related artistic and research areas—are highlighted for their important work and programs. There is also some useful background on the benefits of arts study for senior citizens, and details on the challenges faced by those wishing to offer such opportunities or pursue them. There is much value to be gleaned in appreciating the wisdom of the aged, just as there is in intergenerational understandings and engagement. It is hard to say who benefits from these programs more—the young or the old, the students or teachers, the experts or novices—but the benefits are constructive, critical, and clear.

—CR

* * *

"GRANDMOTHER, speak English!" shouts an exasperated teenager. "*Si, si!*" responds the grandmother agreeably, fumbling her attempt to reach some accommodation with her brash young granddaughter. These lines are from a new play by Wendy Kesselman entitled *Maggie Magalita*, that uses the theatrical medium to explore the generation gap.

The play, winner of the Sharfman Playwriting Award, was presented in the Terrace Theater of the John F. Kennedy Center for the Performing Arts in April as part of the Imagination Celebration, a weeklong event sponsored by the Center's Education Program. The play gave impetus for a discussion about "Older Americans on Stage: Closing the Generation Gap," that explored not just theater but all the arts and the aging.

Dorothy Coones, executive director of the School of Continuing Education, Institute of Gerontology, at the University of Michigan, observed that "there has been an important switch in point of view in the past three years regarding the role of the arts in the lives of older Americans. Heretofore, the *problems* of aging were the focus, and the arts were viewed primarily from the standpoint of therapy, which carries connotations of sickness. Now the arts are viewed as opportunities for involvement, self-satisfaction, and the development of creative capacities."

She went on to say that "The involvement of the elderly in drama is making a difference in how youth perceives them. The arts help to get rid of the stereotypes and myths that surround the senior citizen. The elderly are not necessarily rigid and inflexible, feeble and sickly, unwilling or unable to learn, or lacking in their ability to relate to the young."

Old people need not be estranged from the pleasures of the arts. Indeed, the great talent of artists like Georgia O'Keefe, Artur Rubinstein, Pablo Picasso, and Pablo Casals, to name a few, attests to the continuing contribution and artistic genius that is possible among older people.

HOW WE GROW OLD

Jacqueline Sunderland, executive director of the National Council on Aging, a private agency that has been operating for thirty years, notes that the problem is "How we grow old in a society of the young." She believes that "older Americans are part of our cultural heritage, yet they have often been forgotten. Many older people possess creative abilities that find little opportunity for expression. Yet we have many problems today that demonstrate how both the arts and older people can be mutually enriched when this potential force is tapped."

She says, "I hope we never close the generation gap, but that we illuminate it and make it more understandable. There is much to be learned from these differences. I buried my parents' prejudices, and my children will bury mine. The generation gap is not a new phenomena and not something we can or should erase. There are going to be differences in viewpoint between people who are fourteen and eighty. What we can do is build tolerance.

"The arts can relate people to each other. People from diverse cultures who happen to be over sixty-five can learn to hold hands—physically and mentally—through expressing their ethnicity in dance. They can feel that similar blood flows through other hands. The arts can be a vehicle for this kind of communication and humanization.

"We are not involving older people with the arts in order to make creative artists," Sunderland says. "Some older Americans are already artists. Others have not had the opportunities. Still others need to renew their relationship with their creative potential.

"We have to remember," Sunderland says, "that no other generation in history has lived through so many changes. Those who are over sixty-five today have lived through two world wars, the Korean War and Vietnam, and a major depression. They have seen the world change from horses to cars, to airplanes and rockets to the moon. No other generation of humans has ever seen so much. In many ways they have spent their time on survival. In this sense, the arts for many of these people represent a vast new opportunity."

THE PROFESSIONAL AND THE AGED

The National Council on Aging has worked to bring the professional artist and arts educator to work closer with the aged. "We've had a paucity of professional involvement," Sunderland says. "We need to move toward excellence. It is the professional artist and arts educator who can show us that human potential doesn't stop at some mythical age."

A report of the National Endowment for the Arts that was delivered to the Senate Special Committee on Aging in 1978 says it this way: "Perhaps the most persistent barrier to developing quality arts programs for older Americans is that the public at large, and arts administrators and artists in particular, do not fully understand the relationship of the arts to individuals over sixty-five years of age."

The play and the discussion at the Kennedy Center represent an attempt to acquire and disseminate just this kind of understanding. Along these same lines, the American Theatre Association, with funding from the Center's Alliance for Arts Education, has just completed a report, "Older Americans on Stage," that assembles information about senior adult theater programs in the United States.

The report attempts to probe what is going on in the United States in senior adult theater, that is, theater *by* older Americans—theater in which they actively participate. Some of these are independent groups, like Boston's New Wrinkle Theatre and Oregon's Theatre of Feast, the latter of which has a membership ranging in age from seventy-two to ninety-six.

SENIOR ADULT THEATER GROUPS

Many senior adult theater groups have sprung up as offshoots of community theater groups. Typical of these is Chicago's Free Street Too Theatre, a senior company that tours a group-created production, *To Life,* based on the experience of its members.

What they found in this study is that older people tend to maintain in retirement the habits they acquired when they were younger so that they are not apt to experiment with new kinds of activities. Those who already hold some knowledge of, interest in, or experience with theater are the ones who are most apt to become part of a senior theater group.

While most of these groups are motivated primarily for the pleasure that the activity provides, some have other very specific objectives. Topeka's Barn Players, Maine's Old Age: Tradition Shelved or Shared?, San Francisco's Tale Spinners, and Skokie's Acting Up troupe all illuminate the issue of aging. Other groups have as their main purpose cross-generational contact, therapy or, in the case of Back Alley Theatre's SAGE project in Washington, D.C., professional training. These groups are free to travel and generally do a great deal of touring. In other words, they enjoy performing in front of an appreciative audience.

The report makes it clear that there is a considerable amount of activity in theater among senior citizens in every state. During the discussion at the Kennedy Center, Jack Morrison, executive director of the American Theatre Association and project director for this study, asked, "Does using theater as a social, educational, or therapeutic tool kill it as an art?" The report makes it clear that artistic quality among these groups is often based on criteria that are different from those applied to professional theater: "Success is primarily measured in terms of the amount of participation, the ability to complete projects, and the satisfaction experienced by the participants."

THE QUESTION OF STANDARDS

In the case of the Free Street Too Theatre, significant numbers of professionals have praised its professional quality. But the report states: "Perhaps in the long run it will be generally agreed that no artistic standard should be set."

But whether professional standards are rigidly applied or not, providing opportunities for the aged to participate in the arts and to be guided in these activities by professional artists and arts educators will, no doubt, tap a whole new resource of creative talent in the United States. "I'm convinced," Sunderland says, "that what we are going to witness is a new step in creativity. We're on a treasure hunt, and the surprises only await our providing the right kind of opportunities."

50

THE MANY VS. THE FEW

MUSICAL AMERICA 33 (February 1983)

One of the common catchphrases of the music education profession for many years has been that every child deserves a quality music education. If this were indeed the reality, then perhaps the need for arts advocacy would be a topic of historical interest. It seems that this is obvious, and that those cheering on music education for all would blame anyone but the music teacher. Well, not so fast. Music education programs have been structured for many years whereby the talented few are given the most attention over the uneducated many. When budget cuts and other challenges cause cancellation of programs, those schools with the greatest needs seem to be affected first, and then afterward, the successful ones. While large ensembles and well-regarded school music programs should be given support, there are many students left behind who need musical training, too. To better understand this problem in a clear and direct way, a reading of this article will be helpful. Perhaps you identify with the concerns. Maybe you even know those who are part of the problem, or have seen solutions that work to address the concerns. In the larger picture, the more self-reflection we engage, the smarter the music education profession may be, to move forward by ending the debate of the many versus the few.

—CR

* * *

WHILE IT HAS not yet been achieved, equality of educational opportunity remains a major goal and the dynamic underlying rationale of American public education. In the realm of music education, this ideal is interpreted as "music for every child," and state departments of education, following this line of reasoning, recommend—though seldom mandate—minimum programs of music instruction for all students. Such recommendations are meant to assure that every student in the public schools has some basic access to the study of music.

DIMINISHING OPPORTUNITY

It seems to me that two prevailing trends today are seriously thwarting delivery of this promise to American youth. The first, more obvious than the second, is a lessening of opportunity to study music due to curtailment of music programs. During the current school year in Baltimore public schools, for example, there are thirty-nine fewer music teachers in the elementary schools than there were last year. There are now twenty-six vocal music teachers left to cover 127 elementary schools. These teachers have to service upwards of five schools a week or one whole school a day. The effect: less music instruction for every child. General music is the basic program of music study providing students with the underpinnings for a lifetime of understanding and appreciating music.

In the public schools of Prince George's County (Maryland), instrumental music teachers in the elementary schools were reduced by seventeen this school year. (The school board actually eliminated the entire instrumental music program in the elementary schools last summer, but was forced by community pressures to reinstate it in the fifth and sixth grades.) Twenty instrumental teachers now cover 120 elementary schools, some servicing as many as seven schools a week, none fewer than five. In this school system, fourth graders are no longer offered beginning instrumental study; in fact, no beginning instrumental instruction is being offered this year. Elementary instrumental programs such as this are exploratory in nature, open to all students, and are designed to provide basic knowledge of musical "language."

These are but two instances of cutbacks in music that have been all too quietly undermining music instruction in public schools across the country for the past decade. The result is an enormous disparity of opportunities for music study among school systems. Whereas children in one school are encouraged to explore the rewards of musical study and performance and to acquire a genuine understanding of the enriching satisfactions of music, children in another are offered few, if any, of these opportunities. That one child has music and another doesn't, that one has ample opportunity and another scant, strikes me as anti-egalitarian; it goes against the American grain.

SPECIALIST EMPHASIS

But this inequality is aided—even encouraged—by a second trend, an emphasis on specialism that favors the talented at the expense of the general school population.

When resources begin to dwindle and programs must necessarily be reduced, there is a danger that they will lose their spread and begin to serve only part of the student body.

Music teachers, particularly at the junior and senior high school levels, have always experienced some difficulties in providing adequate and attractive music courses for all students. There is a natural tendency to seek out the talented and the already interested students and provide them with courses tailored to their particular needs. Performance organizations like bands, choruses, and orchestras, for example, generally cater to those who already have demonstrated some ability to sing or to play an instrument.

It is rare to find an instrumental program at the secondary level that offers beginning lessons. An elective class in guitar, which might appeal to numbers of students, is seldom offered. Even music appreciation, a course that is being offered in many high schools, if often geared to those who have already developed an interest or who have acquired a more than ordinary musical background. Electives such as rudiments of music and harmony, where they are offered, are deliberately designed for students with a strong musical background. By and large, then, musical offerings in American high schools favor the talented.

THE PREVAILING TENDENCY

When cuts began to affect music programs during the decade of the '70s, it seemed at first that the idea of serving the many rather than the few would prevail. Some school systems, faced with choices as to what to eliminate, dismantled their string programs. These programs were generally young appendages of the instrumental program that had not yet won a substantial student interest or broad community support. They went with hardly a whimper.

Now, however, cuts in school budgets appear to intensify the already prevalent tendency to favor specialism, particularly the well-entrenched performance organizations. School systems will generally cut music appreciation before they eliminate the band. They will terminate general music (where it is not mandated) before they eliminate their chorus. And in cities that now have a high school of the arts, they will cut musical offerings in the general high schools before they tamper with the programs for their specialized students.

WHITHER THE AUDIENCE?

What do these trends portend? It seems to this observer that we are developing a house with no foundation. We seem more determined than ever to develop artists but couple this with a waning commitment to provide the audience to sustain them. There is no question that we need our bands, choruses, and orchestras, and our specialized schools for the arts, for they are not only the proving ground for developing the nation's musical talent but also a small but musically educated audience.

At the same time, we must also find the way to continue to reach outward to all students, to offer them the possibility of acquiring basic musical understanding. It is not a matter of either/or. Options induced by the devastating choices of curtailment must attend the needs of the many as well as the few. There are opportunities outside the schools for talented students to study music through private lessons and participation in community musical groups. There are few comparable opportunities for the general population of youth to acquire basic musical knowledge and understanding. The schools must sustain that responsibility.

Bibliography

SECTION ONE: MUSIC PEDAGOGY AND SCHOOLING

Fowler, Charles. "National Survey of Musical Performance." *Musical America* 24 (August 1974): 12–13.
—— "Music In Our Schools Day: An Opportunity to Take Stock." *Musical America* 25 (March 1975): 12–14.
—— "The Accountability Dilemma." *Musical America* 26 (August 1976): 8–9.
—— "Arts in the Schools: A Comprehensive View." *Musical America* 31 (December 1981): 10–11.
—— "High Schools of the Arts." *Musical America* 32 (March 1982): 11, 40.
—— "Musical Achievement: Good News & Bad." *Musical America* 32 (May 1982): 12, 24.
—— "A Look into the Crystal Ball." *Musical America* 34 (January 1984): 6–9.
—— "Music: A Basic Intelligence." *Musical America* 34 (June 1984): 12, 14, 40.
—— "The Shameful Neglect of Creativity." *Musical America* 35 (September 1985): 10–12.
—— "Academic Excellence in Teaching the Arts." *Musical America* 36 (August 1986): 6–7, 12.
—— "Evaluation: Pros & Cons." *Musical America* 36 (November 1986): 9–12.
—— "Music in Our Schools: The First 150 Years." *Musical America* 108 (November 1988): 11–14.

SECTION TWO: ADVOCACY AND ARTS EDUCATION POLICY

Fowler, Charles. "Education in the Arts: Getting It All Together." *Musical America* 25 (February 1975): 6–8.
—— "The Role of the National Endowment (for the Arts)." *Musical America* 27 (March 1977): 12, 34.
—— "A New Rationale for the Arts in Education." *Musical America* 27 (September 1977): 13–15.
—— "What's Wrong with Music Education?" *Musical America* 28 (April 1978): 7, 40.

—— "Funding for Arts Programs: The Total is Not So Bleak." *Musical America* 30 (February 1980): 14–15.

—— "Arts Education: Does the Left Hand Know?" *Musical America* 30 (June 1980): 10–11, 37.

—— "Congress and the Arts: Getting With It." *Musical America* 34 (May 1984): 6, 29, 40.

—— "Arts in Basic Education: A Fight for Life?" *Musical America* 34 (August 1984): 13, 18.

—— "Arts Policy in the U.S.: Do We Have One?" *Musical America* 34 (December 1984): 10–13.

—— "Music for Every Child, Every Child for Music." *Musical America* 36 (May 1986): 10–13.

—— "Arts Education Triple Jeopardy." *Musical America* 109 (March 1989): 10–12.

SECTION THREE: ARTS, CULTURE, AND COMMUNITY

Fowler, Charles. "The Smithsonian: Teaching our Musical Heritage." *Musical America* 26 (January 1976): 8–9.

—— "Valuing Our Cultural Treasury." *Musical America* 26 (November 1976): 8–11.

—— "The Community School Movement." *Musical America* 27 (July 1977): 12–13, 40.

—— "Senior Citizens' Symphony Brings Music to Children." *Musical America* 29 (October 1979): 16–17.

—— "Public Universities—The New Cultural Centers." *Musical America* 30 (July 1980): 8–9, 15.

—— "Reaching Kids (Part I): How Symphonies Do It." *Musical America* 35 (February 1985): 11–13, 15.

—— "Reaching Kids (Part II): How Opera Companies Do It." *Musical America* 35 (March 1985): 18–19, 34–35.

—— "Whose Culture Should We Teach?" *Musical America* 108 (July 1988): 14–17.

SECTION FOUR: MUSIC EDUCATION AND PROFESSIONAL REFORM

Fowler, Charles. "The Music Educators National Conference (MENC): David Faces New Goliaths." *Musical America* 26 (April 1976): 8–9.

—— "The Tanglewood Symposium Revisited." *Musical America* 28 (July 1978): 14–15.

—— "Music in Our Schools: An Agenda for the Future." *Musical America* 31 (March 1981): 14, 20.

—— "Changing Schools Through the Arts." *Musical America* 32 (April 1982): 10–11.

—— "The Lack of Professionalism in Higher Education." *Musical America* 32 (June 1982): 14–15.

—— "The Lack of Professionalism in Higher Education—Continued." *Musical America* 32 (September 1982): 13–14.

—— "Music Educators Meet—But Do They Miss the Point?" *Musical America* 34 (September 1984): 11–13, 34.

—— "Are Teachers of the Arts Good Enough?" *Musical America* 35 (October 1985): 8, 10–11, 24.

—— "Educational Reform: Ferment in the Arts." *Musical America* 36 (April 1986): 6–8.

—— "Teacher Overhaul: Can We Do It?" *Musical America* 107 (July 1987): 22, 24, 52, 54–55.

SECTION FIVE: DIVERSITY AND PLURALISM IN MUSIC EDUCATION

Fowler, Charles. "Poverty: An Ingrained Idea." *Musical America* 26 (June 1976): 10–11.

—— "Sex Bias in the Music Room." *Musical America* 26 (December 1976): 8–9.

—— "Special Treatment for the Gifted." *Musical America* 27 (April 1977): 14, 15.

—— "More Arts for the Handicapped." *Musical America* 27 (June 1977): 9–11.

—— "Black Participation at the Kennedy Center: Goals are Set for Cultural Diversity." *Musical America* 29 (August 1979): 16–17, 40.

—— "The Christmas Carol Hassle." *Musical America* 29 (September 1979): 14–16.

—— "Arts by the Handicapped." *Musical America* 29 (November 1979): 12–14.

—— "Older Americans—A New Resource of Creative Talent." *Musical America* 30 (August 1980): 9–12.

—— "The Many vs. the Few." *Musical America* 33 (February 1983): 10, 12.

Index